Blount County Tennessee Chancery Court Records

Book 0 and Book 1

1852–1865

Albert W. Dockter, Jr.

HERITAGE BOOKS
2011

HERITAGE BOOKS
AN IMPRINT OF HERITAGE BOOKS, INC.

Books, CDs, and more—Worldwide

For our listing of thousands of titles see our website
at
www.HeritageBooks.com

Published 2011 by
HERITAGE BOOKS, INC.
Publishing Division
100 Railroad Ave. #104
Westminster, Maryland 21157

Copyright © 1992 Albert W. Dockter, Jr.

Other books by the author:

Blount County, Tennessee Chancery Court Records: Book 0 and Book 1, 1852–1865

Blount County, Tennessee Chancery Court Records: Book 1, Part II, 1866–1869

Estate Settlements of Blount County, Tennessee, Naming Heirs Extracted from: Execution Book II, Chancery Court, February 1872–February 1893; Execution Book II, County Court, April 1893–February 1915; and the Workbook of James A. Greer, Clerk and Master, Chancery Court, 1885–1890

Revolutionary War Veteran William Keeble of Blount County, Tennessee and His Heirs

William Keeble of Blount County, Tennessee

All rights reserved. No part of this book may be reproduced or transmitted in any form or by any means, electronic or mechanical, including photocopying, recording or by any information storage and retrieval system without written permission from the author, except for the inclusion of brief quotations in a review.

International Standard Book Numbers
Paperbound: 978-1-55613-589-7
Clothbound: 978-0-7884-8697-5

I dedicate this first book of the Blount County Chancery Court Records to the officers and members of the Blount County Genealogical and Historical Society in grateful appreciation of their endeavors to assist those seeking to explore their heritage.

CONTENTS

Preface vii

Introduction ix

Chancery Court Records, Book 0 1

Chancery Court Records, Book 1 69

Abbreviations 157

Index 159

PREFACE

The Blount County Genealogical and Historical Society has been kind in printing so much of my Keeble Family research in their Journal. I had sympathy for the readers who were not interested in, yet, another Keeble offspring. I determined that I would find something of value to the entire organization, if at all possible, and dedicate it to the body.

I had little knowledge of the Chancery Court, and knew that few people had looked for genealogical material there. Certainly, the Court should be of historical significance, and so I set about to determine if this was a worthwhile project.

I approached the Clerk and Master and asked him if he knew of the history of the beginnings of the Court in Blount County. He stated that he knew nothing of that information. I requested permission to go to the Chancery Court record repository. (I have since found that his secretaries call it "the dungeon.") This cellar room, damp with the plaster leaching into hair like protuberances on the walls, contains a wealth of information of a bygone era. In modernizing the exterior of the building to provide ramps to the first floor a long "pocket" area next to the old courthouse was left with no drainage. Thus, when rains come from the southeast and pelt down on the building, water runs into this "pocket" and then flows under the windowsill and into this book depository.

I found that Chancery Court had much to offer of a genealogical nature in that if an estate could not be settled because of minor children, or the land was not of a dividable nature, the case was removed from the County Court jurisdiction to Chancery Court for the Chancellor to hear the case and determine if the land should be sold and proceeds divided among the heirs. Minors' interests required the appointment of guardians. Thus, these settlements named the heirs of the deceased person and often gave the names of the deceased person's parents and many times, gave land grant numbers.

The historical nature of the Chancery Court evolved around the fact the Blount County Chancery Court was authorized by the Legislature of Tennessee in 1852. Prior to that time, Blount County citizens were required to go to Kingston in Roane County for redress of their grievances on appeal. (One wonders if a boat trip to Kingston in that day was preferable to a wagon ride to Knoxville.) Many of the cases concerning slaves, land encroachments, rights of way, etc. give an insight as to the customs of the times. The depositions taken from the parties involved give a picture of their speech patterns and idiosyncrasies.

I began copying Book 1 of the Chancery Court Records and suddenly realized that these records had no beginning. Searching a back shelf, I found a leather volume that had "0" on it. This book proved to be the story of the beginning of the Chancery Court in Blount County, Tennessee. The book contained 230 pages, and much of the ink was faded, making it difficult to read. Added to that problem was the difficulty in discerning the scribes' "flowery" capital letters, and indeed, names like BURUM looked like BUSUM, or vice versa.

I determined that since no one had microfilmed this book, I would copy it for posterity. My concern for this book, and others not microfilmed in this cellar depository, was heightened by the senseless burning of the Grundy County Courthouse on May 3, 1990, by two brothers who apparently held a grudge. They destroyed 105 years of records. Should Blount County Courthouse ever have a fire, God forbid, these records in basement rooms would be inundated with water used to fight the fire.

As an organization, we should be promoting a safe repository for all original courthouse records to within recent times and providing the courthouse offices with copies should they need them.

Albert W. Dockter, Jr.

INTRODUCTION

"There was no Chancery Court held in Blount County until 1852. Equity cases arising in Blount County were tried in the Blount County Circuit Court in 1810 and 1811; and before the Supreme Court of Errors and Appeals sitting at Knoxville from 1813 to 1822. Between 1822 and 1824, equity suits not brought in the Circuit Court of Blount County were tried by a Court of Equity held at Knoxville by one of the judges of the Supreme Court of Errors and Appeals. From 1824 to 1831, such cases were tried in a Chancery Court held at Kingston in Roane County. From 1831 to 1833, equity cases in Blount County were tried at Madisonville in Monroe County. From 1833 to 1852, the Chancery Court at Madisonville, and the Chancery Court at Knoxville had concurrent jurisdiction in Blount County equity cases. In 1836, the Circuit Court was divested of jurisdiction in equity cases involving more than $50.00, but since 1852, has had the power to decide all equity cases in which parties did not object to its jurisdiction. In 1852, Blount County was created as a separate Chancery district and provision was made for the court to be held in Maryville.

The Chancery Court is chiefly a court of equity, but also has considerable concurrent jurisdiction with the Probate and Circuit Courts over the appointment and supervision of personal representations and the partition and distribution of estates as well as concurrent jurisdiction with the Circuit Court in all civil cases at law except in liquidated damages. Prior to 1854, the Chancellor, the judge of the Chancery Court, was appointed by the General Assembly. Since then, he has been elected by popular vote. Before 1836, the Chancellor held office during good behavior; since then, he has served for a term of eight years. The Clerk and Master, appointed by the Chancellor, served during good behavior prior to 1836. Since 1836, his term has been limited to six years."

History of Blount County, Tennessee, 1795-1955
Inez E. Burns, Author

CHANCERY COURT

BLOUNT COUNTY, TENNESSEE

Established 1852.

Transcribed in its entirety
by
Albert W. Dockter, Jr.

Editor's Note: Every effort has been made to present accurate transcription of this valuable source of Blount County records. If questions arise, please examine the original found in the storage room of the Blount County Courthouse.

RECORDS BOOK 0 (ZERO)

STATE OF TENNESSEE

Pg. 1 Be it remembered that in pursuance of an Act of the General Assembly passed on the 27th day of February in the year of our Lord One Thousand Eight Hundred and Fifty-Two a Court of Chancery was opened and held at the Courthouse in the town of Maryville on Monday, the 14th of February, being the second Monday of the said month in the year of our Lord One Thousand Eight Hundred and Fifty-Three, Present and Presiding the Hon. THOMAS L. WILLIAMS, Chancellor, a.c. when the following proceedings were heard to wit;-

SAMUEL PRIDE, Esq. having been heretofore by the Chancellor appointed Clerk & Master of the said Court, and was here appearing in open court with his official bonds, heretofore executed, and acknowledged before, and approved by the Chancellor at Chambers, which several bonds are ordered to be entered of record and are as follows: to wit-

Know all men by these presents that we SAMUEL PRIDE, A. C. MONTGOMERY, JOHN E. TOOLE, A. P. TEMPLE and JAMES HENRY are held and severally bound unto the State of Tennessee in the penal sum of ten thousand dollars for the payment of which well and truly by us made, we bind ourselves, our executors and administrators this __ day of October 1852.

Pg. 2 The condition of the above obligation is such as follows: Whereas the above bound SAMUEL PRIDE has this day been appointed by the Chancellor of the Eastern Division of the State, Clerk & Master of the Chancery Court at Maryville, now if the said SAMUEL PRIDE shall safely keep the records of the said court and truly and faithfully discharge and perform all the duties incumbent on him by law as said Clerk & Master then this obligation shall be null and void otherwise remaining in full force and effect.

    SAMUEL PRIDE
    JOHN E. TOOLE
    A. C. MONTGOMERY
    A. P. TEMPLE
    JAMES HENRY

Test: THOMAS L. WILLIAMS

Know all men by these presents that we, SAMUEL PRIDE, JOHN E. TOOLE, A. C. MONTGOMERY, A. P. TEMPLE and JAMES HENRY are jointly and severally held and firmly bound unto the State of Tennessee in the penal sum of ten thousand dollars for the payment of which we have bound ourselves, our heirs, administrators and executors signed with our names and sealed with our seals this __ day of October 1852.

The conditions of the above bound are as follows: The above-bound SAMUEL PRIDE having sometime since been appointed Clerk & Master of the Chancery Court at Maryville, Tennessee, and the Legislature of Tennessee at its last session having passed an act regarding the Clerks of the different courts to give additional bonds have if the said SAMUEL PRIDE shall faithfully account and pay over all monies that have or hereafter come into his hands as commissioner by virtue of any order or decree made by the said Chancery Court to all the real and personal property

Pg. 3   belonging to any persons, as to the estate of any deceased person then shall the above bonds be void otherwise to remain in full force and effect.
(Signatures of the five men again)

Test: THOMAS L. WILLIAMS
...The condition of the above obligation is such that whereas the above-bonded SAMUEL PRIDE has this day been appointed Clerk & Master of the Chancery Court at Maryville for a period of six years... this -- of October 1852.

Pg. 4   He then took upon himself the Oath of Office and entered upon the discharge of the duties thereof. He took upon himself in open court at Maryville on the 14th day of February 1853 an oath to support the Constitution of the United States and of the State of Tennessee, the oath of office and the oath against duelling.

On Page 5 began the lawsuits filed in this newly-established Court of Record.

Pg. 5   SAMUEL HENRY Vs: CHARLOTTE KEYES & O. HEIRS of JOHN KEYES, Dec'd. Feb. 14, 1853. Time to file ans. by June term of court.

COFFIN & WILSON Vs: SAMUEL MCCULLY & O. Parties had compromised suit. Case removed from docket.

C. A. SAFFLE, Gdn. Heirs, petition for sale of lands. Feb. 14, 1853, SAFFLE, Gdn. of minor heirs of JOHN SAFFLE, Dec'd. Heirs: RICHARD M. SAFFLE, SARAH J. SAFFLE and ELIZABETH C. SAFFLE. Owned jointly with JAMES WILSON a tract of land of 5,000 acres. To make contract with JAMES H. GILLESPY to make evaluation.

Pg. 6   JAMES GRAY SMITH Vs: ANN JAMES. Feb. 14, 1853. Bill dismissed. JAMES M. TOOLE and RICHARD I. WILSON pay costs. All bills, all debts due, late.

Pg. 7   WILLIAM JAMES, Dec'd. now due and to be delivered over to Administratrix.

Pg. 8   State of Tennessee Chancery Court held at Courthouse Aug. 8, 1853.

CLEMENTINE A. SAFFLE, Gdn. - Make a report at next term of Court.

ASA AMBRISTER Vs: JAMES M. BRADFORD. Court of opinion demurrer not well-taken, is disallowed. Defdts. required to ans. before Oct. Term of Court.

JAMES GRAY SMITH Vs: ANN JAMES. JOHN E. TOOLE, Esq. took duties of Receiver. To pay pro-rata to creditors of the Maryville concern.

Pg. 9 B. D. BRABSON, THOMAS BRABSON & O. Petition to sell Town Lot. Petition signed by all heirs of JOHN BRABSON, Dec'd. in agreement to sell storehouse and town lot occupied by Major MCTEER and before death of widow of JOHN BRABSON, Dec'd. Court agrees to sale. Heirs have made an agreement with Major WILLIAM MCTEER.

HENRY BUSUM Vs: JAMES HENRY & JOHN F. HENRY & B. D. BRABSON. Dissolve the injunction granted in this cause. B. D. BRABSON permitted to collect his note.

PHILLIS by next friend, JOHN S. CRAIG Vs: JOSIAH D. PUGH & ALEX COOKE. Application by PUGH to take deposition of ALEX COOKE. Granted by Chancellor. PHILLIS be surrendered to JOSIAH D. PUGH. He giving Bond to C&M for $2,800.00.

Pg. 10 HENRY BUSUM Vs: J. & J. F. HENRY & B. D. BRABSON. Attempt to ascertain the value of the services of a Jack, on how many occasions, and report to Court.

C. W. NORWOOD & WIFE Vs: E. & I. W. GEORGE each & O. ROBERT A. TEDFORD is about to remove beyond limits of State. Granted right take deposition of TEDFORD.

Pg. 11 JAMES BERRIRE Vs: MCCLUNG STEELE & O. Aug. 8, 1853, MCCLUNG STEELE and HENRY C. SAFFLE Original vendor - HENRY C. SAFFLE. Sell lot. Pay first SAFFLE, next BERRIRE, then MCCLUNG STEELE.

Pg. 12 JOHN C. GALLAGER Vs: THOMAS J. BLANCHARD. Leave given to file ans. by Oct. Term Ct.

Pg. 13 Maryville, Feb. 13th 1854.
CLEMENTINE A. SAFFLE Vs: WILLIAM MCTEER & O. Asks permission to take deposition from Mrs. C. A. SAFFLE and testimony from TELL. BOOKER who is moving out of State.

ANN JAMES Vs: ROBERT JAMES. Seeks permission to file a Cross-Action.

PHILANCE PARKER Vs: M. C. PARKER. Case be dismissed.

Pg. 14 WILLIAM MCTEER Vs: JOHN T. SMOOT. Amended bill - SANDERS LEEPER now a party thereto.

J. GRAY SMITH Vs: ANN JAMES. Ordered that JOHN E. TOOLE, Receiver and Administrator Estate WILLIAM JAMES, Dec'd. pay to C&M monies collected in Maryville store to be paid out pro-rata to creditors of the Maryville concern.

SUSAN, a woman of color, by her friend JOHN GAMBLE Vs: JAMES PORTER & O. JAMES L. PORTER entitled to possession. Make bond of $200.00 restraining him from removing SUSAN from the limits of the State.

ASA AMBRISTER Vs: JAMES C. BRADFORD. Granted further time to take testimony.

SAMUEL HENRY Vs: CHARLOTTE KEYS & O. Permission to file a cross-bill.

PETER BUSUM Vs: HENRY BUSUM. Case dismissed.

Pg. 15 JAMES PRATER & O. Vs: A. ISH & WILLIAM PRATER, Ex. & Admr. & O. Amend bill. BENJAMIN PRATER a party.

F. HOLMAN & CO. Vs: JOHN L. SMOOT & SAUNDERS LEEPER. Permission to amend bill.

PHILLIS Vs: J. D. PUGH. Time granted to take further testimony and cross-examine SAMUEL JACKSON and retake testimony of JAMES and PENY STEPP.

B. D. BRABSON, THOMAS C. BRABSON & O. Petition to sell town lot in Maryville.

Pg. 16 Monday Nov. 27th, 1854. Chancellor not being in attendance, Court adjourned over until tomorrow. Nov. 28th, 1854.

ANN JAMES Vs: ROBERT JAMES. Suit revived in name of SAMUEL GHORMLY, husband of ANN GHORMLY, formerly ANN JAMES.

LORENZO DONALDSON & S. CUNNINGHAM Vs: MELINDA WATERS, JOHN & WILLIAM WATERS. Ordered that JOHN CLARK be appointed Gdn. minor heirs of E. L. WATERS, Dec'd.

PHILIS, by her friend JOHN S. CRAIG Vs: J. D. PUGH & A. COOK. Case cont'd.

Pg. 17 JAMES NEAL Vs: J. T. HARGIS. Respdt. has until Feb. to file his ans.

C. W. NORWOOD & WIFE Vs: EDWARD GEORGE & I. W. GEORGE & O. Permission to take deposition of ISAAC W. GEORGE one of the Respdts.

C. A. SAFFLE Vs: R. B. CLARK & O. Permission granted Respdt. FOSTER to take deposition of Respdt. CLARK & WILLIAM MCTEER'S ans. filed Nov. 25th, 1854, be received.

HUE WHITTENBURG Vs: A. C. WHITTENBURG. Permission to take testimony of WILLIAM M. BRICKEL, DANIEL WHITTENBURG and JOHN MYERS.

SUSAN, by her next friend, JOHN GAMBLE Vs: JAMES PORTER & O. Cause cont'd.

Pg. 18 F. HOLMAN & O. Vs: JOHN T. SMOOT & L. M. LEEPER. Permission to amend bill.

HUGH HENRY Vs: JOHN HENRY & SAMUEL HENRY. Death of JOHN HENRY admitted. Suit revived against JOHN HENRY, Dec'd. and SAMUEL PRIDE, Admr.

HENRY BUSUM Vs: JOHN F. & J. HENRY & B. D. BRABSON. Case continued.

JAMES GRAY SMITH Vs: ANN JAMES. Report of C&M confirmed in all things.

SAMUEL HENRY Vs: CHARLES KEYS & O. Continued.

Pg. 19 WILLIAM MCTEER Vs: JOHN T. SMOOT & S. M. LEEPER. Sheriff GILLESPY allowed to amend Return to Summons to conform with the facts.

B. D. BRABSON Vs: THOMAS BRABSON & O. To sell town lots. Heirs of JOHN BRABSON, Dec'd. made contract w/WILLIAM MCTEER. He to pay $1,600.00 for storehouse and town lot in Maryville, known as BRABSON'S Storehouse, formerly occupied by BERRY & FOUTE, JOHN BRABSON & CO., I. M. TOOLE & CO. and now occupied by Major MCTEER and to be paid as follows: $400.00 to BENJAMIN BRABSON on condition to sell said lot immediately and before the death of his mother, ELIZABETH BRABSON, wife and widow of JOHN BRABSON, Dec'd. Quote: "Item #22. My will is that my son, BENJAMIN D. BRABSON has the use and benefit of my houses, 7 lots in town of Maryville during lifetime of his mother and at her death, sold by executors and
Pg. 20 money divided among my 8 children: BENJAMIN D. BRABSON, BUSE P. BRABSON, PENELOPE C. BRABSON, JOHN S. MCNUTT and ELIZABETH MCNUTT, THOMAS
Pg. 21 BRABSON, ROBERT H. HODSDEN and MARY HODSDEN, MILTON SHIELDS and PRISCILLA SHIELDS, WILLIAM SCRUGGS and LUCY SCRUGGS, Heirs-at-Law."

JAMES PRATER & O. Vs: WILLIAM PRATER & A. ISH, Ex. of BENJAMIN TROTER. Dec'd. & O. Nov. 28, 1854.

Pg. 22 Division of land according to the Will. Apptd. THOMAS BOYD, JOHN GRIFFITS, HARLAN MATTHEWS and ISAAC D. WEAR to act as surveyors and rep't. next term Ct.

Pg. 23 JAMES M. TULLOCH, SAMUEL T. WOODS, Admr. of SAMUEL THOMPSON, Dec'd. Vs: SAMUEL B. THOMPSON, JAMES WOODS & O. Leave granted take deposition of SAMUEL T. WOODS. Nov. 29, 1854. All questions as to negro boy JIM in possession of SAMUEL B. THOMPSON reserved and parties allowed to take proof who said boy belonged at death of SAMUEL B. THOMPSON, Dec'd. and to his value. C&M determine what advancements made to heirs of Dec'd. prior to his death.

Pg. 24 JAMES BARNES Vs: MCCLUNG STEEL & O. Judge decrees that case be confirmed.

ALEX H. KEITH Vs: ASA WATSON, JAMES BELL & W. C. LILLARD. Leave given JAMES BELL to file a cross-bill.

Pg. 25 ASA AMBRISTER Vs: JAMES C. BRADFORD & WILL W. LAWRENCE. Nov. 29, 1854. Decreed sale of said negroes from BRADFORD to AMBRISTER be void for fraud - Note of $700.00 executed by AMBRISTER to BRADFORD void. BRADFORD to take back negroes from AMBRISTER house and AMBRISTER to deliver up note for sale of said negroes. Determine for Ct.:
1) What has been value of said negroes since they came into Complnt's. possession?
2) Expenses Complnt. incurred keeping the negroes when sick, BRADFORD to pay all costs of case?
T. NIXON VAN DYKE, Chancellor.

Pg. 26 Monday, May 28th, 1855. Chancellor not present. Adjourned until May 29th.

ROBERT JAMES Vs: SAMUEL & ANN GHORMLY, Admr. & O. Leave given Complnt. to amend bill.

JAMES M. TULLOCH & SAMUEL F. WOODS, Admr. & O. of SAMUEL THOMPSON. Dec'd. Vs: SAMUEL B. THOMPSON, Dec'd. Admx. and heirs of SAMUEL B. THOMPSON, Dec'd. order that C&M take and state an account as previously ordered. State value of boy, JIM, at time he was received by SAMUEL B. THOMPSON as well as at time of death of dec'd.

JAMES H. GILLESPY, Ex. Vs: WILL WALLACE & O. Leave granted Complnt. amend bill and account ordered to be taken.

BLANCHARD & VINSANT Vs: SAMUEL T. BICKNELL. Leave granted Respdt. to file ans.

R. L. CATE, Trustee Vs: JAMES WILSON & O. Mrs. SAFFLE and T. C. DEARMOND granted two months to file ans.

Pg. 27 HUGH HENRY of HUGH Vs: SAMUEL & JOHN HENRY. Two months granted SAMUEL PRIDE, Admr. of JOHN HENRY, Dec'd. to file Defense.

C. A. SAFFLE Vs: R. B. CLARK & O. Clark has time to file ans. Parties have five months to start testimony.

C. W. NORWOOD & WIFE Vs: I. W. & E. GEORGE, Extr. & O. C&M to take account:
1) What amts. came into hands of I. EDWARD and ISAAC W. GEORGE as Extrs. of SAMUEL GEORGE, Dec'd., and time rec'd.?
2) What amts. were dispersed and to whom?
3) What amt. pd. to widow or rec'd. by her from estate of her husband SAMUEL GEORGE, Dec'd.?
4) What amt. of property and money was, or should have been rec'd. as Admr. for BARBARY GEORGE?
5) What amt. paid debts of BARBARY GEORGE?
6) What amts. distributed to each heir and legatee in accordance with Will of said SAMUEL GEORGE, Dec'd.?

Pg. 28 C&M to report what amt. due Complnt. MALINDA NORWOOD and balance of Heirs and Legatees.

JAMES PRATER & O. Vs: A. ISH & W. PRATER, Ex. of B. PRATER, Dec'd. Time given to report C&M.

HENRY BUSUM Vs: J. & J. F. HENRY & B. D. BRABSON. Case cont'd.

I. GRAY SMITH Vs: ANN JAMES. Case cont'd.

JAMES BARNES Vs: M. STEELE & O. Titles to be made purchasers when money pd.

PHILIS, by next friend, JOHN S. CRAIG Vs: J. D. PUGH & O. Case cont'd.

Pg. 29 SAMUEL & ANN GHORMLY Vs: ROBERT JAMES & O. Cont'd. for 5 mos.

WILLIAM PRESSLEY Vs: J. & J. F. HENRY. Asks permission to amend Bill.

SAMUEL PRIDE, Admr. of JOHN HENRY, Dec'd. Vs: WILLIAM MCTEER & O. Motion to to dismiss Bill. Motion overruled by Ct.

ELI NUNN, Admr. Vs: JOHN E. TOOLE, Trustee & O. Complnt. entitled to relief. Title to said negroes divested from Respdt. and rested in Complnt. as personal rep. of ELIZABETH, Dec'd. and Respdt. be relieved of liability on account of his Trust upon payment of balance. The marriage contract be declared at an end. C&M give acct. of monies handled.

Pg. 30   JOHN R. HAYS Vs: JOHN MCCLAIN, Admr. & O. Respdt. required to rely on amends for defense.

WILLIAM MCTEER Vs: JOHN T. SMOOT & S. M. LEEPER. Bill of Complnt. MCTEER dismissed at his cost. Respdt. SMOOT having left for parts unknown.

B. D. and T. C. BRABSON, Ex parte Extr. of JOHN BRABSON, Dec'd. Rep't. confirmed. Purchaser MCTEER to pay all costs.

JAMES ANDERSON, Extr. & C. Vs: ABIJAH W. EMMETT. Respdt. given 2 mos. to file ans.

Pg. 31   JAMES PRATER & O. Vs: A. ISH & W. PRATER, Extr. of B. PRATER, Dec'd. May 30, 1855. Loan-out money on hand for 6 mos. at 6% interest.

LORENZO DONALDSON & SARAH CUNNINGHAM Vs: MATILDA WATERS. Complnts. entitled relief. LORENZO entitled to, and is owner of, remainder of tract of Land mentioned in Bill after 100 A. is struck off to Widow and Heirs of said E. L. WATERS, Dec'd. to wit: MATILDA WATERS, JOHN WATERS and WILLIAM WATERS.

F. POPE, PORTER MCCULLOCH and WILLIAM MCTEER, SR. Appointed Comm'rs. to divide said land. 100 A. to said Widow & Heirs on end next to JOHN MCCULLOCH. Make Plat. Complnt. DONALDSON pay all costs.

SAMUEL & ANN GHORMLY & O. Vs: ROBERT JAMES & O. Petition - ROBERT JAMES enter as Defdt. with all rights of other Defdts.

Pg. 32 ROBERT JAMES Vs: SAMUEL & ANN GHORMLY, Admrs. Two mos. to file ans.

HENRY WHITTENBURGER Vs: AMBROSE C. WHITTENBURGER. A. C. WHITTENBURGER rec'd. land in Deed as Vendor and understood to perform conditions mentioned in Deed. Respdt. is bound to support and maintain Complnt. and Wife during their lifetime and land conveyed by said Deed bound in Equity for support of said HENRY and his Wife. A. C. WHITTENBURGER ordered to perform conditions of Contract. C&M determine value of land and products. i.e. Worth per annum to support HENRY and Wife decently.
1) What amt. has A. C. WHITTENBURGER furnished toward that support?
2) What amt. due HENRY and Wife to date?
Rep't. next term of Ct. AMBROSE WHITTENBURGER to pay all costs of Ct.

Pg. 33 ASA AMBRISTER Vs: JAMES C. BRADFORD & W. W. LAWRENCE. May 30, 1855. Complnt. AMBRISTER recover from BRADFORD $600.00 with add'l. sum of $77.40, 6% interest, since money was paid to BRADFORD and the $188.91, the amt. C&M reports at this time, in all $866.38 & BRADFORD to pay all costs.

Pg. 34 PETER GIBSON Vs: JOHN GAULT & H. H. CARUTHERS Extr. & C. Wednesday, May 31, 1855. MARGARET STERLING departed this life at time alleged in Complnt's. Bill having published her last Will & Test. bequeathing a part of Estate to synod of church she belonged to. That part of Estate in hands of JOHN GAULT & H. H. CARUTHERS, $326.00. Appears to satisfaction of Ct. that PETER GIBSON, GAVIN MCMILLAN, THOMAS FLOVEL, JAMES COOK, JAMES C. MCMILLAN, ALEX WEIR, ROBERT REID, HUGH MCMILLAN, JOHN ORR, Trustees of the Western Literary and Theological Seminary of Reformed Presbyterian Church is Inc. and made by Laws of State of Ohio, a body politic and corporate and authorized to recover the bequest. Respdt. JOHN GAULT and H. H. CARUTHERS, Ex. of said MARGARET, Dec'd. money be paid to C&M to forward to Seminary. Sum of $30.00 to J. I. WRIGHT & W. L. EKIN as fees for services and council.

Pg. 35   SUSAN, b/n/f/JOHN GAMBLE Vs: JAMES L. PORTER. Continued by consent of parties.

SAMUEL HENRY Vs: MARGERY KEYS & O. Continued by consent of parties.

SAMUEL & ANN GHORMLY by Admrs. & C. (Insolvent Bills) Vs: ROBERT JAMES & O. In this case THOMAS JAMES, ISOBEL JAMES, ROBERT SHEPHERD and WIFE are made parties and have until next term of Ct. to file ans.

JAMES M. TULLOCH & SAMUEL TULLOCH, Admrs. & O. Vs: SAMUEL B. THOMPSON & O. Testimony of JOHN RIDER, Respdt. and SAMUEL G. WORD, Complnt. be taken in this case.

Pg. 36   J. C. GALLAGHER Vs: THOMAS J. BLANCHARD. Wed. May 30, 1855. Desires C&M take and state an acc't. between parties showing:
1) What amt. of partnership came into hands of each?
2) What each got separately?
3) What dispersements were made?
4) What amt. of tools, labor or money furnished by each to benefit firm and balance remaining?

ALEXANDER H. KEITH Vs: JAMES BELL, IRA WATSON, WILLIAM C. LILLARD & JAMES BELL Vs: ALEXANDER H. KEITH, IRA WATSON & W. C. LILLARD. Bill and Cross-Bill.

Pg. 37   Aug. 23, 1853. WILLIAM C. LILLARD bought of JAMES BELL his lease of Montvale Springs in Blount County and executed obligations for $1,000.00 to BELL signed by ALEX H. KEITH as Security. On Nov. 25, 1853, IRA WATSON entered an agreement with W. C. LILLARD in writing "that the said WATSON shall release to said LILLARD from lease he purchased from JAMES BELL on Montvale Springs property. WATSON receiving the old
Pg. 38   furniture that was rec'd. from BELL. WATSON has paid BELL $1,000.00. WATSON further agreed to assume

payments of promissory notes of $1,000.00 each. Oct. 10th, 1854, and Oct. 10th, 1855. JAMES BELL to recover of ALEXANDER KEITH, IRA WATSON and W. C. LILLARD $2,135.00, two notes plus interest. ALEXANDER KEITH to recover of IRA WATSON $2,135.00, the amt. of decree in favor of said BELL. Respdt. WATSON to pay all costs of suit-at-law in Kingston in the Circuit Court.

JAMES H. GILLESPY Vs: HEIRS of MATTHEW WALLACE, Dec'd. C&M make an account and report cash value of boy, JEFFERSON, mentioned in the pleadings.

Pg. 39   JAMES NEIL Vs: JOHN T. HARGUS. May 30, 1855. Misunderstanding in area of land purchased. Complnt. entitled to relief and to have title to that part of land divided out of Respdt. and vested to Complnt. and Heirs upon said sum of money paid.

Pg. 40   JAMES H. GILLESPY, Ex. & O. Vs: HEIRS of MATTHEW WALLACE, Dec'd. Last Will & Test. of MATTHEW WALLACE, Dec'd. boy, JEFFERSON, to be sold by Ex. at public or private sale. If sold for less than $800.00 at private sale take bond and security for purchase money and retain lien on boy until purchase money pd. Ct. asks:
1) Who were the original heirs of Legatee under said Will?
2) Who, if any, are dead who have died intestate?
3) Who are the minors, if any, who are the present legatees and distributees under Will?
4) What amt. of funds has come to the Ex., and what amt. been dispersed and to whom?

Pg. 41   Nov. 27th, 1855. L. DONALDSON & O. Vs: MATILDA WATERS & HEIRS. Report of Comm'rs., all things being undisputed to, were confirmed and case referred to the Rules to take acc't.

HENRY WHITTENBURGER Vs: A. C. WHITTENBURGER. The parties had settled all matters of dispute. Cont'd. to next term of Ct. Parties to present terms of settlement.

Pg. 42   SAMUEL PRIDE, Admr. of JOHN HENRY, Dec'd. Vs: WILLIAM MCTEER & O. Respdt. be required to make report as Rec'vr. at next term of Ct.

N. S. PECK & O. Vs: JAMES A. AIKEN. Cause cont'd.

ELI NUNN, Admr. Vs: JOHN E. TOOLE, Trustee. Upon rep't. of C&M, all things confirmed.

HENRY BUSUM Vs: J. & J. F. HENRY & O. Trial cont'd. due to absence of Respdt.

JOHN C. GALLAHER Vs: THOMAS J. BLANCHARD. Cont'd. to next term of Ct.

Pg. 43 C. A. SAFFLE Vs: ROBERT CLARK & O. Cont'd. to next term of Ct.

JAMES NEAL Vs: JOHN T. HARGUS. Ordered that same be confirmed in all things.

PHILLIS, a woman of color, b/n/f/J. S. CRAIG Vs: JOSIAH D. PUGH & A. COOK. Case cont'd. due to absence of Complnt's. Sol.

SUSAN, a woman of color, b/n/f/JOHN GAMBLE Vs: JAMES PORTER & O. Nov. 29, 1855. It appears to Ct., A. B. GAMBLE had no title to Complnt. to causing? ALLEN GARNER but title to her was in Respdt. JAMES MCCONNEL and that in her husband's carry-over to JAMES PORTER giving him title to Complnt. It is ordered that Complnt's. bill be dismissed and JOHN GAMBLE n/f/and ANDREW CRISWELL, his Security, pay costs.

Pg. 44 JAMES H. GILLESPY, Ex. of M. WALLACE, Dec'd. Vs: Legatees of Dec'd. WALLACE. Nov. 28, 1855. Aug. 4, 1855, Ex. sold slave, JEFFERSON, to JAMES M. TOOLE, for $1.000.00 on credit of 9 mos. w/int. and rec'd. note of J. M. TOOLE, WILLIAM TOOLE and JOHN E. TOOLE as Securities. All rights and title which Legatees of MATTHEW WALLACE had in said slave be divested out of them and vested in JAMES M. TOOLE, forever. Funds to be pd. to C&M for distribution to heirs. Rep't. to next term of Ct. amt. of settlements.

Pg. 45 JOSEPH MISER, Admr. Vs: MICHAEL & P. M. BOWERMAN. Compromise settlement read in Ct. Parties met at House of WILLIAM BRICKELL. After mature consideration and compromise and peace to wit: P. M. BOWER-

Pg. 46 MAN pay to JOSEPH MISER, Admr., $150.00 and release JOSEPH and Estate of GEORGE MISER, SR., Dec'd. from any and all claims and that title to the 4 slaves mentioned in the Bill in this case be settled forever. Be vested into P. M. BOWERMAN and his Heirs forever. BOWERMAN pay 1/2 costs, JOSEPH MISER the other 1/2. GEORGE MISER, Dec'd. Four slaves: DAVIS, PLEASANT, ABBY and LUCRETIA be divested in said PLEASANT M. BOWERMAN forever.

JAMES PRATER, BENJAMIN PRATER, HUGH PRATER & LAFAYETTE PRATER Vs: WILLIAM PRATER & ALEXANDER ISH in their own right & as Ex. of Last Will & Test. of BENJAMIN PRATER, Dec'd. ELIZABETH ISH, DANIEL D. BERRY and LETTITIA BERRY, GEORGE W. PRATER, JOSIAH K. JOHNSON and CLARISSA JOHNSON, NANCY GILBERT, BENJAMIN F. PRATER, JAMES PRATER, JOHN PRATER AND WILLIAM PRATER. Nov. 28, 1855.

Pg. 47 To make division of lands. ISAAC D. WEAR did not act as one of Comm'rs. and WILLIAM L. HEADRICK acted with other members of Commission. Surveyed. HEADRICK is Public Surveyor for the County of Roane. "We divided the lands according to the Will of BENJAMIN PRATER, Dec'd. into 7 lots drawn as follows, to wit: Lot #1 was drawn by the heirs of THOMAS PRATER, Dec'd. and is bounded on Bank of Holston River 174 A. Lot #2 drawn by CLARISSA JOHNSON, wife of JOSIAH JOHNSON... is bounded... on

Pg. 48 river bank containing 247 1/2 A. Lot #3 drawn by LETTITIA BERRY, wife of ----- BERRY, formerly LETTITIA DANFORTH and is bounded by... bank of river and Ferry Road containing 219 3/4 A. Lot #4 was drawn by SAMUEL PRATER, Dec'd. Heirs, bounded on bank of

Pg. 49 Holston River containing 143 3/4 A. Lot #5 drawn by WILLIAM PRATER... bounded... bank of river... containing 406 A. Lot #6 was drawn by ELIZABETH ISH, wife of ALEXANDER ISH, bounded by... bank of river containing 459 1/2 A., also an island of 8 A. belonging to Lot #6, and known as Cove Island. Lot #7 drawn by GEORGE

Pg. 50 PRATER bounded... bank of river containing 253 1/2 A. Also Lot #7 contains an island of 30 A. known as Booth Island. Witness: THOMAS BOYD, JOHN GRIFFITH, JAMES GRIFFITS, HARLEN MATTHEWS, WILL L. HEADRICK, Surveyor. Lot #1 from BENJAMIN PRATER, Dec'd. to Heirs of THOMAS PRATER, Dec'd., to wit: NANCY

GILBERT, BENJAMIN F. PRATER, JAMES PRATER, JOHN PRATER and WILLIAM PRATER and their heirs and assigns, forever. Lot #2 from BENJAMIN PRATER, Dec'd. to be vested in CLARISSA JOHNSON, her heirs and assigns forever.

Pg. 51   Lot #3 from BENJAMIN PRATER, Dec'd. to LETTETIA BERRY, her heirs and assigns, forever. Lot #4 from BENJAMIN PRATER, Dec'd. to SAMUEL PRATER, Dec'd. to wit: JAMES PRATER, BENJAMIN PRATER, HUGH PRATER & LAFAYETTE PRATER, their Heirs and assigns forever. Lot #5 from BENJAMIN PRATER, Dec'd. to WILLIAM PRATER, his heirs and assigns forever. Lot #6 from BENJAMIN PRATER, Dec'd. to ELIZABETH ISH, her heirs and assigns forever. Lot #7 from BENJAMIN PRATER. Dec'd. to GEORGE W. PRATER his heirs and assigns forever.

Pg. 52   It is ordered that the foregoing portion of this Decree for Registration in the County of Roane in which said County the said lands lie. The gross aggregate of the Personal Estate to be distributed in money, debts, rents, proceeds of sales. The death of GEORGE S. GILBERT is admitted and the suit as to him abates.

Pg. 53   JAMES G. SMITH Vs: ANN JAMES, Admx. Nov. 28, 1855. The Recv'r. to make full rep't. to C&M what rec'd., what paid out. Clerk will rep't. debts due from Maryville concern with names of creditors and amt. of their claims. Nothing further to be pd. until other creditors of concern shall have rec'd. an equal share. Clerk will pay out to creditors upon this principle.

Pg. 54   WILLIAM MORTON Vs: JOHN MORTON, Ex. & O. In 1852 WILLIAM MORTON, the Elder, died in Blount County having made his last Will & Test., appt'd. JOHN MORTON, his Extr. No settlement to date. C&M to take and state an acc't. If settlement of Extr. made with Clerk of C. C. this suit will be disregarded.

SAMUEL PRIDE, Admr. JOHN HENRY, Dec'd. Vs: WILLIAM MCTEER & O. WILLIAM MCTEER acts as Recv'r. Rep't. next term Ct. What effects of the firms: MCTEER, PRIDE & HENRY and MCTEER, HENRY & CO. came into his hands, or were in his hands at time of filing of this Bill?

Goods, Debts, Account Monies, and disposition of same. WILLIAM A. WALKER appt'd. a Spec. Comm'r. to show:
1) Stock vested in businesses.
2) Profits and Debts.

Pg. 55 ELI NUNN, Admr. of MARTHA E. NUNN Vs: JOHN E. TOOLE, Trustee. Trust funds in hands of Trustee has been disposed of and distributed leaving bal. of $46.71 for Trustee for Services and Ct. Costs.

Pg. 56 JAMES NEAL Vs: JOHN T. HARGUS. The Title to the undivided half of the tract of land lying in the 1st Civil District Blount County on waters of Nine Mile Creek - a tract granted by State of Tennessee to IBIJAH CONGER - 150 A. bounded by MATTHEW HOUSTON'S land known as the Old Forge Place then joining land formerly owned by MATTHEW MCGHEE to a stake w/CHRISTIAN BEST entry thence to HUFFSTETLER line - thence to vacant land and then DOWNEY'S entry. Offered $47.85 for the land. If not purchased in 2 mos. to be sold by C&M at Public Sale.

Pg. 57 C. W. NORWOOD & wife Vs: E. & I. W. GEORGE, Ex. & C. Case cont'd.

JOHN R. HAYS Vs: JOHN MCCLAIN, Admr. Cause remanded to the Rules and action dissolved by Respdt. giving bond with security to refund.

PHILLIS, b/n/f/JOHN S. CRAIG Vs: J. D. PUGH & O. Case cont'd.

BLANCHARD & VINSANT Vs: JAMES T. BICKNELL. Leave given Respdt. to file ans.

ROBERT JAMES Vs: ANN GHORMLY. Judgement set aside and leave given to file ans.

Pg. 58 SAMUEL HENRY Vs: CHARLOTTA KEYS & O. Cause cont'd.

JAMES M. TULLOCH & SAMUEL WOODS, Adm. & C. Vs: HEIRS of SAMUEL THOMPSON, Dec'd. Suit is revived against JOHN E. TOOLE, Admr. of LEROY F. THOMPSON.

Pg. 59   JAMES M. TULLOCH & SAM T. WOODS, Admrs. of SAMUEL THOMPSON, Dec'd. Vs: SAMUEL THOMPSON, Dec'd. The Dec'd. had given to his heirs in his lifetime, to wit: JUNE WOODS had been advanced $125.00. NANCY THOMPSON, $125.00. MARY A. HALL, $125.00. JOHN RIDER, husband of DORCUS THOMPSON, $125.00. WILLIAM N. THOMPSON, $125.00. SAMUEL B. THOMPSON, $130.00 and negro boy, JIM, of the value of $350.00 at time of advancement. LEROY T. THOMPSON, $500.00. Ordered by the Ct. that said heirs be charged respectively with the sums advanced. Ct. orders remainder of distribution of estate be made equally.

SAMUEL & ANN GHORMLY, Admrs. of WILLIAM JAMES, Dec'd. Vs: ROBERT JAMES & O. ROBERT JAMES & O. Vs: ANN & SAMUEL GHORMLY, Admrs. of WILLIAM JAMES, Dec'd. Testimony taken in either case shall be read in evidence in all causes between parties. Petition of HYATT MCBURNEY & CO., LANNICAN & BRICKMYER filed this day.

Pg. 60   SUSAN, a woman of color, b/n/f/JOHN GAMBLE Vs: JAMES PORTER & MOSES MCCONNELL & HIS WIFE, JANE. Complnt. by her council excepted to reading of deposition of Respdt. MOSES MCCONNELL and his wife, JANE MCCONNELL for incompetency of the witnesses and because they were Defdts., which objection was allowed. Complnt. may appeal to next term of Supreme Ct. in Knoxville, Tenn. second Mon. of Sept. next.

Pg. 61   R. L. CATES, TRUSTEE & O. Vs: JAMES WILSON & O. Nov. 29, 1855. Respdt. WILSON to admit Ans. of C. A. SAFFLE, Gdn., contains a true statement of facts. Respdt. DEARMOND not pay compound Int. and that JAMES WILSON assign of said DEARMOND is entitled to residue of said funds in hands of Complnt. CATES. SAFFELL appealed to next term Ct. to be held in Knoxville in Sept. Appeal granted.

Pg. 62   Circuit Court, January Term 1856. Feb. 1, 1856, Ct. was opened by Hon. E. ALEXANDER, presiding.

N. S. PECK Vs: JAMES M. AIKEN & O. This case came up for consideration w/E. ALEXANDER presiding it having been certified to the Circuit Judge on acc't. of the incompetency of the Hon. Chancellor of this Division. Plaintiff has leave to amend his Bill and costs of amendment reserved for future consideration of Ct. Cause remanded to the Rules for taking testimony and depositions.

Pg. 63 No entries on this page.

Pg. 64 May 26, 1856. Chancery Ct. opened. Hon. Chancellor LUCKERY presiding. (SETH W. LUCKY)

C. A. SAFFLE, Ex Parte. Case cont'd.

SAMUEL HENRY Vs: CHARLOTTA KEYS & O. Cause cont'd.

C. W. & M. NORWOOD Vs: E. & I. W. GEORGE, Ex. Complnt. MATILDA NORWOOD indisposed. Her testimony has not been taken. Case cont'd.

BLANCHARD & VINSANT Vs: SAMUEL BICKNELL. Respdt. allowed 2 mos. to file Cross-Bill.

H. C. SAFFLE & BRO. Vs: WILLIAM MCTEER. Leave granted Respdt. to file ans.

JEREMIAH DOTSON Vs: JOHN EVERETT. Leave granted Respdt. to file ans.

Pg. 65 F. H. HOLMAN Vs: JOHN T. SMOOT & S. LEEPER. Cause remanded to Rules.

SAMUEL & ANN GHORMLY, Admrs. Vs: ROBERT JAMES. Cause remanded to Rules.

SAMUEL PRIDE, Admr. JOHN HENRY, Dec'd. Vs: WILLIAM MCTEER. Cause cont'd.

JOHN HAYS Vs: JOHN MCCLAIN, Admr. of SAMUEL DOUTHETT. Death of Respdt. admitted.

Pg. 66 WILLIAM MCTEER Vs: WILLIAM M. & J. STEELE. Parties compromised - agreed to dismiss suit.

HENRY WHITTENBERGER Vs: A. C. WHITTENBERGER. Matter had been compromised.

SAMUEL & ANN GHORMLY, Admrs. WILLIAM JAMES, Dec'd. Vs: ROBERT JAMES. Ordered that Complnt. give Security for prosecution of this suit.

Pg. 67 HENRY BUSUM Vs: J. & J. F. HENRY. May 27, 1856. Judge is of opinion that Complnt. and Respdts. in early season of 1847 stood the Jack "General Taylor," named in pleading in partnership. (Difficulties developed - cost of maintenance, fees for service, who retained same. Ct. requests information as to situation prior to July 15, 1847, and following that date.) Long detailed proceedings condensed in parentheses.

Pg. 68 LORENZO DONALDSON & SARAH CUNNINGHAM Vs: MATILDA WATERS, JOHN WATERS & WILLIAM WATERS, Heirs-at-Law of E. L. WATERS, Dec'd. REV. F. POPE, Surveyor, R. P. MCCULLOCH & WILLIAM MCTEER, SR. appt'd. to divide land. Laid off to L. DONALDSON, 100 A. bounded by JOHN MCCULLOCH, J. BLACK, corner to BLACK and CHANDLER, corner to CHANDLER and ROGERS then PORTER MCCULLOCH. Land divested out of E. L. WATERS, Dec'd. and into L. D. DONALDSON and Heirs, forever. Widow and Heirs are: MATILDA WATERS, JOHN WATERS and WILLIAM WATERS.

WILLIAM MORTON Vs: JOHN MORTON, Ex. & O. May 29, 1856. Sale of land necessary for division. Complnt. allowed to introduce proof of rents of land for 1853-1854.

Pg. 70 JAMES NEAL Vs: JOHN T. HARGUS. Land sold at Courthouse door on Mar. 29, 1856. JOHN E. TOOLE and WILLIAM D. MCGINLEY became purchasers, for $130.00. Land divested from Respdt. HARGIS and Complnt. NEAL and vested in JOHN E. TOOLE and W. D. MCGINLEY.

Pg. 71 JAMES BONHAM Vs: EPHRAIM LINK. To file a paper - a Certificate of JAMES W. CAMPBELL, Clerk of District Ct. of the U.S. for Eastern Div. of Tennessee. Filed as Exhibit "C".

PHILIS, a woman of color, b/n/f/JOHN S. CRAIG Vs: J. D. PUGH & A. COOK. Complnt. not entitled to relief she seeks. She is neither free nor in-law entitled to be free. Bill dismissed - each party paying own costs. No amt.

allowed Respdt. for hire of negro pending suit.

Pg. 72 CLEMENTINE A. SAFFELL Vs: WILLIAM MCTEER, FOSTER & PIERCE & ROBERT B. CLARK. Final Decree, May 29, 1856. Respdt. CLARK undertook brickwork on dwelling house, for Complnt. CLARK embarassed w/debt. Respdt. MCTEER lent him money and materials.
Pg. 73 MCTEER asked for lien in writing. CLARK confessed a Judgement to Respdt. FOSTER. Garnishment served on Complnt., determine what CLARK due. Complnt. not credited by CLARK w/amt. debt due FOSTER & PIERCE, CLARK removed to Illinois. CLARK sent bill owed by Complnt. to FOSTER & PIERCE for their collection from Complnt. MCTEER insisting on balance of $131.40 due
Pg. 74 him. Complnt. to pay MCTEER. Costs to be paid by HORACE FOSTER. FOSTER & PIERCE appeal to next term of Supreme Ct. in Knoxville Sept. next.

Pg. 75 JAMES PRATER & O. Vs: ALEX ISH, Ex. & O. May 28, 1856. Since last Ct., WILLIAM PRATER has departed this life. HUGH B. LEEPER and MARY PRATER appt'd. Admr. and Admx. Financial considerations. Chancellor has
Pg. 76 found aggregate of Estate to be $41,476.33. After expenses - for distribution among Legatees - $36,200.64, giving to each $5,171.66 Heirs of THOMAS PRATER,
Pg. 77 Dec'd. w/interest $5,018.70. J. K. JOHNSON rec'd. $5,151.50. LETITIA BERRY rec'd. $4,946.00. GEORGE W. PRATER rec'd. $5,575.00 - which is over and above his share and he must account to executors. WILLIAM PRATER $4,985.39 which leaves due his estate $186.28. ALEXANDER ISH $4,940.00 leaves him due the sum of $231.66.

Pg. 78 JAMES M. TULLOCH & SAMUEL T. WOODS, Admr. Vs: Heirs of SAMUEL THOMPSON, Dec'd. Total amt. of Estate- $11,659.91. Balance for distribution - $4,084.90. To JANE WOODS $125.00, NANCY THOMPSON $125.00, MARY A. HALL $125.00, JOHN RIDER $125.00, WILLIAM
Pg. 79 N. THOMPSON $125.00, SAMUEL B. THOMPSON
Pg. 80 $130.00 plus negro boy $350.00, LEROY THOMPSON $500.00. $1605.00 had been advanced to Legatees. (Two add'l. lists of dispersements to these heirs were given.)

Pg. 81 HUGH HENRY, JR. Vs: SAMUEL PRIDE, Admr. THOMAS HENRY, Dec'd. & SAMUEL HENRY. Clerk authorized to take testimony of SAMUEL HENRY, Respdt. Chancellor requests C&M to state amt. of Estate which came into his hands.

Pg. 82   A. ISH, JESSE KERR & O. Vs: KNOXVILLE & CHARLESTON R.R. CO. 4 mos. to file ans.

MOSES GAMBLE & O. Vs: E. NUNN & O. Time granted to file ans.

C. W. NORWOOD & WIFE Vs: E. &. I. W. GEORGE, Ex. & O. WILLIAM JOHNSON and wife, AMANDA JOHNSON, Leave given to file Cross-Bill.

Pg. 83   JAMES BARNES Vs: MCCLUNG STEEL & O. Final Decree. Lot purchase money pd. BARNES directed title be vested in ALEXANDER KENNEDY. Lot on Main St. divested out of WILEY MCDONALD, F. MCDONALD and MCCLUNG STEEL and be vested in ALEXANDER KENNEDY and his Heirs forever.

J. GRAY SMITH Vs: ANN JAMES, Admr. C&M to distribute funds in his hands.

Pg. 84   WILLIAM MORTON Vs: JOHN MORTON Ex. & C. Chancellor of opinion H. MAYNARD, Sol. for Complnt., have fee out of money coming. Ordered $25.00 be pd. Sol.

JOHN ALEXANDER & O. Vs: ANDREW FURGUSON. Leave given Respdt. to file ans.

JAMES S. BONHAM Vs: EPHRAIM LINK. Injunction dissolved. Respdt. permitted to proceed to judgement if he desires. Shall file with C&M.

Pg. 85   C. W. NORWOOD & WIFE Vs: E. &. I. W. GEORGE. WILLIAM JOHNSON and wife, AMANDA, allowed to answer Bill and introduce other issues. Proceed to take proof.

JOHN R. HAYS Vs: JOHN MCCLAIN, Admr. Allowed to revive this case, agnst. ANDREW MCCLAIN and ALEXANDER MCCLAIN, Admrs. of said JOHN MCCLAIN and also agnst. the Admr. *de bonus nom* of SAMUEL DOUTHET, Dec'd.

Pg. 86 JAMES H. GILLESPY, Ex. & C. Vs: HEIRS of MATTHEW WALLACE, Dec'd. Extr. has $4,827.18 subject to deduction of $300.00 - reasonable compensation for his services. Extr. pd. JESSE WALLACE, one of Legatees, $295.00, and has paid to C&M $1,048.66, the amt. purchase money for boy, JEFF, sold by order of Ct. w/interest. Tract of land and town Lots #44 and #45 to be sold at public auction to highest bidder.

BLANCHARD & VINSANT Vs: J. T. BICKNELL. Leave granted Respdt. file Cross Bill.

Pg. 87 N. S. PECK & O. Vs: JAMES AIKIN & O. Leave granted Respdts. to file Ans.

R. I. WILSON Vs: WILLIAM MCTEER & O. Injunction dissolved. Requested actions not taken.

JAMES ANDERSON, Admr. Vs: ABIJAH EVERETT. Case remanded to Rules for taking testimony.

Pg. 88 Nov. 24, 1856. Chancellor VAN DYKE presiding.
JOHN ALEXANDER Vs: ANDREW FERGUSON. Case cont'd. and remanded to Rules for testimony.

C. A. SAFFELL, Executor Partition - to use in this case Dr. JAMES H. GILLESPY, pay all costs and it is dismissed by Petition.

SAMUEL & ANN GHORMLY, Admrs. Ex. WILLIAM JAMES, Dec'd. Vs: ROBERT JAMES. Cont'd. and remanded to Rules.

C. W. NORWOOD & WIFE Vs: E. &. I. W. GEORGE, ex. us. Cont'd. and remanded to Rules.

WILLIAM PRESSLEY Vs: J. &. J. F. HENRY & O. Case cont'd. by consent of parties.

Pg. 89 ASA AMBRISTER Vs: ALEX KENNEDY. Complnt. ordered to file terms of compromise.

DAVID KEY & O. Vs: H. T. COX & O. Complnt. compromised w/Defdt. Received sum of $22.07 in full out of his claim agnst. H. T. COX and PETER KEY, Extrs. Estate of PETER KEY, Dec'd.

HUGH HENRY Vs: SAMUEL PRIDE, Admr. JOHN HENRY, Dec'd. Previous order revived and case remanded to the Rules.

Pg. 90 J. H. BONHAM Vs: EPHRAIM LINK. Cause cont'd.

JOHN EVERETT Vs: JAMES HENRY. Leave given to file Ans.

R. L. CATES Vs: T. G. DEARMOND, C. A. SAFFELL & O. The Judgement of the Supreme Ct. affirming the decree of this Ct. C&M proceed to take an account ordered.

H. C. SAFFLE & BRO. Vs: WILLIAM MCTEER. Leave granted to file his ans.

H. HARTZELL & J. G. WALLACE Vs: the HEIRS of G. S. GILBERTS LOTTY?. Permission granted WILLIAM A. WALKER to file his claims against Estate of G. S. GILBERT and A. L. and S. GILBERT.

Pg. 91 ALEXANDER ISH & O. Vs: KNOXVILLE & CHARLESTON R.R. & CHAIRMAN OF C. C. OF BLOUNT COUNTY. Defdt. has 10 days to file Ans. Process of Subpoena to answer issue to STEPHEN J. MCREYNOLDS, County Judge for County of Blount.

Pg. 92 F. HOLMAN & CO. Vs: SAUNDERS M. LEEPER & JOHN T. SMOOT. Nov. 24, 1856. Complnt. Bill be dismissed and Respdt. recover of FRANCIS HOLMAN and JOSEPH WHEELER and HORACE MAYNARD their Security all costs of this cause.

JEREMIAH DOTSON Vs: JOHN EVERETT. Complnt. paid Respdt. money for a town lot. Respdt. did not sign over title. Complnt. entitled to title. Respdt. has no rights to rents or profits of said lot. Lot situated in Louisville - adjoining lot of JAMES WILSON and known as Lot #5 in street leading from FOSTER'S Brick Shop to Holston River. Vested out of JOHN EVERETT into JEREMIAH DOTSON and heirs forever.

Pg. 93 HENRY BUSUM Vs: J. & J. F. HENRY & O. Set aside earlier report. Determine number of Jennies and Mares were put to Jack while in posseslon of Complnt. and price.
1) What amt. of money and property rec'd. for services?
Pg. 94 2) What amt. of money rec'd. by Respdt. for services during this time?
3) Cost of maintaining Jack. Ascertain what amt., if anything, Complnt. due for keeping Jack after expiration of season?

SAMUEL PRIDE, Admr. JOHN HENRY Vs: WILLIAM MCTEER & O. Leave given to take exceptions to Comm'rs. rep't. as WILLIAM MCTEER failed to make rep't. as required. MCTEER has 2 mos. to file rep't.

H. HEARTSELL & J. G. WALLACE, Admrs. & C. Vs: HEIRS & CREDITORS of G. S. GILBERT & O. By motion of M. H. WILLIAMS by Sol., leave granted him to file petition asking to be made party defendant to suit.

Pg. 95 WILLIAM WALLACE, Admr. SAMUEL D. HENDERSON Vs: SAM WALLACE, S. A. HENDERSON & O. C&M to take acc't. personal assets of estate of SAMUEL D. HENDERSON, Dec'd.

HIRAM HARTZELL & JESSE G. WALLACE, Admrs. of G. S., A. L. & S. S. GILBERT, Dec'd. Vs: H. A. SAFFLE, NANCY GILBERT & O. Nov. 26, 1856. Acc't. to be taken ascertaining indebtedness of the several estates and amt. of personal assets belonging to same. Also to take testimony that it be practical that the undivided tract of land belonging to the estates of A. L., S. S. GILBERT and to DAVID GILBERT, minor heir of GEORGE S. GILBERT, in which the interests of A. L. and S. S. GILBERT are under
Pg. 96 2 Deeds of Trust, or to advantage that whole property be sold. Rep't. to next term of Ct.

STEPHEN J. MCREYNOLDS Vs: JOHN STRANGE & O. Ordered that JAMES A. MCCAMY one of the Respdts. be appt'd. Rec'vr. w/Personal Bond and Security of $1.000.00. Acc't. for goods 7 assets. Ascertain indebtedness of JOHN STRANGE and amt. due him.

Pg. 97 WILLIAM MORTON Vs: JOHN MORTON, Extr. of WILLIAM MORTON, Dec'd. Nov. 25, 1856. Tract of land on Six Miles Creek joining lands of MICHAEL GARDNER and O. was sold on Aug. 8, 1856, to JOHN MORTON, as highest bidder for $455.00. He has paid $46.50 and has due as his share of personal estate and $5.00 directed by the Will of WILLIAM MORTON to be paid to him $12.63 also due JAMES MORTON $12.63 and JOSEPH MORTON $12.63 and also due SILAS MORTON $12.63 and A. H. MORTON $12.63 and JOSEPH MORTON $12.63 and also due DAVID MORTON as his share of personal estate $7.63. There is due Complnt. WILLIAM MORTON $61.61. Respdt. JOHN MORTON bought undivided interest of all the Heirs.

Pg. 98 JAMES PRATER & O. Vs: ALEX ISH & WILLIAM PRATER, Extrs. & C. Heirs and children of SAMUEL PRATER, Dec'd. entitled to interest in sum of $1,500.00. Ordered that BENJAMIN PRATER pay interest on said sum to C&M.

MARGARET HENRY Vs: SAMUEL HENRY & JOHN W. MALCOMB. Complnt. not due relief. Her bill to be dismissed. Defdt. recover of plaintiff and her Security, P. D. HAMONTREE and JAMES HAMONTREE, the costs of cause.

JAMES H. GILLESPY, Extr. & C. Vs: HEIRS of MATTHEW WALLACE. Ordered that Extr. of MATTHEW WALLACE pay into C&M all monies w/which he is chargeable. Any add'l. parties necessary to enable Ct. make final decree may be brought into Ct. by process of publication.

Pg. 99 MOSES GAMBLE & O. Vs: ELI NUNN & O. Cause of Judgement set aside. Respdts. filed Ans. Case cont'd.

WILLIAM WALLACE, Admr. & C. Vs: SARAH HENDERSON & O. Nov. 26, 1856. Admr. proceed sell property and negro boy, ANDERSON, belonging to said estate, at public sale. It appears debts are $4,516.05; Admr. ordered to pay creditors funds accruing from said sale entered in Deed of Trust executed by SAMUEL D. HENDERSON, Feb. 5, 1855, to ANDREW MCCLAIN in the order of payment therein specified. Any residue pd. to C&M, C&M to take acc't. showing:

1) Amt. personal assets of said estate in hands of C&M.
2) What dispersements made heretofore.
3) Amt. indebtedness of estate.
4) Admr. enter into a bond in amt. of $2,000.00.

SAMUEL HENRY Vs: MOSES KEYES & O. Nov. 26, 1856. Bill and Cross Bill appeared to his Honor that Respdt's. ancestor and WILLIAM LOWRY were principals and Complnt. was Security to an obligation given to JAMES HOUSTON to wit: HAYWOOD BURNETT, ROBERT **Pg. 100** TEDFORD, Extr. of said HOUSTON, Dec'd. for sum of $789.29 plus costs of suit, on May 22, 1848, a motion having before that time been made in Circuit Ct. by SAMUEL HENRY Vs: WILLIAM MCTEER & MOSES KEYES, Extr. of JOHN KEYES, Dec'd. for $1,090.37 the amt. pd. by SAMUEL HENRY on the Judgement rendered **Pg. 101** agnst. him and LOWRY. Ct. found HENRY was Security of JOHN KEYES and WILLIAM LOWRY in obligation above described. Judgement was rendered against MCTEER & KEYES as Extr. of JOHN KEYES, Dec'd., for $1,090.37 plus court costs. On Aug. 13, 1850, order issued from Circuit Ct. returnable 4th Mon. Sept. 1850, commanding sheriff notify Respdts. - Heirs-at-law of JOHN KEYES, Dec'd. - to show cause why lands descended to them from their father should not be sold to satisfy judgement. On May 30, 1851, same was admitted to Jury who found for Complnt. Ordered that SAMUEL HENRY have execution agnst. said lands and execution was raised on tract of land July 25, 1851, situated in Blount County on waters of Crooked Creek in 14th Civil District adjoining lands of **Pg. 102** SAMUEL HENRY and O. containing 240 A. which were owned by JOHN KEYES, Dec'd. and which descended to heirs-at-law. Tract sold by Sheriff on Sept. 20, 1851, for $500.00. Complnt. became owner and later raised his bid to $1,000.00 and entered in satisfaction. Then an alias execution was issued on said Judgement and was levied by the Sheriff on Dec. 2, 1851, on three other tracts of land in District 12 adjoining lands of J. H. ROWAN, GEORGE CALDWELL, HEDRICK and O. - in all 239 A. plus 80 A. sold to MARTIN HARPER and one sold to **Pg. 103** Complnt. of 60 A. MARTIN HARPER pd. $210.00. Complnt. pd. $315.00. Sheriff failed to give notice. Complnt. not entitled to land for that reason, as tenant on land not notified. C&M to sell land at public auction. Respdts. appealed to Supreme Ct. in Knoxville second

Mon. in Sept. next.

HEARTSELL & WALLACE, Admr. A. L. GILBERT & O. Vs: NANCY GILBERT & O. Complnt. has leave to amend bill making other parties Defdts.

Pg. 104 Court adjourned Thurs., Nov. 27th, 1856. Hon. T. NIXON VAN DYKE.

Pg. 105 May 25, 26, and 27, 1857. Chancellor did not appear... SAMUEL PRIDE, C&M.

Pg. 106 July 6 and 7, 1857. Special Term of Ct. Chancellor still not in attendance. Adjourned.

July 8, 1857. Since VAN DYKE did not appear, WILLIAM G. SWAN, Judge of Circuit Ct. by interchange w/Chancellor T. NIXON VAN DYKE since Circuit Ct. in recess.

JOHN HAYS Vs: SAMUEL DOUTHET'S HEIRS. Process ordered agnst. ISAAC T. DOUTHET of Blount County and GEORGE MONTGOMERY of Knox County, Admrs. of SAMUEL DOUTHET, Dec'd. Show why suit should not be revived agnst. them.

Pg. 107 JAMES PRATER & O. Vs: A. ISH Extr. & O. Previous order of Ct. revived for C&M to rep't.

S. J. MCREYNOLDS Vs: JOHN A. SNIDER & O. Ordered that all things be confirmed.

E. E. CONER Vs: JOHN EVERETT. Parties settled dispute and suit to be dismissed.

JEREMIAH DOTSON Vs: JOHN EVERETT. Judgement against Respdt. EVERETT sum of $20.00 and court costs.

R. L. MCNUTT & O. Vs: JOHN EVERETT. Suit compromised. Suit dismissed costs to Complnt.

Pg. 108 P. T. SILER & O. Vs: E. EVERETT & S. R. CAMERON. July 8, 1857. SAMUEL R. CAMERON, a nonresident of State. Publication to be made requiring him to appear and plead answer or demur to said Bill as judgement will be taken agnst. him.

Pg. 109 S. J. MCREYNOLDS, Admr. Estate of WILSON SNIDER, Dec'd. Vs: DORCAS SNIDER, ISABELL SNIDER, JOHN SNIDER, & BETSY JANE SNIDER, Minor Heirs of WILSON SNIDER, Dec'd. & O. Ans. of SAMUEL CLEMENS, Gdn. of minor heirs of WILSON SNYDER, Dec'd. and Judgement agnst. ELINOR SNIDER, the widow of said WILSON SNIDER, Dec'd. Land was sold for $170.00. NAPOLIAN B. MCCLAIN, Purchaser. MCCLAIN paid purchase money. Before purchase money became due, S. J. MCREYNOLDS was elected and commissioned County Judge for Blount County and thus became incompetent to render vesting title to purchaser. Court is pleased to Order and Decree all interest of DORCAS SNYDER, JOHN SNIDER, ISABELL SNIDER and BETSY JANE SNYDER, minor heirs of WILSON SNYDER, Dec'd. in the land containing 50 A. District 8, on waters of Crooked Creek adjoining lands of JOSEPH MARTIN, Dec'd., N. B. MCCLAIN, JOHN RUSSELL and O. late entry granted by State of Tennessee to JOEL HILL by Grant #12101, Dated

Pg. 110 Dec. 7, 1825. This land to be given to N. B. MCCLAIN for Registration. Since MCREYNOLDS can no longer handle Administration, that duty turned over to C&M.

WILLIAM WALLACE, Admr. Vs: WIDOW, HEIRS, & CREDITORS of SAMUEL D. HENDERSON, Dec'd. July 8, 1857. JOHN BOGLE, to act as Surveyor and RICHARD I. WILSON and JEFFERSON STONE be appointed Comm'rs. to lay off and apprise to SARAH HENDERSON, widow, 1/3 real estate to include the mansion house, if required by the said Sarah, and report to next term of Ct. The personal assets have been exhausted in paying debts and

Pg. 111 a large balance yet owing. Necessary to sell residue of estate after assignment of Dower. Admr. to expose to public sale on premises all lands in pleadings mentioned.

JAMES H. GILLESPY, Extr. & C. Vs: WILLIAM WALLACE & O. C&M to lend out money until next term Ct.

Pg. 112 WALLACE & HEARTSELL, Extrs. & C. Vs: HEIRS & CREDITORS of GILBERTS. July 8, 1857. The 60-70 A. tract of land near Louisville cannot be divided in usual way without injury to those interested in it. C&M permitted to divide land into lots, if advantageous, so as to produce the most amt. of money. Offer first as one tract -

Pg. 113 then as lots. C&M report next term Ct. amt. assets in hands of H. T. COX belonging to GILBERTS deposited with him as collateral security. The Master will also rep't. in like manner as to collateral deposited w/WILLIAM HENDERSON.

JAMES WILSON Vs: SAMUEL PRIDE, Admr. MR. HENRY, Dec'd. & SARAH HENRY, WIDOW & ANN BROWN & O. Heirs of JOHN HENRY, Dec'd. July 9, 1857. Respdts. given time to Ans.

Pg. 114 JAMES A. HOUSTON & CO. Vs: P. P. HOUSTON, MARY A. HOUSTON & MARY E. HOUSTON. Time to amend Bill.

JAMES S. BONHAM Vs: EPHRAIM LINK. Cause remanded to Rules generally.

SAMUEL W. O'CONNER & O. Vs: ELI MYERS & O. Permission granted to file Ans.

Pg. 115 SAMUEL GHORMLY & WIFE Vs: ROBERT JAMES. Permission to take deposition of J. GRAY SMITH to be read in evidence in this case.

SAMUEL PRIDE, Admr. of JOHN HENRY, Dec'd. Vs: WILLIAM MCTEER & O. Leave granted Complnt. to take testimony to be read in evidence in this case.

J. T. BICKNELL Vs: BLANCHARD & VINSANT. Judgement set aside and leave to Ans. granted.

GEORGE DAVIS Vs: JOHN MCNALLY. Leave granted to file Ans.

RICHARD M. SAFFELL & O. Vs: JAMES WILSON & O. Have until Oct. Term to file Ans.

N. S. PECK & O. Vs: J. M. AIKIN & O. Cause cont'd. for taking testimony generally.

Pg. 116 Court adjourned July 9, 1857. WILLIAM G. SWAN, Judge.

Pg. 117 July 28, 1857. Special Term of Chancery Court. His Hon. T. N. VAN DYKE presiding.

TELLINGHAST & O. Vs: MCTEER, PRIDE & O. Leave granted for CLARK HESSER & CO. for the use of KENT, E. B. STODDARD & CO., JAMES A. JACKIN, Admrs. W. P. WILSTOCK, G. P. PENN, THEODORE CAMPBELL MCCAULY, JAMES E. BROWN, F. HOLIMAN CO. and JOSIAS GAMBLE to file their petitions to become Respdts. in this case.

JAMES H. GILLESPY, Extr. Vs: HEIRS of M. WALLACE. The Order under terms of Ct. revived.

A. ISH, J. KERR & O. Vs: KNOXVILLE-CHARLESTON R.R. Remanded to rules for taking testimony.

Pg. 118 H. HEARTSELL & J. G. WALLACE Vs: HEIRS of G. S., A. L. & S. S. GILBERT. Previous order to be opened to permit C&M to dispose of land and town lots belonging to GEORGE S. GILBERT in same manner as lands owned by A. L. & S. S. GILBERT.

Pg. 119 Circuit Court of Blount County, Tennessee. Sept. 29, 1857. Ct. opened by the Hon. JAMES M. WELCKER, Judge of the 2nd Judicial Circuit Court sitting to supply the incompetency of the Hon. T. N. VAN DYKE, Chancellor.

N. S. PECK & O. Vs: JAMES M. AIKIN & O. Case cont'd. to allow retaking depositions of JOHN L. PAYNE and ABRAHAM EDDINGTON. Depositions to be taken in Monroe County.

Pg. 120 Nov. 23, 1857. Court met. T. NIXON VAN DYKE presiding. J. GRAY SMITH Vs: ANN JAMES. Case cont'd.

JAMES PRATER & O. Vs: ALEX ISH, Extr. Nov. 24, 1857. Extr. has settled Will & Estate - Cause confirmed. There remains unaccounted for and undisposed $768.68 of which sum of $31.66 is due LETETIA BERRY and the sum $529.07 due to Heirs of SAMUEL PRATER under
Pg. 121 former decree. Remaining funds divided equally to 7 legatees. It appears the $768.68 has been paid by the Extr. to office of C&M. He shall satisfy Heirs equally.

P. T. SILER & O. Vs: EVERETT & CAMERON. C&M to

rep't. how much remains unpaid of purchase money for tract of land purchased from Respdt. EVERETT from Respdt. CAMERON and how much due upon demand.

I. SIMERLY & WIFE & O. Vs: JOHN EVERETT & O. Plea wholly insufficient and doesn't present a bar to Complnts. claim to relief. The same is overruled and Defdt. ordered to ans.

Nov. 25, 1857. HUGH HENRY of HUGH Vs: SAMUEL PRIDE, Admr. The death of Complnt. admitted.

Pg. 122 JOHN R. HAYS Vs: SAMUEL DOUTHET, Extr. Ordered on motion of Complnts. case revived agnst. ISAAC S. DOUTHET and GEORGE MONTGOMERY as Admrs. of SAMUEL DOUTHET, Dec'd.

JAMES PORTER & O. Vs: WILLIAM A. SPENCER & O. Leave given Complnts. to amend their bill.

MAD. COX & J. M. HENRY Vs: MCTEER & O. Leave granted to amend Bill.

WILLIAM JOHNSTON & WIFE Vs: ED GEORGE & O. One mo. given to plead Ans.

ROBERT WEIR Vs: JAMES D. WEIR & O. One mo. given to plead Ans.

GEORGE DAVIS Vs: JOHN MCNALLY. Remanded to Rules for 5 mos. for taking testimony.

S. J. MCREYNOLDS Vs: HEIRS of M. SNIDER, Dec'd. Former order on C&M relieved to make Settlement with Admr. and rep't.

SAMUEL PRIDE Vs: WILLIAM MCTEER & O. Two mos. allowance to file Ans.

Pg. 123 Wed., Nov. 25, 1857. HIRAM HEARTSELL & J. G. WALLACE, Admrs. Vs: HEIRS of GILBERTS & O. Cause to be heard upon exception of C. A. WILLIAMS to the rep't. of Master as to his claim which exception is sustained to allow claim of C. A. WILLIAMS to rest as a charge upon estate of GEORGE GILBERT and A. L.

GILBERT and S. GILBERT as well as on the assets of A. L. GILBERT and BRO.

P. T. SILER & O. Vs: EVERETT & CAMERON. Respdt. EVERETT purchased from Respdt. CAMERON a tract of land, took title, but has not paid for land or obtained legal title. Owes Complnt. SILER, $568.44 and costs; and CAMERON, $230.00. Also due Complnt. MAYNARD, $29.82; MARY WEST, $97.18; and State of Tennessee, $31.66. In all Respdt. EVERETT owes $974.10. He has no monies available - only the land. Respdt. given 4 mos. to pay or land sold.

Pg. 124 SAMUEL PRIDE, Admr. Vs: WILLIAM MCTEER & O. An acc't. to be taken w/WILLIAM MCTEER to show:
1) What amt. effects came into his hands as Recv'r.?
2) What portion applied to payment of his individual liabilities?
3) What debts of firm MCTEER, PRIDE & HENRY & CO. were paid after date of Recv'rship. out of his individual means?
Ordered JAMES A. COFFIN, app'td. Comm'r. to take said acc't. If he fails, THOMAS N. CLARK be app'td. w/powers of a C&M to require production of books, papers, vouchers, and interrogate parties.

Pg. 125 R. I. WILSON Vs: WILLIAM MCTEER et al. Judgment entered agnst. Defdt. for want of Answer.

Pg. 126 S. W. & M. E. O'CONNER Vs: ELIZABETH MYERS. Nov. 26, 1857. Respdt. required to site all acc't. books and other papers asked by Complnt. bill at C&M office in 10 days.

H. T. COX Vs: A. P. BOWERMAN & O. Respdt. has leave to plead Answer to Complnt. Bill.

JAMES H. TEDFORD Vs: JAMES WILSON & O. Respdt. entered notion for dissolution of Injunction.

T. D. TILLINGHAST Vs: JOHN HENRY'S HEIRS. Leave granted WILLIAM WALLACE, Treas. of Maryville College, to become party to said bill and file claims agnst. said Estate, also LAURELL & CO. and WILLIAM YATES, JR. have leave to file their claims and be party Defdts. to this case and in like manner S. G. PORTER and STEPHENS and LAVITT.

MARY C. FERGUSON & O. Vs: JOHN MCCULLY & WIFE & O. Leave granted Respdt. D. GOODLINK 2 mos. to file Answer.

Pg. 127 JAMES HENRY n/f/WILLIAM PRESSLEY, a man of color, & O. Vs: J. F. & JAMES HENRY. Complnt. came and suggested parties had settled, or about to settle, matters involved in this case. To advise at next term of Ct.

RODERICK MCKENSEY Vs: JESSE KERR. Case remanded to Rules for taking testimony.

JAMES H. GILLESPY, Extr. Vs: HEIRS of M. WALLACE, Dec'd. Cont'd. next term Ct.

J. BONHAM Vs: E. LINK. Cont'd. until next term Ct. Remanded to Rules for taking testimony.

JOHN ALEXANDER Vs: ANDREW FERGUSON. Cause cont'd. on affidavit of Complnt.

H. HEARTZELL & J. G. WALLACE, Admrs. of G. S. & A. L. & S. S. GILBERT, Dec'd. Vs: SAMUEL K. FINLEY. Remanded to rules until next term Ct. to take proof.

Pg. 128 Thurs., Nov. 26th, 1857. JAMES PORTER & O. Vs: WILLIAM A. SPENCER & O. Motion to dissolve Injunction. WILLIAM A. SPENCER to take judgement on note and be allowed to collect Judgement.

J. T. BICKNELL Vs: BLANCHARD & VINSANT. Judgement taken agnst. Defdts. Is set aside upon Defdts. paying cost of Cross Bill.

Pg. 129 JAMES H. GILLESPY Extr. & C. Vs: WILLIAM WALLACE & O. Heirs of MATTHEW WALLACE, Dec'd. Complnts. permitted to amend their bill as to make Admr. of ELIZABETH CAMPBELL, Dec'd., a party by coming forward and filing his Answer.

R. M. SAFFELL & O. Vs: JAMES WILSON & O. HENRY C. SAFFELL has 2 mos. to file Answer.

JOHN EVERETT Vs: JAMES HENRY. Master to hear proof and rep't. if Respdt. can make title and comply with requirements of his contract.

C. A. NORWOOD & WIFE Vs: E. & I. W. GEORGE & O. Vs: WILLIAM S. JOHNSON & WIFE Vs: E. & I. W. GEORGE. These causes refer to winding up of same Estates, between same parties and should be heard together.

Pg. 130 Fri., Nov. 27th, 1857. SAMUEL & ANN GHORMLY, Extr. & Extx. of WILLIAM JAMES, Dec'd. Vs: ROBERT JAMES & O. C&M to:
1) What assets have come to Admx. for her belonging to Estate of WILLIAM JAMES?
2) Liabilities existed at death of WILLIAM JAMES and to whom owed?
3) What amt. of assets dispersed and to whom?
4) What amt. of claims if any there are?
Master to hear proof. WILLIAM JAMES owned a tract of land. Complnt. ANN GHORMLY, being widow, entitled to Dower. Ct. orders JAMES C. WRIGHT, JAMES BARNES and J. C. M. BOGLE to be Comm'rs. survey land and assign Dower. Rep't. Ct.

Pg. 131 ANN GHORMLY, Admx. WILLIAM JAMES, Dec'd. & SAMUEL GHORMLY, her HUSBAND Vs: ROBERT JAMES. Complnt. intestate and ROBERT JAMES, Respdt. were partners in certain mercantile, wool carding and cotton spinning and own manufacturing establishments at Chilhowee in Blount County, Tennessee, and in livestock, grist and saw mill and farming operations at same place. Ct. of opinion and decrees that the instrument set up by Respdt. ROBERT JAMES dated Jan. 10, 1852, purporting to be agreement signed by WILLIAM JAMES is a forgery as to his signature. C&M to take and state an acc't.
1) What amt. of Capital Stock invested by each party in said partnership, at what time and what in?
2) What partnership assets in hand at death of intestate?
3) What did assets consist of and what disposition?
4) What outstanding liabilities of partnership?

Pg. 132 5) What amt. goods purchased by firm and how disposed of?
6) What amt. of either or both parties have been withdrawn and appropriated for their own use?

Respdt. appeals to Supreme Ct. in Knoxville.

ROBERT JAMES & O. Vs: SAMUEL & ANN GHORMLY, Admr. & Admx. & C. Motion to dissolve injunction heretofore granted. The equity is fully met. Defdt. allowed to collect debts specified. The said SAMUEL and ANN GHORMLY, Admr. and Admx., recover from ROBERT JAMES, ROBERT SHEPHERD, ELIZABETH SHEPHERD (formerly ELIZABETH JAMES), ISABELLA JAMES and HENRY JAMES, the Security in the injunction, the sum of $3,873.96 being the amt. of debts mentioned in bill for which execution may issue upon refunding bond.

Pg. 133 JAMES HENRY & O. Vs: ALEX KENNEDY & O. Respdt. asks for dissolving of injunction. KENNEDY allowed to proceed at-law for collection of his note.

(This item crossed out.)
H. HEARTSELL & I. G. WALLACE, Admrs. of GILBERTS Vs: HEIRS & CREDITORS of A. L. GILBERT & O. O. P. TEMPLE, Atty., for certain of the creditors has reason to suspect that H. T. COX in addition to the 10% charge agnst. Estate of A. L. GILBERT & BRO. for collecting collaterals left in his hands has also charged commissions for his services, as Agent of EAKIN & CO. of Nashville. Requests C&M take deposition from member of EAKIN firm on this point. (This above item completely crossed out on page.)

Pg. 134 JAMES H. TEDFORD Vs: JAMES WILSON & O. Requests dissolution of injunction.

HENRY BUSUM Vs: J. & J. F. HENRY.
1) State number of Mares and Jennets put to the Jack during spring and fall seasons and price of such liasons.
2) Show he has used diligence to collect debts for services.
3) Show in what case Respdt. interfered w/Complnt. by making other contracts.
4) Show value of bridge rec'd. by Respdt. and take bal. between parties.

Pg. 135 H. BUSUM Vs: J. F. HENRY. Nov. 27, 1857. Settlement of partnership acc'ts. There is due Respdt., $125.50. Complnt. BUSUM to pay that amt. and Ct. costs. BUSUM appeals to next term of Supreme Ct. in Knoxville.

Pg. 136 ALEXANDER ISH & O. Vs: KNOXVILLE & CHARLESTON R. R. CO. Nov. 27, 1857. Proof of exhibits called for - Papers and Books.
1) Two articles of contract entered into by KNOXVILLE & CHARLESTON R. R. CO. and the BLUE RIDGE R. R. CO. on July 8, 1853 and on Mar. 1, 1854. Entries in books of record showing the subscription of $120,000.00 of stock by the Chairman of County Ct. of Blount County, Tennessee and entry of Jan. 14, 1856 showing loss of the original books and organization of the said Company on June 28, 1853. Chancellor decrees there is no equity in Complnt's. Bill and dismisses the same. Further ordered that Complnt. together w/JOHN GRIFFITHS, their Security, pay costs of this cause. Complnt. prays an appeal to Supreme Ct. in Knoxville Sept. next. The Clerk will copy into the record the two articles of contract and the said entries from the record book of the KNOXVILLE & CHARLESTON R. R. CO. and also the affidavit of WILLIAM WALLACE showing the loss of the original record book of Respdt. It is agreed in said book of records there is no entry preceeding the said subscription of $120,000 by the Chairman of the County Ct. of Blount County.

Pg. 137 H. HEARTZELL & J. G. WALLACE, Admrs. of GILBERTS & O. Vs: HEIRS & CREDITORS of A. L. GILBERT & O. C&M to take deposition from someone of EAKIN & CO. of Nashville, in whose name the deed of trust in the pleadings mentioned was made by A. L. GILBERT and S. S. GILBERT and what collaterals were left in hands of H. T. COX, Trustee.
1) Did COX have any beneficial interest in said debt?
2) What percent of any sum he charged them for collecting same?
3) C&M to hear proof and rep't. whether there was any arrangement made by A. L. GILBERT & BRO. for the payment of any other claim.
Clerk also determine what amt. of monies pd. by GEORGE S. GILBERT in his lifetime as charged in Bill of
Pg. 138 C. H. SAFFELL in a certain land trade. Determine also any claim C. H. SAFFELL has agnst. GEORGE S. GILBERT'S Estate subject to be set off agnst. payment of GILBERT to SAFFELL.

C&M to determine whether note executed as charged by

A. L. GILBERT and S. S. GILBERT for $1,000.00 has been pd. to NANCY GILBERT. Does NANCY GILBERT have any claim upon said lot?

Pg. 139 Since Surveyor hasn't described land to date, cont'd. until next term of Ct. Sale of said lands to HENRY C. SAFFELL who becomes purchaser to amt. of $3,530.73 and SAFFELL is the regular Gdn. of DAVID GILBERT, a Minor, and entitled to 1/3 of monies from sale of portions of said land.

SAFFELL to be credited on notes executed by him for the purchase and interest from DAVID'S share to be used for DAVID'S needs.

S. J. MCREYNOLDS Vs: JACOB SUMMY & O. Motion granted to amend bill by Complnt. and make JONATHAN HAMMOND of the firm HAMMOND & HENRY, JOHN GAMBLE of the firm GAMBLE & GEORGE and JAMES HENRY of JOHN, Trustee, Parties to the same.

R. I. WILSON Vs: W. H. NEWBOLD & O. On this cause on affidavit made JOHN S. M. PRIDE and SAMUEL PRIDE, Admrs. of JOHN HENRY, Dec'd. have leave to file Answer.

Pg. 140 JAMES WILSON Vs: HEIRS & WIDOW of JOHN HENRY, Dec'd. & SAMUEL PRIDE, Admr. of JOHN HENRY. Nov. 27, 1857. Since SAMUEL PRIDE a party to suit, as C&M. Ct. appoints WILLIAM A. WALKER, a Spec. Comm'r. to take account and ascertain:
1) What amt. assets come to hands of SAMUEL PRIDE, Admr. JOHN HENRY?
2) What amt. of assets dispersed and what amt. on hands?
3) Will it be necessary to sell land, or any part thereof, to pay Complnt. judgement?
4) What amt. yet due on judgement?
5) What amt. of individual debts and of partnership debts yet outstanding?
Creditors of JOHN HENRY, Dec'd. allowed to become parties to this suit. The minor Heirs of JOHN HENRY, Dec'd. be required to file Answer to Complnt's. Bill.

Pg. 141 H. HEARTSELL & J. G. WALLACE, Admrs. of GILBERTS & O. Vs: HEIRS & CREDITORS & C. SAMUEL R.

ROGERS allowed to be made party Defdt. to said bill he being surviving partner of ROGERS & BOYD.

JOHN HAYS Vs: SAMUEL DOUTHET, Admr. In this case it is admitted that GEORGE C. MONTGOMERY and ISAAC T. DOUTHET are Admrs. of SAMUEL DOUTHET, Dec'd. by assent. Case revived agnst. them.

H. T. COX Vs: WILL COX & JOSEPH MCCULLY. C&M to determine whether payment for tract of land specified in pleadings has been paid.

H. T. COX Vs: W. M. COX & JOSEPH MCCULLY. Nov. 27, 1857. Defdt. JOSEPH MCCULLY is endebted to Complnt. for $533.71, balance of consideration money for tract of land described in pleadings. If bal. not pd. in 4 mos. - full amt. land to be sold in public sale.

Pg. 142 J. A. HOUSTON & CO. Vs: P. P. HOUSTON & O. Complnt's. bill to be dismissed and Complnt. JAMES A. HOUSTON, SAMUEL L. YEAROUT, JOHN L. CRAIG, F. M. HOOD and JAMES W. HAMMINS, their Security, pay all costs for which execution may issue.

JAMES ANDERSON, Extr. & C. Vs: A. W. EMETT. A. W. EMMETT had contracted with said Testator on Dec. 11, 1850, for a tract of land in mountains near Tuckaleechee Cove adjoining lands of Heirs of JOHN MYERS, Dec'd., WILLIAM MYERS and DANIEL DUNN and bounded on one side by the Old Indian Boundary Line in 15th Civil Dis-
Pg. 143 trict of Blount County and by terms of memorandum, the Respdt. EMMETT was to pay for said land in property and it appears on memorandum that EMMETT pd. on Dec. 12, 1850, sum of $36.94 on said contract. Land to be sold upon decree and purchaser to have a good title and no right of redemption by EMMETT. C&M to determine if EMMETT pd. anything above the $36.94 pd. His funds to be returned to him. C&M to determine what rents and profits EMMETT has enjoyed and advise. Clerk to advertise and make sale.

Pg. 144 P. T. SILER & O. Vs: L. R. CAMERON & O. CAMERON has leave to file a Cross Bill.

WILLIAM WALLACE, Admr. SAMUEL D. HENDERSON,

Pg. 145 Dec'd. by A. MCCLAIN & O. Nov. 27, 1857. Sell tract of land belonging to SAMUEL D. HENDERSON, Dec'd. Dower to be transferred to SARAH A. HENDERSON, widow of intestate. Land on waters of Little River containing 250 A. and apparently 1/3 of the value of real estate of deceased. Land be divested out of Heirs of SAMUEL D. HENDERSON and vested into SARAH A. HENDERSON together w/all appurtenances for and during the term of her natural life. C&M to make title to lands sold to SAMUEL MCCAMY by the Comm'rs. and also to STEPHEN S. PORTER another purchaser of same. (The other 2/3 of the land).

Pg. 146 MOSES GAMBLE & O. Vs: ELI NUNN & O. Complnts. were necessary parties to suit of ELI NUNN Vs: JOHN E. TOOLE. Ct. being of opinion that the marriage articles exhibited in this cause and in former suit entered into by ELI NUNN and Respdt. and his now Dec'd. wife, MARTHA E. NUNN, formerly MARTHA E. THOMPSON excluded the right of the said husband to any portion of the property settled upon the said wife. MARTHA E. made no disposition of her property and that Complnts. at her death were entitled to the same as her heirs-at-law. It is further ordered that on the -- day of Nov. 185-, the Decree was void and that the same be reversed - and for naught.

Pg. 147 It further appearing to the Ct. from the Bill, the Answer of MCTEER and NUNN and other proof that Defdt. WILLIAM MCTEER after the said Void Decree purchased the said negroes mentioned in the Bill-To-Wit: MILLY, ELIZABETH and CLOE is in fact an innocent purchaser. It is Ordered, Judged and Decreed that any title said MCTEER may hold or claim to said negroes and title of negroes be divested of the said MCTEER, NUNN and JOHN E. TOOLE and vested in Complnts. and ordered that MCTEER and his Security, JOHN SINGLETON, be ordered to surrender up said negroes in 20 days to C&M. Master to hire out the same until further order of this Ct. It appears to Ct. that ELI NUNN did, during the life of his wife purchase a certain house and 2 lots in Maryville on East side of Pistol Creek of one SAMUEL LEA with the funds of said MARTHA E., his wife, specified in the same marriage agreement, for which he took titles in his own name.

Pg. 148 Ct. of opinion NUNN held said property in trust for his wife. Ordered that Complnts. are entitled to same as heirs-at-law of said MARTHA E. NUNN and that title of said lots be divested out of ELI NUNN and vested in Complnts. C&M to take acc't.

1) What amt. of funds specified in said marriage articles came to hand of said NUNN or JOHN E. TOOLE - in what did they consist? What disposition of them?

2) Who has had possession from death of MARTHA of the negroes? What a reasonable hire of same?

ELI NUNN prays for appeal to Supreme Ct. in Knoxville at next term.

Pg. 149 JAMES H. GILLESPY, Extr. & C. Vs: HEIRS of MATTHEW WALLACE. Nov. 27, 1857. Ordered by Chancellor that C&M collect monies belonging to said estate and have them in readiness at next term of Ct.

Pg. 150 Jan. 29, 1858. Hon. JAMES M. WELCKER, Judge 2nd Judicial Circuit, sitting in supply due to incompetency of the Hon. VAN DYKE.

NICHOLAS S. PECK & O. Vs: JAMES M. EAKIN & O. Jan. 30, 1858. Cause cont'd. to next term Ct.

Pg. 151 May 24, 1858. T. NIXON VAN DYKE presiding.

WILLIAM PRESSLY & O. Vs: J. & J. T. HENRY & O. Case dismissed. Complnt. pay costs.

SAMUEL PRIDE, Admr. Vs: WILLIAM MCTEER & O. DANIEL D. FOUTE appt'd. Comm'r. to take and state said acc't. and rep't. next term of Ct.

Pg. 152 R. M. SAFFLE Vs: JAMES WILSON & O. Cause cont'd. Death of CLEMENTINE A. SAFFLE one of Respdts. suggested and admitted. Cause is revived agnst. SAMUEL L. YEAROUT, her Admr.

S. J. MCREYNOLDS, Admr. of WILSON SNIDER, Dec'd. Vs: ELENOR SNIDER & O. The same is in all things ordered to be confirmed and Complnt. pay all costs.

Pg. 153 MAD. COX & J. MCHENRY Vs: WILLIAM MCTEER & O. Leave granted Respdts. to file Answer.

C. W. NORWOOD & WIFE Vs: ED. & I. W. GEORGE & O. Cases to be blended and to be tried WILLIAM S. JOHNSTON & WIFE Vs: E. & I. W. GEORGE & O. together. To be cont'd.

HUGH HENRY & O. Vs: SAMUEL PRIDE, Admr. Cause cont'd. by consent.

JAMES E. SIMERLY & WIFE Vs: JOHN EVERETT & O. Complnt. given new bond w/sufficient Security. Former Securities released.

JAMES WILSON Vs: HEIRS of JOHN HENRY, Dec'd. WILLIAM A. WALKER continue as Spec. Comm'r. to take and state same and rep't. next term of Ct.

Pg. 154 SAMUEL PRIDE Vs: WILLIAM MCTEER & O. Death of ISAAC N. RANKIN as Respdt. suggested.

S. J. MCREYNOLDS Vs: JOHN STRANGE & O. Recv'r. JAMES A. MCCAMY rep't. next term Ct., Amt. of debts due firm of GRAHAM, STRANGE & CO.

JOHN EVERETT Vs: JAMES HENRY. Bills, Answers, Exhibits, Proof and Rep't. being excepted to by Complnt.
Pg. 155 It appearing to Ct. that at April Term Ct. for Knox County for year 1853, upon a bill filed by THOMAS M. ROOKER and his wife, ELIZABETH, agnst. HENRY C. SAFFELL and O., Extrs. of last Will of SAMUEL SAFFELL, Dec'd., the rights and title of a lot of land in controversy, together with divers other lots, or tracts, was divested out of ELIZABETH SAFFELL and vested in ALEXANDER ISH, as Trustee, for the sole and separate use of ELIZABETH ROOKER with powers to said trustee. When he is satisfied that the wants and comforts of ELIZABETH ROOKER and her position in society requires it - to dispose of a sufficiency of said real estate and invest in a negro woman, or girl to assist her in her domestic affairs and take title of said negro in himself. It appears to Ct.
ALEXANDER ISH declined accepting the land trust and Respdt., in this case was appt'd. in his place and Respdt. purchased from beneficiary and her husband the land in controversy and sold same to Complnt. Ct. feels Respdt. not able to make to Complnt. a good and sufficient title. Ct. decrees that contract between Complnt. and Respdt.

be recinded. Respdt. be perpetually enjoined from collecting judgement agnst. Complnt. for purchase money.

Pg. 156 P. T. SILER & O. Vs: EPP EVERETT & O. May 28, 1858. Lands sold to MARION CAMERON for $796.00. Money to be collected by C&M.

RODERICK MCKENZIE Vs: JESSE KERR. May 26, 1858. Decreed by Chancellor. Complnt. Bill be dismissed. Respdt. collect from Complnt. and WILLIAM WALLACE, his Security. Complnt. appeals to Supreme Ct. in Knoxville.

Pg. 157 The C&M, SAMUEL PRIDE, having appt'd. THOMAS A. POPE his Deputy Clerk and Master of the County Court, he appeared in open Ct. this day and was sworn in as such. May 26, 1858.

JOSEPH H. TEDFORD Vs: JAMES WILSON & O. This cause cont'd. by consent of parties.

BLANCHARD & VINSANT Vs: SAMUEL T. BECKNELL. It admitted by THOMAS J. BLANCHARD and Defdt. this cause has been compromised. BLANCHARD pay costs of original bill and Respdt. S. T. BICKNELL pay Cross Bill costs. Case settled.

Pg. 158 H. HEARTSELL & J. G. WALLACE, Admrs. Vs: HEIRS & CREDITORS of GEORGE S., A. L. & S. S. GILBERT, Dec'd. Chancellor pleased to rep't., item of $181.82 - compensation retained by H. T. COX for executing Deed of Trust made by A. L. and S. S. GILBERT to secure Nashville debts is sustained. COX to be examined on oath to matter of $423.63 which he has pd. out of collaterals placed in his hands. Admr. ordered to collect debts of estates they represent and pay into Ct. all monies on
Pg. 159 hand. C&M has authority to modify any of his reports heretofore made. C&M to hear proof as to money due from A. L. and S. S. GILBERT to Mrs. NANCY E. GILBERT and what interest she may have in lot in controversy. Part in case concerning SAMUEL K. FINLEY is remanded to the Rules for lacking further proof.

JAMES ANDERSON, Admr. Vs: A. W. EMMETT. Cause cont'd.

Pg. 160 ROBERT WEAR Vs: J. D. WEAR & O. May 27, 1858. His honor doesn't know if sale of land and slaves necessary to make distribution among heirs.
Therefore, determine:
1) Whether land can be equally divided among heirs.
2) Whether the slaves can be equally divided among heirs.
3) Whether necessary to sell slaves and land.
4) What the slaves and land are currently worth?
5) Whether the girl, TILDA, was intended by Intestate, HUGH WEAR, as an advancement to his daughter, MARTHA MCCONNELL, or was she a loan. When did she go into possession of Mrs. MCCONNELL, and what was her value at the time?

Pg. 161 GEORGE DAVIS Vs: JOHN MCNELLY. Deed of conveyance from Complnt. to Respdt. dated June 15, 1849, was executed without consideration and was procured by fraudulent representations of Respdt. and not intended to be operative between the parties. Complnt. entitled to the relief prayed for. Decreed said Deed be delivered up to Complnt. and cancelled and all rights of Respdt. in and to land described, to wit: 190 A. as follows: Bank of creek to a corner in original survey of 344 A. made for BENJAMIN TIPTON in Blount County and divested out of JOHN MCNALLY and vested in GEORGE DAVIS.

Pg. 162 JOHN MCNALLY appeals to next term of Supreme Court in Knoxville.

JOHN R. HAYS Vs: J. T. DOUTHET & GEORGE MONTGOMERY, Admrs. of L. DOUTHET, Dec'd. Case cont'd.

Pg. 163 J. GRAY SMITH Vs: ANN JAMES. In all things confirmed. Recv'r. ordered to pay all monies by him collected to C&M to be distributed as heretofore directed.

RICHARD M. SAFFELL Vs: JAMES WILSON & O. Since filing of bill, ELIZABETH SAFFELL, one of Complnts., has married J. C. M. BOBLE. Ordered that he be made a party Complnt.

Pg. 164 JOHN ALEXANDER & WIFE & O. Vs: ANDREW FERGUSON. Transcript of a Decree of Chancery Ct. at Greeneville had an evidence by Complnts. Complnts. not entitied to relief they sought. Bill be dismissed and they to pay all costs. Complnt. requests appeal to Supreme Ct. in Knoxville.

JAMES PORTER & O. Vs: WILLIAM A. SPENCER & O. May 28, 1858. Granted Respdt. SPENCER to proceed to judgement in Circuit Ct. of Knox County.

MARY C. FERGUSON & O. Vs: DENNISON GOODLINK & WIFE. Given leave to take depositions of JOHN MCCULLY and his wife and report to next court.

Pg. 165 JAMES HENRY & O. Vs: ALEXANDER KENNEDY & O. KENNEDY requests filing of Cross Bill.

H. T. COX Vs: JOSEPH MCCULLY & W. M. COX. H. T. COX was highest and best bidder in land sale. Purchase money paid. Land be divested out of WILLESTON M. COX and invested in H. T. COX. Costs to be paid out of proceeds of sale.

Pg. 166 JAMES PORTER & O. Vs: W. A. SPENCER & O. It is suggested that JAMES THOMPSON one of the Sureties in the injunction and prosecution bonds is a material witness for the Complnt. Ordered by Ct. that Complnts. have leave to substitute new and other bonds. Original bondsmen hereby discharged.

H. T. COX Vs: R. P. BOWERMAN & O. May 28, 1858.
1) What amt. of funds ought to have come to hands of said trustee, R. P. BOWERMAN, in execution of said trust arising from collection of debts in the sale of real and personal estate?
2) What debts have been paid by said trustee out of funds and to whom paid?
3) Whether there remain any debts uncollected or any
Pg. 167 property undisposed of?

SAMUEL W. & M. E. O'CONNER Vs: ELIZABETH MYERS & O. It appearing MARY ANN O'CONNER, the mother of the Complnt. was one of the legatees of PHILIP MYERS, Dec'd. and MARY ANN departed this life in the year ---- and that her personal rep. is not a party but is a necessary party to these proceedings. Complnt. has leave to amend their bill so as to make her personal rep. a party

Complnt. and prosecute suit as such.

Pg. 168 JAMES HENRY & O. Vs: ALEX KENNEDY & O. ALEXANDER MCCLAIN, one of the Sureties in the Prosecution Bond is a material witness for Complnt. and it is ordered that Complnt. has leave to substitute new and other bonds. Original bondsmen discharged.

JAMES H. GILLESPY, Extr. & C. Vs: LEGATEES of MATTHEW WALLACE. May 28, 1858. C&M to refigure his acc't. allowing credit of $25.00 to the Extr. for taxes in 1852 and that he will not charge interest on advancement made to JESSE WALLACE, one of the Legatees.

Pg. 169 C&M to have all monies loaned out at hand for next term of Ct., and as to the question raised in the pleadings as to the right of the child of the negro woman named AILCY born after the making of the Will but before the death of the Testator, the Chancellor is pleased to declare that the Testator died testate as to said child and that the same passed under the general cessionary clause of the said Will to the tenant, for life, the wife of the said Testator, and he so decrees.

Pg. 170 JAMES L. BONHAM Vs: EPHRAIM LINK. May 25, 1858. Judge orders that the Complnt's. bill be dismissed and that the injunction be dissolved and that EPHRAIM LINK, Respdt., recover of Complnt. JAMES L. BONHAM and CHARLES P. SAFFLE, his Security, in the injunction. Bond $282.48 being the amt. of Judgement enjoined in this case with interest thereon.

CIRCUIT COURT, Maryville, Tennessee, June 1, 1858. The Hon. JAMES M. WELCHER, Judge of the Judicial Circuit of Tennessee, sitting to supply the incompetency of Hon. T. NIXON VAN DYKE.

NICHOLAS S. PECK & O. Vs: JAMES M. AIKIN & O. Complnts. are entitled to relief sought. The ejectment suit at law now pending in Circuit Ct. of Blount County, of JAMES M. AIKIN Vs: Complnts. be dismissed and Respdt.

Pg. 171 be enjoined from further proceedings w/suit for the recovery of said land and that JAMES M. AIKIN and SOLOMAN WILSON pay all costs of suit-at-law. JAMES M. AIKIN appeals to Supreme Ct. of Tennessee in Knoxville.

Pg. 172 J. GRAY SMITH Vs: ANN JAMES, Admx. Cont'd. by consent of parties.

C. W. NORWOOD & WIFE Vs: ED. & I. W. GEORGE, Extrs. Cont'd. by consent of parties.

WILLIAM S. JOHNSTON et al. Vs: ED. & I. W. GEORGE, Extrs. Cont'd. by consent of parties.

S. J. MCREYNOLDS Vs: JOHN A. STRANGE & CO. Leave granted for Recv'r. to make rep't.

WILLIAM & JESSE ELLMORE Vs: EPP. EVERETT. Leave to file Answer.

C. W. MCGHEE, Extr. Vs: BELL RUSSELL. Leave to file Answer.

DAVID CUNNIGHAM, Extr. Vs: ALBERT CUNNINGHAM. Leave to file Answer. Both parties to take proof before Answer filed.

Pg. 173 ROBERTSON, HUDSON & PULLIAM Vs: S. J. MCREYNOLDS & O. Nov. 22, 1858. Leave granted Respdt. to file Answer.

JOHN GRIFFETH & JOHN EAKIN Vs: the WIDOW & HEIRS of GEORGE MCKAY, Dec'd. & JOHN RHEA. In this cause the Ct. appt'd. JOHN C. MCCAY, Gdn. of JAMES D., DAVID C., WILLIAM M., MARGERY E., WILLIAM W. MCKAY, minor children of GEORGE MCKAY, Dec'd. who are Respdts. in this case.

H. HARTZELL & J. C. WALLACE Vs: HEIRS of G. S. GILBERT, Dec'd. & O. On motion of the C&M ordered to make rep't. of fee to T. C. LEGAN, Atty., for Admrs.

NICHOLAS BREWER, Admr. Vs: RHODA CHAMBERS & O. Leave to file Answer.

J. B. LIPPENCOTT & O. Vs: S. J. MCREYNOLDS et al. Leave granted to plead Answer.

Pg. 174 JOHN HARPER Vs: A. C. MONTGOMERY. Nov. 23, 1858. Bill dismissed and Respdt. recover of Complnt. and his

Surety, ELIJAH NELSON.

JEREMIAH SIMERLY & WIFE Vs: JOHN EVERETT & O. Lands asked to be partitioned are adversely held by CATHERINE EVERETT, one of the Respdts. and that title is disputed and not clear. Complnts. bill dismissed and Respdt. recovers of the Plaintiff all costs for which execution may issue. The bill is dismissed without prejudice to Complnt. of any right they may have to sue at law.

Pg. 175 WOOD, ABBOTT & CO. Vs: COX & DEVER. Respdts. have not filed Answer as ordered in July 1857 term. Two mos. to file or in contempt. of Ct.

T. D. TILLINGHAST Vs: WILLIAM MCTEER & O. Cause revived against WILLIAM J. HENRY, Admr. of MARGARET STANFORD by consent of parties. (This item was stricken from the record.)

SAMUEL PRIDE Vs: WILLIAM MCTEER & O. Cont'd. by consent of parties and HENRY MILLER is appt'd. Admr. for ISAAC N. RANKIN, Dec'd. a nonresident Respdt.

JAMES HENRY et al. Vs: ALEXANDER KENNEDY et al. One month granted to Respdt. J. M. TOOLE to file his answer to cross bill.

JAMES PORTER et al. Vs: WILLIAM A. SPENCER et al. Cont'd. to next term of Ct.

RICH I. WILSON Vs: WILLIAM MCTEER & O. This cause dismissed by Complnt. paying costs. (The above item was stricken from the record.)

MAD. COX & J. M. HENRY Vs: WILLIAM MCTEER & O. Leave granted Respdt. until Jan. Circuit Ct. to file answer.

Pg. 176 JOSEPH TEDFORD Vs: JAMES WILSON. Injunction be dissolved by Respdt. giving a bond w/security.

H. C. SAFFELL Vs. WILLIAM MCTEER. Cont'd. by consent of parties.

B. F. DUNCAN Vs: D. L. TRUNDLE & O. Cont'd. by consent for Complnt. to amend bill and make WILLIAM P.

CANNON a party Defdt.

G. G. O'CONNER, Gdn. Vs: JOHN C. MYERS & O. Suggested that JOHN BROWN one of the Securities is a material witness. Complnt. ordered by Ct. has leave to substitute new securities. Original sureties are hereby discharged.

Pg. 177 P. L. SILER & O. Vs: SAMUEL R. CAMERON & O. MARION CAMERON who purchased the lands mentioned in pleadings at sale made by C&M, applied on Nov. 23, 1858, for a writ of possession to put him in possession of the land by him purchased. Case remains in Ct. undisposed of. The Ct. orders and directs a writ of possession issue to the Sheriff of Blount County that he put said purchaser into possession of said lands. One note due of MARION CAMERON fell due 15th day of Nov. 1858 and remains unpaid. C&M to recover from MARION CAMERON and HENRY MYERS, his security $398.00 Principal and $12.40 Int.

SAMUEL PRIDE, Admr. of JOHN HENRY, Dec'd. Vs: WILLIAM MCTEER & O.
1) What amt. of debts outstanding and unpaid against the several firms of MCTEER, PRIDE & HENRY and MCTEER, HENRY & CO. on 1st of Jan. 1855?
2) What amt. of said liabilities have been pd. since that time by Recv'r. and when pd.?
Pg. 178 3) What amt. of said debts remain unsatisfied, to whom due and amt. of each?

JOHN R. HAYES Vs: JOHN MCCLAIN, Admr. & DOUTHETT & MONTGOMERY et al. Nov. 23, 1858. It appears to Ct. that there is no equity in Complnts. bill and that the allegations of the same have been fully met and denied. Complnt. bill be dismissed and Complnt. pay all costs accruing and that execution issue against JOHN R. HAYES and J. A. HAYES, JAMES L. BONHAM and M. L. TEFFETELLER for the same.
Compltnt. by his Sol., prays an appeal to next term of Supreme Ct. in Knoxville. (In small print) J. A. HAYS, JAMES S. BONHAM, M. L. TEFFETELLER uniting in the junctive bond eight in cause of taking the first appointive of WASHINGTON ISBILL, which may be excepted and excluded.

T. D. TILLINGHAST Vs: WILLIAM MCTEER & O. In this cause it is suggested and admitted that MARGARET J. STANFORD one of the Defdts. in this cause has departed this life. By consent of parties it is ordered that said cause stand revived against WILLIAM J. HENRY who has been appt'd. Admr. MARGARET died leaving two minor children who are nonresidents of this state. Their names are unknown and they to be made parties Defdts. to this cause when their names are discovered and publication be made as to them. Further ordered that judgement Pro Confesso be taken against ALBERT G. DUNN and RACHEL DUNN, JOHN B. DUNN and MARY DUNN, his Wife, WILLIAM J. HENRY, SAMUEL HENRY, L. L. STANFORD and ALEXANDER MCCLAIN, Gdn. of SAMUEL HENRY, WILLIAM MCTEER and JOHN L. M. PRIDE for want of Ans. Cause remanded to the rules for taking proof.

Pg. 179 W. L. JOHNSON & WIFE Vs: E. & I. W. GEORGE & O. It appearing from the allegation that MARY ELIZABETH ANDERSON and BARBARY REBECCA ANDERSON are both minors and they have no regular Gdn., and they have been regularly served with process and further appearing that ROMULUS BADGETT, DAVID BADGETT and SAMUEL BADGETT and CLEMENTINE BADGETT are minors and have no regular Gdn. It is ordered that S. J. REYNOLDS be appointed Gdn. for said minors, that he be required to file their Ans. and C&M to notify him of his appointment. Furthermore ordered that on application of Complnts. that judgement Pro Confesso against CHARLES W. NORWOOD and MALINDA, his wife, and JAMES M. ANDERSON and JAMES THOMPSON for want of an Ans. and against JAMES L. ANDERSON, NANCY M. WRIGHT and ----- WRIGHT, DONALD BADGETT, SAMUEL BADGETT who are nonresidents and to whom publication has been duly made. Further ordered that Alias Process issue to Hamilton County to be served on EDMOND J. ANDERSON and to Roane County to be served on MARTHA and WILLIAM FOUTE and it further appearing that BARBARY ANDERSON has intermarried with ROBERT WEAR of Blount County, it is ordered that ROBERT WEAR be made a party defendant to this cause and process of subpoena issue to notify him.

Pg. 180 SUSAN HOOD, Extr. & O. Vs: HEIRS of JOHN HOOD, Dec'd. Nov. 23, 1858. The sale of land made by Complnt. SUSAN HOOD in her bill mentioned to wit: 156 A. more or less in Blount County adjoining lands of ELKANY JOHNSON, JOSEPH BRODDY and O. and same upon which JOHN HOOD, Dec'd. resided up to the time of his death. SUSAN in and by Last Will and Testament fulfilled her duties as Admx. sold to LEWIS RUSSELL for $1,200.00 was a fair and adequate consideration and the purchase money has been pd. Sale confirmed and out of hands of heirs of JOHN HOOD, Dec'd. to wit: SARAH A. HOOD, SAMUEL B. HOOD, HUGH A. HOOD, HESTER A. HOOD, FRANCIS J. HOOD and MARGARET R. HOOD.

Pg. 181 RICHARD J. WILSON Vs: WILLIAM MCTEER et als. Complnt. dismisses his bill. Complnt. and JOHN M. COFFIN, his security pay all costs for which execution may issue.

J. H. GILLESPY, Extr. & C. of MATTHEW WALLACE Vs: LEGATEES of M. WALLACE. Master proceed to make distribution of funds in his hands. Sum of $1,962.20 in hands of C&M. On application, leave granted to the heirs of ELIZABETH CAMPBELL, Dec'd. to file a cross bill in this cause in order to bring in the security of J. H. GILLESPY, the Extr. of MARTHA WALLACE, Dec'd.

Pg. 182 W. S. PORTER Vs: WILLIAM MCTEER & L. D. FRANKLIN. Have until Jan. Term to file Ans.

JAMES PORTER Vs: WILLIAM MCTEER et als. On application leave granted to Respdt. SAMUEL PRIDE one month to file Ans.

RICHARD M. SAFFELL & O. Vs: JAMES WILSON & O. Complnt. exception to the Ans. of HENRY C. SAFFLE. JAMES WILSON is ordered to deposit in office of Clerk of this Ct. the books of the firm WILSON & SAFFELL within two months for inspection of Complnts. and their council.

Pg. 183 Wed., Nov. 24, 1858.
SAMUEL PRIDE, Admr. of JOHN HENRY, Dec'd. Vs: WILLIAM MCTEER & O. This day came DANIEL FOUT and filed his rep't. in this cause which on motion of Complnts.' Sol. for sufficient reasons apparent on face of

rep't. is set aside and AZSO A. BARNES, Esq. is appt'd. Spec. Comm'r. in place of DANIEL FOUT to take said rep't. and amend decree and said commission will report to next term of this Ct.

JOHN ALEXANDER & WIFE & O. Vs: ANDREW FERGUSON. A certified copy of the decree of the Supreme Ct. filed in this cause declaring the title of the lands in Complnts. as heirs of RHODA DUNCAN and remanding this cause to this Ct. for purpose of having an account taken of the estate. C&M will show the annual balance of the rents of said tract of land since the death of RHODA DUNCAN. He will show proof of betterments on said land, since death of JOSEPH DUNCAN by the Defdt. ANDREW FERGUSON. It is further considered by the Ct. that a writ of possession from the Ct. on the application of the Complnt. or either of them, to put Complnt. in possession.

Pg. 184 CHARLES NORWOOD & WIFE Vs: E. & I. W. GEORGE & O. It being suggested in this cause that BARBARA ANDERSON, one of the Respdts. has intermarried since the filing of the bill with ROBERT WEAR of Blount County, ROBERT WEAR to be made a party Defdt. and that process of subpoena issue to notify him.

W. E. BROWNING Vs: EDMOND WAYMAN, JOHN CUMMINGS & JOHN M. HEISKILL. Nov. 24, 1858. Ct. orders and decrees that the equity of the bill is fully met and the claim of the Complnt. of a lien is not supported by the proof. Ct. further decrees that the Complnt. bill be reissued and the Respdt. recover of him, the said W. E. BROWNING all the costs for which execution is awarded but this decree is not to effect the rt. of said Complnt. to sue-at-law for any claim he may have agnst. Respdt. for work done.

Pg. 185 J. SIMMERLY & WIFE & O. Vs: JOHN EVERETT & O. On application of Complnts. by their Sol. for sufficient reasons shown the decree in this cause entered on yesterday is vacated and for nothing held and Complnts. are allowed to amend their bill in payment of all costs of the cause which amendment is filed and that Respdts. to recover of Complnt. all costs in this cause.

MOSES GAMBLE & WIFE, A. F. GAMBLE, L. M. THOMPSON, ROBERT MCKAMY & WIFE, L. F. MCKAMY Vs: ELI NUNN, JOHN E. TOOLE & O. Certified copy of Supreme Ct. decree which is as follows, to wit: Heard at Sept. Term 1858 at Knoxville.

Sat., Oct. 11, 1858.
MOSES GAMBLE & WIFE, A. F. GAMBLE, L. M. THOMPSON, ROBERT MCKAMY & WIFE, L. F. MCKAMY Vs: ELI NUNN, JOHN E. TOOLE & O. Heard before ARCHIBALD WRIGHT, Hon. ROBERT J. MCKINNEY and Hon. ROBERT L. CAROTHERS; from the transcript of the record from Chancery Ct. at Maryville Ct. is of the opinion there was no error in the decree of the Chancellor and the same is in all things confirmed. ELI NUNN is by the provisions of the marriage contract made between him and his wife MARTHA E. before their marriage, to wit: on the 11th day of July 1858 (1838?), entirely excluded from any interest in the property and effects of his said wife

Pg. 186 both before and after the death of his said wife and that the same contract was in full force at death of same MARTHA E. NUNN and the property and effects that belonged to MARTHA E. NUNN on the date of her marriage to ELI NUNN descended to the Complnts. as the heirs-at-law of the said MARTHA E. NUNN and that they are entitled to the same. The Ct. is also of the opinion that the decree of the Chancery Ct. in Maryville in the case of ELI NUNN was Complnt. and JOHN E. TOOLE was Respdt. which declared that ELI NUNN was entitled to the property that belonged to his said wife at the date of their marriage is fraudulent and made without making Complnts. in this suit parties to the same. It is therefore considered by the Ct. that the said decree be annulled, vacated and for nothing held. It is further decreed that the slave MILLY and her two children ELIZABETH and CLOE specified in the pleadings be divested out of JOHN E. TOOLE, Trustee & C. of ELI NUNN and WILLIAM MCTEER and be vested in Complnts. and heirs. It also appears that ELI NUNN purchased, with the effects of his said wife, a town lot from one SAMUEL LEE in Maryville, Tennessee. - in East Maryville bounded by Pistol Creek on N. in the W. by College St. near the new bridge on the S. by Broad St. containing @ 1/2 A. and took title in his

Pg. 187 name. It is therefore considered by the Ct. that title to the house and lot be divested out of said ELI NUNN and be vested in Complnts. and heirs in fee simple.

The Ct. is also of the opinion and so declares that Respdt. WILLIAM MCTEER took no title to said slaves by virtue of his purchase under said decree of Chancellor of Chancery Ct. at Maryville. It is further ordered by Ct. that the Master take and state an acc't. and ascertain:
1) What amt. of money, notes and effects and property specified in said tract deeded to JOHN E. TOOLE came to the hands of JOHN E. TOOLE and ELI NUNN or either of them and what deposition made by them of the same?
2) Who has had the possession of the said negroes since the death of MARTHA E. NUNN and what would be a reasonable rent for the house and lot and for hire of the said negroes?
3) What would be a reasonable compensation to JOHN E. TOOLE for his services of taking care of said property specified in said past deed and in collecting any debts specified in the same part?
It appears to Ct. WILLIAM MCTEER has paid ELI NUNN $301.00, part of the purchase money agreed for payment of said negroes.

Pg. 188 WILLIAM MCTEER to recover for the heir of JOHN BAXTER to him and his assigns the said sum of $301.00 with a further sum of $45.15 the interest therein from the 1st day of April 1851 (or 1857?) the time when the same was pd. Cost of Ct. taken from funds in controversy. CARICK W. NELSON, Clerk of Supreme Ct. in Knoxville, 23rd Nov. 1858.

WALLACE & HEARTSELL, Admr. Vs: HEIRS of GEORGE S. GILBERT & S. S. GILBERT. H. T. COX had pd. out $423.26 in claims agnst. estate. Ct. awards him $423.26 from the estate. C&M to collect residue of said claims. A.

Pg. 189 L. GILBERT & BRO. had purchased a lot described in the pleadings in Concord, Knox County, Tennessee. and erected a building thereon but title of said lot was made to Respdt. FINLEY & FINLEY had pd. the purchase money therefore. Decreed by Ct. that the equitable title to lot and appurtenances was in the said A. L. GILBERT & BROS. but that FINLEY is entitled to be re-imbursed for his purchase money. NANCY E. GILBERT is the legal owner of the lot in the town of Louisville known as the 3 Square lot, but she was in fact only a Mortgagee thereon

Pg. 190 and the equitable title remains in said A. L. GILBERT & BROS. Master to sell two lots mentioned above. It is further appearing to the Ct. that the claims known in the records as the Nashville Claims in the hands of H. T. COX was first secured by a Deed of Trust on the lands of said GILBERTS and that they were further secured by the collaterals placed in the hands of said COX and that Messrs. A. M. and J. G. WALLACE, creditors of A. L. GILBERT & BROS. were secured by a second mortgage on the same lands. Ordered by Ct. the Nashville Claims will be first pd. from the collaterals in COX'S hands and Nashville lands to be first pd. out of sale of lands. Then general creditors are entitled to be pd. and pd. Pro Rata.

Pg. 191 Ct. wants to know what amt. pd. by SAMUEL K. FINLEY for Concord lot.

Due THOMAS C. LYON, Sol. for Complnt. $100.00.
On the 25th day of Nov. 1855, A. M. and J. G. WALLACE made an assignment evidenced by a deed on file for a supplimentary amt. of money due them on the part of said mortgagees as deeds of trust and said creditors be substituted to all the rts. of the said A. M. and J. G. WALLACE arising from sale of said lands.

Pg. 192 SAMUEL PRIDE, C&M. Vs: JAMES HENRY & WILLIAM HENDERSON, W. B. TAYLOR, H. T. COX, B. L. WARREN, H. C. SAFFLE, DANIEL TAYLOR & H. T. COX, NANCY E. GILBERT & H. FOSTER, WILLIAM HENDERSON & JAMES HENRY. Two notes executed by JAMES HENRY and WILLIAM HENDERSON as follows: Six mos. after date w/interest we promise to pay SAMUEL PRIDE, C&M. $603.33 in payment of storehouse, dwelling house and 1 A. of land belonging to the estate of A. L., S. S. GILBERT, Dec'd. and DAVID GILBERT, a minor heir of GEORGE GILBERT, Dec'd. Oct. 9, 1857.
        JAMES HENRY
        WILLIAM HENDERSON

1 yr. after date - $603.33.

Pgs. 193-198 (Notes on all the above people taken.)

Pg. 198 S. J. MCREYNOLDS Vs: JACOB SUMMEY, MILLY ANN HENRY et al. Nov. 23, 1858. Final hearing on Bill and Ans. of JACOB SUMMEY, JAMES HENRY, JONATHAN

Pg. 199 HAMMOND and JOHN GAMBLE against MILLY ANN HENRY. The Ct. being satisfied that the deed from JACOB SUMMEY to MILLIE ANN HENRY for the land set forth in the bill, although absolute on its face securing the payment of the several sums of money hereinafter mentioned to MILLIE ANN HENRY. It appears from pleadings that on the 17th day of May 1857, MILLIE ANN HENRY pd. for JACOB SUMMEY to Messrs. HAMMOND and HENRY $104.72, to Messrs. GAMBLE and GEORGE $15.38. On the 17th day of May 1857, JACOB SUMMEY was indebted to MILLY ANN HENRY in the sum of $25.00 all amounting to $145.10 which was all the money pd. by MILLIE ANN HENRY for said land and that S. J. MCREYNOLDS recovered a judgement before SAMUEL YEAROUT, Esq. on the 13th June 1857, against JACOB SUMMEY for $84.70 and costs of suit to enforce collection of said judgement he attended said land. Ct. pleased to order and decree the said deed from JACOB SUMMEY to MILLIE ANN HENRY for the land set forth in the pleadings is hereby declared a mortgage only to secure the several sums of money. C&M to sell land at public sale. Proceeds of sale distributed first to payment of costs of the cause, then to MILLY ANN HENRY the sum of $145.10 w/interest from 17th May 1857. Thirdly, to J. M.

Pg. 200 MCREYNOLDS $84.70 and costs of suit w/interest from 13th June 1857. Remainder pd. to JACOB SUMMEY.

WALLACE & HEARTSELL, Admrs. Vs: HEIRS & CREDITORS of the GILBERTS. B. F. OWENS had become purchaser under the sale of said lands ordered in this cause. Lots #3, 14, 2, 15 at the price of $100.00 but he had failed and refused to execute his note. Two-thirds of money now due and owing. Land to be resold if he doesn't execute note within 2 wks.

Pg. 201 ROBERT WEAR et al. Vs: JAMES D. WEAR et al. Nov. 1858. Agreed to continue cause. Master to hear any proof either party may desire.

JAMES HENRY, Admr. Estate of HUGH HENRY, Dec'd. Vs: SAMUEL PRIDE, Admr. Estate of JOHN HENRY. Nov. 23, 1858. Judge pleased to decree that Respdts. Exceptions 1, 2, 4, 5, 6, 7, 8, be overruled and disallowed and 3rd exception be sustained. Alter and modify his rep't. as to calculate interest of actual rents until the said ward arrived at her majority and after that time he will calculate interest in the balance as ascertained to be in the hands of his guardian at simple interest.

Pg. 202 N. BREWER, Gdn. of JOHN CHAMBERS, Lunatic Vs: RHODA CHAMBERS et al. On petition of JAMES THOMPSON, HORACE MAYNARD, WILLIAM MARCUM, JAMES M. WHEELER, B. D. BRABSON, and J. M. TOOLE, surviving partners of the firm BRABSON & TOOLE, R. J. WILSON and JOHN M. COFFIN late partners under the name and style of WILSON & COFFIN, JAMES M. TOOLE, ELIZABETH BRICKEY and JAMES COTTER, Extr. of the last Will and Testament of WILLIAM COTTER, Dec'd. they are allowed to become parties Respdt. to this suit with leave to file their claims which they have agnst. the said JOHN CHAMBERS with the C&M of this Ct., and by consent of parties, WILLIAM WALKER is appt'd. Gdn. for the minor children of said lunatic.
1) What amt. of debts due and owing by said JOHN CHAMBERS?
2) What value of his personal assets in hands of Gdn. belonging to his ward?
3) What several tracts of land in pleadings are worth?
4) Whether it will be necessary to sell personal property for the said comfort of said lunatic or his family for payment of debts?

Pg. 203 MARY C. FERGUSON & JANE W. GOODLINK Vs: JOSEPH D. GOODLINK & JOHN MCCULLY & WIFE. Nov. 23, 1858. In this cause the Will of MICHAEL GOODLINK, Dec'd. exhibited in Ct. and giving a construction to the 4th clause of same. His Honor Orders, Judges and Decrees that it was the intention of the Testator in the 4th clause to vest in his said daughters, MARY MARGORITE, MARTHA and JANE a rt. to the balance of his plantation as tenants-in-common charged with the support of their sister FRANCIS during her natural life and that on the death of MICHAEL, the Testator, they each became possessed of a joint and individual interest in said lands, and that on death of MARGARETTE, the mother of Respdt. JOSEPH D. GOODLINK the undivided interest which she held in said lands descends to the said JOSEPH as her only heir-at-law. And it appearing that FRANCIS is now dead, His Honor Orders, Judges and Decrees that lands mentioned in the 4th clause is now equal and undivided estate in fee simple of Complnts. MARY C. FERGUSON, JANE W. GOODLINK and the Respdts. MARTHA MCCULLY and JOSEPH W. GOODLINK. Chancellor of opinion this is not a proper case for an acc't.

Pg. 204 This is disallowed. Costs of case can be equally divided by the parties.

MARY C. FERGUSON and JANE W. GOODLINK appeal to Supreme Ct. in Knoxville next term Ct.

MOSES GAMBLE & WIFE & O. Vs: ELI NUNN et al. Recorded from transcript of Supreme Ct. Knoxville. Orders an acc't. be taken by the Master and a writ of possession issue to place the Complnts. in possession of the town lots in E. Maryville and M. rep't. to next term Ct. Further ordered and recorded that GEORGE BROWN, WILLIAM D. MCGINLEY and JESSE G. WALLACE have a lien on the property recovered in this suit for their respective fees.

CHARLES A. SAFFELL Vs: JAMES D. BONHAM. Motion - Came the Complnt. by his Sol., A. A. TEMPLE, pressed the Ct. for a decree agnst. Defdt. for money pd. as his security. It appears to the Chancellor that on Jan. 29, 1856 the Complnt. executed a bond before the C&M jointly with EPHRIAM LINK for prosecution of a suit brought by the said Defdt. agnst. LINK in this Ct. On May 8, 1858, a decree was pronounced by Chancellor agnst. Complnt. Upon the said bond in pain of the said LINK for sum of $282.58 beside certain costs that he hath incurred. On the 23rd of Nov. 1858, the said Compltnt. pd. upon the said judgement in part the sum of $257.50 which expended the funds.

Pg. 205 JOHN R. HAYS Vs: JOHN MCCLAIN, Admr. & DOUTHETT. Appealed to Supreme Ct. Knoxville, Tennessee.

HARTSELL & WALLACE, Admr. Vs: HEIRS & CREDITORS of G. S. GILBERT, Dec'd. Complnts. asked to amend their bill so as to make THOMAS F. SAFFELL of the same County as a party Defdt.

Pg. 206 May 23, 1859.

WILLIAM WALLACE, Admr. of L. D. HENDERSON, Dec'd. Vs: SARAH A. HENDERSON & O. C&M to take testimony what fees should be allowed and pd. THOMAS C. LYON and JESSE G. WALLACE, Sol., for the Admr. and rep't. to Ct.

WILLIAM C. & RICHARD L. CRESWELL Vs: ANDREW CRESWELL & O. and ANDREW CRESWELL Vs: RICHARD CRESWELL & O. Leave granted Defdts. to file Ans.

H. C. SAFFLE & BROS. Vs: WILLIAM MCTEER. Case cont'd.

S. R. CAMERON Vs: P. T. SILER. Case cont'd.

JESSE & WILLIAM ELMORE Vs: EPP EVERETT. Case cont'd.

Pg. 207 WILLIAM S. PORTER Vs: L. D. FRANKLIN. Case cont'd.

WILLIAM WALLACE, Admr. of S. D. HENDERSON, Dec'd. Vs: HEIRS & CREDITORS OF S. D. HENDERSON, Dec'd. May 23, 1859. Admr. has disposed of Personal Property embraced and set forth in the deed of trust for sum of $3,080.07 appropriated for payment of debts leaving balance of $911.54. The land after assignment of dower was sold for $6,776.00 and the negro boy ANSEN was sold for $1,528.00. The money has been pd. for residue of said debts ordered that the fees of THOMAS C. LYON and JESSE G. WALLACE, Sols. for Complnt. and payment of costs in this case - that the Admr. account to C&M funds remaining in his hands. It appears that SAMUEL WALLACE became the purchaser of the negro boy ANSEN and has pd. the purchase money. C&M execute a proper conveyance to him for said boy.

Pg. 208 ESTHER HARDIN Vs: HEIRS-AT-LAW of JOHN HARDIN, Dec'd. Two mos. to file Ans.

HUDSON, ROBERTSON & PULLIAM & O. Vs: S. J. MCREYNOLDS & O. Debt of Complnt. has been pd. The parties agreed that case be dismissed.

JOHN GRIFFITTS, Extr. Vs: HEIRS of E. KEENE & O. & J. B. JACKSON Vs: HEIRS of E. KEENE, Dec'd. Remanded to rules for taking testimony.

Pg. 209 B. F. DUNCAN Vs: DANIEL L. TRUNDLE et al. May 24, 1859. Respdt. to have 2 mos. to Ans.

DAVID CUNNINGHAM, Admr. Vs: ALFRED CUNNINGHAM. Remanded to rules for taking testimony.

SAMUEL PRIDE, Admr. Vs. WILLIAM MCTEER & O. Ordered that parties of reference make report to show:
1) What compensation WILLIAM MCTEER shall be allowed as Rec'vr. and the expenses of Rec'vrship?
2) What loss sustained on the loss of bacon and other produce belonging to the firm of MCTEER, PRIDE & HENRY and also MCTEER, HENRY & CO.?
3) What discount or loss may have been sustained in the collection of bad debts or doubtful debts? MCTEER to make list of all judgements and notes which came into his hands as Rec'vr., as assets of the several firms.

Pg. 210 S. J. MCREYNOLDS Vs: JACOB SUMMEY, MILLEY A. HENRY & O. May 23, 1859. On the 11th day of Mar. 1859, C&M sold land as directed by earlier Ct. and S. J. MCREYNOLDS became purchaser for sum of $350.50. Used WILLIAM WALLACE as security. Court pleased to order, adjudge and decree all rights - title interest that JACOB SUMMEY has in said tract of land containing by estimation 124 A. in Blount County, Tennessee, and Civil District #14 on waters of Ellejoy Creek known as the E. half of the Old Dutch JOHN GARNER farm adjoining the lands of the heirs of JOHN HENRY, Dec'd. GEORGE LATHAM, WILLIAM ELDIDGE, A. DUNLAP & O. be divested out of him and into S. J. MCREYNOLDS and his heirs and assigns, forever.

Pg. 211 SAMUEL PRIDE, C&M. Vs: MARION CAMERON & HENRY MYERS. MARION CAMERON and HENRY MYERS are indebted to SAMUEL PRIDE, C&M. by note: $398.00 of
Pg. 212 May 15, 1858. Note remains due and unpaid plus $24.48 interest.

SAMUEL PRIDE, C&M. Vs: JAMES HENRY & WILLIAM HENDERSON. Latter two indebted to C&M $603.33 due in 18 mos. for store and dwelling house and 1 A. of land belonging and sold as property of A. L. and S. S. GILBERT, Dec'd. and DAVID GILBERT, minor heir of GEORGE GILBERT, Dec'd. Oct. 9th, 1857. Said note remains due and unpaid with $58.83 interest. May 24, 1859.

SAMUEL PRIDE, C&M. Vs: WILLIAM HENDERSON & JAMES HENRY. $37.33 pd. for 1/4 A. of land fronting the store and dwelling house of the late A. L. and S. S. GILBERT and O. sold as the property of GEORGE L. GILBERT, Dec'd. ($3.54 interest) May 30, 1859.

Pg. 213 B. W. & J. P. FORCE & CO. Vs: J. A. HOUSTON & CO. & S. J. MCREYNOLDS. Complnt. dismissed this bill as to S. J. MCREYNOLDS the same having been filed agnst. him by mistake. Complnt. assumes all costs of making MCREYNOLDS a party.

CHARLES M. MCGHEE Vs: BARKLY RUSSELL. Leave granted to amend Complnt.'s bill.

Pg. 214 DAVID CAMPBELL et al. Vs: J. H. GILLESPY, Extr. et als. Leave granted Respdt. to file Ans.

RICHARD M. SAFFLE Vs. JAMES WILSON & O. On affidavit case cont'd. Books and Papers of said firm WILSON & SAFFLE have not been filed. Respdt. has 1 mo. to do so.

JAMES W. HAMIL & O. Vs: JOHN EVERETT and JOHN EVERETT Vs: JAMES W. HAMIL & O. Both parties have 2 mos. to file Ans.

Pg. 215 DAVID L. STOUT Vs: AMANDA HOOD. May 30, 1859. Amt. of purchase money due upon house and lot described, not given. C&M to take and state an acc't. in this case and the unpaid purchase money yet due. May 31st, 1859.

CHAMBERLAIN MILER CO. & O. Vs: S. J. MCREYNOLDS & O. Complnts. by Sol. dismiss their suit. As to J. B. LIPPENCOTT & CO. assume 1/3rd of cost.

J. B. LIPPENCOTT & CO. & O. Vs: S. J. MCREYNOLDS & O. In this cause JAMES W. HUMES, Sol. for Complnt., makes oath that he is informed and believes S. J. MCREYNOLDS in disobedience and violation of the injunction of the Ct. - did continue to sell and dispose of the property of said firm included in a deed of trust executed by S. J. MCREYNOLDS & CO. to WILLIAM L. HUTTON, trustee on the 4th day of Nov. 1857. and S. J. MCREYNOLDS did a part, if not the whole of the proceeds and merchandise belonging to the said MCREYNOLDS & CO. Remanded to the next term of Ct. (This entire item stricken from the page.)

Pg. 216 JOHN GRIFFETT & JOHN EAKIN, Extrs. of GEORGE MCKAY, Dec'd. Vs: JOHN P. RHEA & O. May 30, 1859. JANE MCKAY, Widow, and MARY ANN and ROBERT MCKAY are nonresidents of Tennessee and publication was made in newspaper for four successive weeks requiring nonresidents to Ans. the bill filed agnst. them. They failed to Ans. Complnts. JOHN EAKIN and JOHN GRIFFITHS, Extrs. of GEORGE MCKAY, Dec'd. were empowered and directed by Will of Testator to sell lands of which GEORGE MCKAY was seized and possessed at the time of
Pg. 217 his death. 127 1/2 A. corner w/JAMES HUNT'S lands to JOHN GREER'S lands to a hickory on JOHN RHEA'S line to GEORGE DUNCAN'S line to J. HUNT'S line with the consent of the family of said GEORGE MCKAY to enable them to remove from the State of Tennessee. The family did consent to and did desire the sale of said described lands so far as it could consent and the Extrs. in pursuance of the provisions of the Will sold said described land in month of Feb. 1856 to one JOHN P. RHEA for sum of $1,147.50 which has all been pd. Ct. declares sum of $1,147.50 a fair consideration. The MCKAY family has moved to the state of Iowa soon after the sale of the land, but because it appears to the Ct. that a part of the family were minors at the time of the said sale and unable to give their consent to the sale, the Ct. is pleased to satisfy and confirm said sale and decree that all rights, title, claim and interest the said widow's children of the said GEORGE MCKAY, Dec'd. the said JOHN GRIFFITS and JOHN EAKIN, Extrs. & C. be divested out of them in JOHN P. RHEA, Complnt. pay costs of proceeds out of sale of said lands.

Pg. 218 T. D. TILLINGHAST Vs: HEIRS & CREDITORS of JOHN HENRY, Dec'd. and JAMES WILSON Vs: HEIRS of JOHN HENRY. On motion of Complnt. T. D. TILLINGHAST by his Sol. ordered by Ct. these two causes to be heard together.

S. J. MCREYNOLDS Vs: GRISHAM STRANGE & CO. Unable to make full rep't. ordered that rep't. be rec'd. and order be cont'd. to file supplimental rep't.

MOSES GAMBLE & O. Vs: ELI NUNN & O. May 30, 1859. ELI NUNN has $235.10 belonging to Estate of his dec'd. wife, MARTHA ELIZABETH, after deducting expenditures made by the said NUNN in the purchase of property mentioned in the pleadings and it appears to Ct. that rents and profits of the property and the hire of the negroes mentioned in pleadings since the death of MARTHA E. and until the negroes came into hands of C&M amounted to $356.82 yet due from said NUNN. Ordered that Complnt. recover of said ELI NUNN, $591.92.

Pg. 219

C. W. NORWOOD & WIFE Vs: EDWARD GEORGE & O. and W. S. JOHNSON & WIFE Vs: EDWARD GEORGE & O. Sheriff reports ROBERT WEAR has been served w/process more than 10 days before regular term of Ct. and has failed to Ans. On application Judgement is entered agnst. him. It further appearing to the Ct. from return of Sheriff that CLEMENTINE BADGETT is a nonresident of this state. Ordered that publication be made as to CLEMENTINE BADGETT a Defdt.

JOSEPH H. TEDFORD Vs: JAMES WILSON & O. May 31, 1859. No equity in Complnts. bill. The Ct. orders and decrees that the bill in this case be dismissed and Complnt. pay costs.

Pg. 220 HENRY MILLER b/n/f/FLORA J. FAGG. Leave granted to Ans. petition as to make NEWTON GOODWIN of Arkansas and JULIUS N. FAGG, a minor, resident of Blount County parties and that publication be made to the nonresident.

T. D. TILLINGHAST Vs: WILL MCTEER & O. On motion of their Sol., JOHN C. CHILDS and his wife, JANE CHILDS, ANN BOWEN and JAMES HENRY given rt. to file an amended Ans. It is ordered that notice served on J. G. WALLACE and JOHN E. TOOLE shall be sufficient to take depositions on behalf of Respdts. and that a notice in SAMUEL PRIDE and JAMES HENRY shall be sufficient to take depositions on behalf of Complnts.

JAMES PORTER Vs. SAMUEL PRIDE, Admr. JOHN L. M. PRIDE, WILLIAM J. HENRY, WILLIAM MCTEER. The heirs-at-law of JOHN HENRY, Dec'd. interested in the subject matter in controversy. One of said heirs, he and such others of the heirs as may choose are permitted to make themselves party Defdts. and file Ans.

Pg. 221 SAMUEL PRIDE Vs: WILLIAM MCTEER & O. Judgement taken agnst. WILLIAM MCTEER, WILLIAM P. L. CUMINGS, R. P. BOWERMAN, ALEXANDER KENNEDY, JAMES HENRY, H. T. COX, WILLIAM A. SPENCER, JAMES M. TOOLE, WILLIAM PORTER, JAMES MCCAMY, DAVID CHANDLER, WILLIAM KIDD, ANDREW MCCLAIN, JOHN SINGLETON, JAMES PORTER, WILLIAM J. HENRY, SAMUEL MCKINSEY, WILLIAM D. MCGINLEY, PETER L. DARYLL, HENRY WILLIAM DARRYLL and KENNY MILLER, Admr. of ISAAC D. RANKIN, HENRY H. (JAFRIES?) for want of Ans.

Pg. 222 DAVID L. STOUT Vs: AMANDA HOOD. May 31, 1859. There is yet due of the purchase money the sum of $274.48. The Ct. declares to be a lien on the house and lot in town of Morganton, Blount County, Tennessee. Lot #9 containing 1/2 A. and joins lots of JOHN CAULSON, THOMAS and SAMUEL HENLEY & O. AMANDA HOOD to have 4 mos. to pay said sum w/int. and declare a lien to the Master of the Ct. If not pd. by then, C&M to sell land.

W. S. JOHNSON Vs: ED. GEORGE & O. Ordered that process be issued to Hamilton County to serve on EDWARD J. ANDERSON and to Roane County to be served on WILLIAM and MARTHA FOUTE.

J. B. LIPPINCOTT, Atty. & O. Vs: S. J. MCREYNOLDS & CO. Complnts. Atty. states MCREYNOLDS has violated the injunction upon him. Ct. orders an attachment for contempt of said process be issued agnst. MCREYNOLDS.

Pg. 223 JOSEPH H. TEDFORD Vs: JAMES WILSON et al. Complnt. prays an appeal to next term of Supreme Ct., Second Mon. in Sept. next. Knoxville, Tennessee.

Wed., June 1, 1859, JAMES W. HAMIL & O. Vs: JOHN

EVERETT/JOHN EVERETT Vs: JAMES W. HAMIL. Two mos. to file ans.

Pg. 224 JAMES HENRY, Admr. of HUGH HENRY, Dec'd. Vs: SAMUEL PRIDE, Admr. of JOHN HENRY, Dec'd. On rep't. of W. D. MCGINLEY, Spec. Comm'r., 415 exceptions sustained and balance of exceptions overruled. It appearing that there remained in the hands of Respdts.' intestate JOHN HENRY, Dec'd., $964.18 due and owing and to the Complnts.' intestate which has issue been accounted for or pd. over. It is ordered adjudged and decreed that the said Complnt. JAMES HENRY, Admr. of HUGH HENRY, Dec'd. recover of said SAMUEL PRIDE, Admr. of JOHN HENRY, Dec'd. which has come to his hands of the JOHN HENRY estate to be administered the said sum of $964.18 and the cost of cause for which execution may issue to be levied of the goods and chattels rights and credits. SAMUEL PRIDE, Admr. to be administered. Respdt. prays an appeal to next term of Supreme Ct. in Knoxville.

MOSES GAMBLE & O. Vs: ELI NUNN & O. Complnts. in
Pg. 225 this cause who are of age have compromised the matters in controversy out of the rents of houses and hire of slaves with ELI NUNN and have agreed to release their interest in the decree pronounced. W. D. WALKER is app'td. Spec. Comm'r. to take examination of ANGELINE GAMBLE, wife of MOSES GAMBLE and of LOUISA F., wife of ROBERT MCKAMY touching the execution of the release and in consent with executed releases.

H. HEARTSELL & J. G. WALLACE, Admr. of GEORGE S. GILBERT, A. L. GILBERT & S. S. GILBERT, Dec'd. Vs: HEIRS & CREDITORS of said ESTATE. May 30, 1859. On exceptions of Respdt. H. C. SAFFELL, Gdn. of DAVID GILBERT, to said report: 1st and 2nd exceptions overruled, 3rd exception is sustained. C&M to make rep't. as to what would be a reasonable allowance to be pd. Respdt. for services as Gdn. in taking and collecting rents
Pg. 226 of property mentioned in the pleadings. Said Gdn. has rec'd. of rents and profits of the lands, belonging to the estate of A. L. GILBERT and S. S. GILBERT the sum of $249.74. SAFFELL has rec'd. full amt. of proceeds of sale of DAVID GILBERT'S undivided interest in said lands from C&M. Costs of case $57.54. C&M to recover from

H. C. SAFFLE $312.89 for which execution may issue. It appears to Ct. that in the lifetime of said GEORGE S. GILBERT he purchased of claimant SAFFELL a tract of land containing about 40 A. mentioned in pleadings which the said C. H. SAFFELL executed his bond to the said GEORGE S. GILBERT for title and pd. SAFFELL $300.00 and a good and sufficient conveyance of 10 A. of land belonging to GEORGE S.'s minor children. When the said children should attain the age of 21 years that the said agreement on the part of the said GEORGE S. cannot

Pg. 227 be complied with as is Ordered, judged and decreed that the said contract of sale be recinded and for nothing held that although the title and interest the heirs might have vested out of them and into H. C. SAFFELL, C. H. SAFFELL refund the sum of $300.00 to the C&M. Tract of land has been possession of the said GEORGE S. GILBERT. Ordered that the rents and profits of the same be set off agnst. whatever interest may have accrued on the $300.00. It appears to the Ct. that GEORGE S. GILBERT died siezed and possessed of a town lot in the town of Louisville on the street leading by FOSTER'S store to the

Pg. 228 river adjoining the lots of H. C. SAFFELL, L. D. CARTER and O. which was purchased by said GILBERT of SAMUEL SAFFELL, Dec'd. and known and described as the BOYD lot which yet remains unsold. C&M to sell lot. C&M to take proof and rep't. what would be a reasonable allowance for JESSE G. WALLACE and H. HEARTSELL, Admrs. to be pd. out of respective estates. Respdt. L. K. FINLEY pd. of the purchase money on the lot in Concord, Knox County, Tennessee mentioned in the pleadings the

Pg. 229 sum of $150.00 w/interest of $30.62 and FINLEY has also pd. a debt of A. L. and S. S. GILBERT to Messr. H. L. FRENCH & SON as security the sum of $245.78 in which interest $66.10 making in all pd. $492.56. Master sold lot to FINLEY for $213.30. Land divested out of A. L. and S. S. GILBERT and into FINLEY. Due and owing to NANCY GILBERT from A. L. GILBERT and S. S. GILBERT the sum of $375.71, which was a lien on a lot in the town of Louisville adjoining lots C. P. SAFFELL and O. purchased by A. L. and S. S. GILBERT of C. P. SAFFELL and conveyed in trust to NANCY GILBERT called the third corner lot into court and agrees to take said lot in full satisfaction of her said claim. It is ordered that C&M execute to NANCY E. GILBERT a proper conveyance. C&M to take proof what would be a reasonable allowance for W. D. MCGINLEY for services as Trustee.

ROBERT WEAR & O. Vs: JAMES D. WEAR & O. DAVID and ISABELLA WEAR are minors and have been regularly served w/process but are not answered the bill by themselves or Gdns. The order was heretofore requiring an acc't. are therefore recinded and on motion leave is granted Complnt. to amend his bill so as to show that the said minors were over 14 yrs. of age at the commencement of this suit and to ask that they be required to Ans. the bill to the end that all parties may be before the Ct. which amendment is made and therefore the Ans. of the said minors were filed.

Pg. 230 SAMUEL PRIDE Vs. WILLIAM MCTEER & O. Final Decree - This case came to be finally heard on this 31st day of May 1859 before Hon. T. NIXON VAN DYKE, Chancellor, upon the bill and Ans. and Exhibit A to the original bill and judgement Pro Confesso taken as to all the Defdts. except S. S. PORTER from all which it appears that on the 21st day of Mar. 1854 one WILLIAM P. L. CUMMINGS conveyed by deed of tract date in Exhibit A three lots of land in the town of Maryville, known in the plan of said town as Lots #7, 8 and 40. No. 40 situated on Main St. Nos. 7 and 8 situated in back street and bounded by College St., the town commons and JAMES WILSON. Said lots were sold to SAMUEL PRIDE and WILLIAM MCTEER of the first part, WILLIAM C. WALLACE and SAMUEL W. WALLACE of the second part and WILLIAM MCTEER of the 3rd part for which they pd. for said property in the proportions following: That is today: $300.00 by the said PRIDE and MCTEER, $600.00 by the said WILLIAM C. and SAMUEL WALLACE, and $600.00 by the said WILLIAM MCTEER and it further appears that on the 21st of Aug. 1855, the said WILLIAM MCTEER became the purchaser and owner of the interest in said property of the said W. C. and S. W. WALLACE and it further appears that on the 29th of Jan. 1856, the said MCTEER conveyed said lots in trust to R. P. BOWERMAN for the benefit of ALEXANDER KENNEDY, JAMES HENRY and O. who are Defdts. in this cause. And it further appears that at the Sept. term 1855 at the Circuit Ct. of Blount County divers judgements were rendered agnst. the said WILLIAM MCTEER as surviving partner of MCTEER, PRIDE & HENRY on which executions were issued and levied on the interest of said MCTEER in said property, which was sold on the 1st day of Sept. 1856, by the Sheriff of Blount County and which sale Defdts. S. S. PORTER became the purchaser of Lots #7 and 8 and RANKIN DURYEA & CO. became the purchaser of Lot #40 and it appears that at the time of filing the bill in this case the said R. P. BOWERMAN as Trustee aforesaid had advertised the property for sale by virtue of said deed of trust.

CHANCERY COURT
BLOUNT COUNTY, TENNESSEE
MINUTE BOOK I

Chancery Court - 4th Monday, November 1859.

Pg. 1   T. D. TILLINGHAST Vs: WILLIAM MCTEER & O. Motion - SAMUEL PRIOR by his Sol. by consent of Complnt. council.

S. W. O'CONNER, for wards, as heirs of PHILIP MYERS.

L. GRAY SMITH Vs: ANN JAMES, Admx.

GREENE FARMER & O. Vs: JAMES WATTERS & JOSIAS GAMBLE, Extrs. of ENOCH WATTERS, Dec'd. (Add names to original bill. - LEWIS C. FARMER, LERENAH C. FARMER, SARAH A. FARMER, RULINA A. FARMER and GREEN FARMER - last four have a Gdn. appointed for them, they being minors - and to add: MARY STEPHENS, formerly MARY TATE and her husband, JOHN STEPHENS. Above are nonresidents of Tennessee together with O. whose names appear in original bill.)

Pg. 2   C. W. & M. R. NORWOOD Vs: ED. & I. W. GEORGE, Extrs. & WILLIAM J. JOHNSON & WIFE Vs: E. GEORGE, Extr. On motion, the death of ELIZABETH ANDERSON is admitted. - subpoena issued to Sheriff of Warren County against E. J. ANDERSON.
Court adjourned.   T. NIXON VAN DYKE, Chancellor

Chancery Court - Tues., Nov. 29, 1859.

JOHN EVERETT Vs: JAMES W. HAMIL & O. Motion to

dissolve injunction.

S. J. MCREYNOLDS Vs: GRESHAM STRANGE. Rep't. next term Ct. collections and disbursements.

JOHN EVERETT Vs: JAMES W. HAMIL. Complnt. to give security for costs.

RICHARD DEARMAND Vs: JAMES CLARK & O. One of Respdts. is Extr. of JAMES CLARKE, Dec'd. Ans. of HARVEY P. CLARKE. Tract of land which JAMES CLARKE, Dec'd. bound himself on 11 Mar. 1850, to make title to Complnt. DEARMAND. 12th Civil District consists of 100 A. Joins land of JOHN P. HOOKE & O. DEARMAND pd. $300.00 is shown by admission of said Extr. HARVEY P. CLARKE. CAMPBELL DEARMAND gets title. RICHARD DEARMAND and security pay C.C.

Pg. 3 Be it remembered that at Superior Ct. begun and held for Eastern Division, Tennessee, at Knoxville, 2nd Monday of Sept. 1859, the following decrees were pronounced by said Ct. Oct. 4, 1859 - Blount County Chancery Court.

JOSEPH TEDFORD Vs: JAMES WILSON et al. JOSEPH TEDFORD and WILLIAM MCTEER on Jan. 8, 1856, entered a written contract/TEDFORD bound himself to give his labor and that of his wife, in managing a farm, for said MCTEER for $350.00 a yr. After raising a crop, the crop and other property taken by Sheriff of Blount County to satisfy judgement in favor of JAMES WILSON agnst. MCTEER & JESSE KERR. JOSEPH TEDFORD has a lien upon proceeds of farm, so raised by him and his family. Ct. orders JOSEPH TEDFORD have and retain lien for his labor - wages in corn, wheat and oats.

Pg. 4 CARRICK W. NELSON - Clerk of the Supreme Ct. - Eastern Div. State of Tenn. at Knoxville certify above. C. W. NELSON, Clerk - F. M. MCFALL, D. Clerk.

Pg. 5 B. W. & I. P. FORCE & CO. Vs: J. A. HOUSTON & CO. & O. J. A. HOUSTON, SAMUEL YEAROUT, JOHN S. CRAIG, G. P. RUTLEDGE, WILLIAM WALLACE, T. I. WILSON, JOHN COFFIN, SAMUEL F. COWAN and ALEXANDER MCNUTT, COOK BAILEY & CO. and ROCKFORD MFG. CO. - CHAMBERLAIN MILER & CO.

S. J. MCREYNOLDS on motion of SAMUEL A. ROGERS was sworn as a Sol.

Pg. 6 WILLIAM & JESS ELLMORE Vs: EPP EVERETT. Con't. to next term.

JAMES BONHAM Vs: EPHRIAM LINK. CHARLES P. SAFFLE. Case taken to Supreme Ct., Tennessee.

DAVID L. STOUT Vs: AMANDA HOOD. Nov. 28, 1859. Purchased house and land Lot #9 in plan - Town of Morganton, Blount County, Tennessee, adjoining lots of LABE COULSON, THOMAS HENLEY & O., DAVID L. STOUT, his Security, W. G. MCKENSEY.

Pg. 7 R. B. DOUGLAS & O. Vs: S. J. MCREYNOLDS & O. S. and D. GHORMALY and SAMUEL T. BECKNALL - time to file Ans.

MAD. COX & J. MCHENRY Vs: WILLIAM MCTEER & O. Consent and Marriage of ANN E. HANNUM and her husband, FIELDING POPE.

THOMAS C. SARTAIN & WIFE Vs: W. W. BAYLESS & O. Nov. 29, 1859. Division of slaves. Sale is necessary.

Pg. 8 JAMES KEYS Vs: WILLIAM M. STEELE & BRO. JAMES STEELE a nonresident. Publication to be made in papers.

Pg. 9 SAMUEL PRIDE Vs: WILLIAM MCTEER, P. L. CUMMINGS. Fri., Oct. 14, 1859. WILLIAM CUMMINGS, SAMUEL PRIDE, WILLIAM MCTEER, WILLIAM C. and SAMUEL W. WALLACE. Debt. to Maryville College.

Pg. 10 S. M. WELLS Vs: JOHN W. STEELE. Time to file Ans.

SAMUEL & ANN GHORMLEY, Adm. & Admx. of WILLIAM JAMES, Dec'd. Vs: ROBERT JAMES. Supreme Ct. agreed with lower Ct. ruling in case.

Pg. 11 Settlement of partnership - WILLIAM JAMES and ROBERT JAMES - WILLIAM JAMES intestate. ROBERT JAMES and his Security, JAMES HENRY.

SAMUEL & ANN GHORMLEY, Admr. & Admx. of WILLIAM

JAMES, Dec'd. Vs: ROBERT JAMES & O. Insolvent bill.

Pg. 12 Hon. T. NIXON VAN DYKE, Chancellor, presiding. Wed., Nov. 30, 1859.

MOSES GAMBLE & O. Vs: ELI NUNN & O. W. A. WALKER to take exam and be advised personally.

B. W. & J. P. FORCE & CO. and ROBERTSON, HUDSON & PULLIAM Vs: J. A. HOUSTON & CO. & O. Ans. of JOHN N. TEDFORD, J. C. M. BOGLE, SAMUEL YEAROUT, JOHN S. CRAIG. Plaintiffs recovered judgement in U.S. Circuit Ct. in Knoxville.

Pg. 13 RICHARD S. ROBERTSON, CHARLES C. HUDSON, ROBERT W. PULLIAM, WILLIAM D. RANKIN, PLES. M. CRAIGMILES, HUGH MCD. MCELRATH, JOHN H. CRAIGMILES recovered judgements Vs: SAMUEL L. YEAROUT. YEAROUT lands adjoining lands of WILLIAM H. THOMPSON, JOHN W. FROW, ANDREW EARLY and O. 9th District on waters of Pistol Creek Farm on which ISAAC YEAROUT resided at death. Personal property of SAMUEL L. YEAROUT. Also sell right and interest of JOHN S. CRAIG, Dec'd. and JOHN TEDFORD, and also 4 town lots in Maryville.

Pg. 14 ROBERT WEAR Vs: JAMES D. WEAR & O. Necessity to sell land and negroes for purpose of distribution among heirs of HUGH WEAR, Dec'd. Widow's Dower, except for negro girl TILDA, RACHEL and her two children, TOM, WILLIAM SAM, PETER, MARY and infant son, AMY, LOTTY to be sold to the highest bidder. RACHEL and her two Ch. and MARY and her Ch. each sold as one lot. To rep't. to Ct. if girl TILDA was intended by HUGH WEAR as an advancement to his daughter, MARTHA MCCONNELL, or was she a loan? Ct. needs to know expenses required in caring and providing for negroes in relation to the property.

Pg. 15 ROBERT WEAR Vs: JAMES D. WEAR & O. Cont'd. Necessity to sell land and negroes to settle estate.

Pg. 16 P. F. SILER et al. Vs: CAMERON & EVERETT. C&M to loan out funds until next term Ct.

Pg. 17   H. HEARTSELL & J. G. WALLACE, Admrs. GILBERTS Vs: HEIRS & CREDITORS of GILBERTS. Judgement agnst. J. S. BONHAM. Feb. 7, 1857. Levied on lot in town of Louisville. - Main Street adjoining land of W. T. HEARTSELL, opposite side Street ABRAM HEARTSELL, where JAMES D. TEMPLE resides. Judgement agnst. JOSHUA O. and JOHN R. HAYS in town of Louisville, a back lot adjoining lands of H. T. COX where S. B. HEART resides.

Pg. 18   Allow H. HEARTSELL $500.00 and JESSE G. WALLACE $250.00 compensation for services.

R. M. SAFFELL & O. Vs: JAMES WILSON & O. Books of firm WILSON and SAFFELL as evidence. Complnts.' father, JOHN SAFFELL and JAMES WILSON were bus. partners, merchandizing in Maryville many yrs. In yr. 1841, partnership dissolved by death of JOHN SAFFELL. 1842 settlement made fully w/J. H. GILLEPSY and H. C. SAFFELL, Admr. Estate of JOHN SAFFELL.

Pg. 19   Respdt. WILSON and JOHN SAFFELL had undivided interest in 3 tracts of land: Gibson Tract, 100 A. in Stewart Tract and a Mt. tract of 5,000 A., all unpartitioned. Calls for sale of land. No other complaint.

H. & B. DOUGLAS & O. Vs: S. J. MCREYNOLDS & O. One of Respdts., ESTHER HARDIN, intermarried w/HUGH B. LEEPER. He to be made party to suit.

Pg. 20   B. F. DUNCAN Vs: D. L. TRUNDLE et al. Respdt. WILLIAM H. CANNON - No equity in Complnt. bill. Injunction dissolved. 29th Nov. 1859.

THOMAS C. SARTAIN & WIFE Vs: WILLIAM BAYLESS et al. Nov. 30, 1859. Necessity to sell slaves to settle Est. of SARAH BAYLESS, Dec'd. for distribution among heirs. Slaves MARY, SAM, PRESTON, and HANNAH be sold in 12 mos. time w/interest to highest bidder. 5% down taking a note and good security. Woman, HANNAH, and Ch. to be sold as one.

Pg. 21   P. T. SILER, HORACE MAYNARD, MARY A. WEST. Admr. STATE of TENNESSEE Vs: EPAPHRODITUS EVERETT & SAMUEL R. CAMERON. Nov. 30, 1859. MARY A. WEST, Admx. Money due CAMERON for tract of land. EVERETT to pay bills.

Pg. 22 JAMES PORTER et al. Vs: WILLIAM A. SPENCER et al. Nov. 30, 1859. Ruling of the Supreme Ct. Knoxville, 2nd Mon. in Nov. JAMES PORTER, JAMES M. HENRY, JAMES MCCAMY, WILLIAM D. MCGINLEY, WILLIAM I. HENRY, P. M. BOWERMAN, JOHN SINGLETON Vs: WILLIAM A. SPENCER, WILLIAM MCTEER et al. WILLIAM A. SPENCER a note or bond for $8,500.00 due 12 mos. after date. A Deed of Trust made by said MCTEER for security of said obligation.

Pg. 23 Problem be remanded from Supreme Ct. Knoxville to Chancery Court, Blount County.

Pg. 24 JAMES HENRY et. al. Vs: ALEXANDER KENNEDY & O. JAMES HENRY, JOHN SINGLETON, ANDREW MCCLAIN et al. Vs: ALEXANDER KENNEDY, WILLIAM MCTEER & WILLIAM S. SPENCER. (Supreme Ct. Knoxville - same $8,000.00 of earlier case - costs equally divided between parties - case remanded to Maryville and Chancery Ct.)

Pg. 25 DAVID & CLAIBORNE CUNNINGHAM Vs: ALFRED CUNNINGHAM et al. MOSES CUNNINGHAM to ALFRED CUNNINGHAM. ALFRED took advantage of his father's extreme age and imbecility by fraud and undue influence.

Pg. 26 ALFRED CUNNINGHAM supposed to have pd. his father $700.00. Need proof. What advancements in money or property, if any, ever made by MOSES CUNNINGHAM to any of his children? Court needs to determine these facts.

J. EVERETT Vs: JAMES HAMILL & JAMES M. SCOTT. Action overruled.

A. NORWOOD & WIFE Vs: E. GEORGE et al. and W. S. JOHNSON & WIFE Vs: E. GEORGE et al. Suggested to Ct. that EDWARD J. ANDERSON is a nonresident. Unable to locate him. Ct. pleased to direct that publication be made as to him.

Pg. 27 J. H. GILLESPY, Admr. of MATTHEW WALLACE, Dec'd. & DAVID CAMPBELL, Admr. of ELIZABETH CAMPBELL, Dec'd. Vs: JAMES H. GILLESPY et als. Case heard Nov. 30, 1859. JAMES H. GILLESPY filed complaint as Extr. of Estate of MATTHEW WALLACE, Dec'd. Filed bill in March.

1855 for final settlement of Estate. In hands of Extr. $6,353.07 plus property accounted for $4,396.87 in Nov. 1858. Ct. ordered distribution among legatees under the Will leaving sum of $1,962.20 at that time still in hands of Extr. He has failed to pay over. In 1858, Term of Ct. (Nov.) leave granted Complnt. in X Bill to bring ALEXANDER MCNUTT, HUGH BOGLE, WILLIAM C. GILLESPY, and CAMPBELL GILLESPY, Securities on said bond, into cause.

Pg. 28 Complnts. entitled to relief they prayed for.

Ct. adjourned until tomorrow morning, 8:00 AM.
T. NIXON VAN DYKE, Chancellor
Ct. met pursuant to adjournment.

JAMES TAYLOR et al. Vs: JAMES WALKER et al. SAMUEL PRIDE permitted to file X bill.

Pg. 29 ANN & SAMUEL GHORMLY, Adm. of WILLIAM JAMES, Dec'd. Vs: ROBERT JAMES. Complnts. granted permission to file amended bill. Ordered C&M to take testimony and rep't. what is a reasonable compensation for THOMAS C. LYON, GEORGE BROWN, JOHN E. TOOLE, JESSE G. WALLACE for services as council in this litigation on behalf of estate of WILLIAM JAMES.

Pg. 30 SAMUEL PRIDE, Admr. of JOHN HENRY, Dec'd. Vs: WILLIAM MCTEER et al. Respdt. MCTEER allowed 5% commission on one and 15% on another and on no other sums. Must acc't. for what interest rec'd. for money held from sale of goods and property belonging to firm of MCTEER, PRIDE & HENRY, or MCTEER, HENRY & CO. Advise Ct. what amts. pd. out.

Pg. 31 H. T. COX Vs: R. P. BOWERMAN et al. Cont'd. to next term of Ct.

R. L. CATES & W. D. MCGINLEY, Extrs. & C. Vs: WILLIAM AMBRISTER et al. Leave granted to Defdts. BETSY and MORIAH who are slaves, and RILEY and HENRY also slaves and minors to appear and Ans. b/n/f a Gdn. at litem JAMES W. HUME and leave further granted to file Ans. at next term of Ct. ASA AMBRISTER, one of the Resdts. not having been served w/process comes into Ct.

by his Sol. and asks to enter his appearance, which is allowed.

M. L. TEFFETELLER Vs: JOHN R. HAYS & J. O. HAYS. Jdgmt. by motion. M. L. TEFFETELLER by Sol. moved Ct. for jdgmt. agnst. JOHN R. & JOSHUA O. HAYS. Appearing to Ct. from receipt of W. H. SWAN, Deputy Sherriff of Knox County, and endorsement of said SWAN, Feb. 28, 1859, pd. $41.89 in full agnst. JOHN R. and JOSHUA O. HAYS as Security upon a bond for prosecution of a suit between JOHN R. and JOSHUA HAYS, Complnts. and J. T. DOUTHET and GEORGE MONTGOMERY, Admrs. of SAMUEL DOUTHET, Dec'd. as Respdts. O.A.D. that judgement be rendered agnst. JOHN R. HAYS and J. O. HAYS in favor of TEFFETELLER for the sum of $41.89 plus costs.

Pg. 32 WILLIAM M. STEELE, Admr. Est. of MARY ANN O'CONNER Vs: ELIZABETH DAVIS et al. Nov. 30, 1859. Complnt. entitled to relief sought. C&M to take an acc't.
1) What personal Est. of PHILIP MYERS, Dec'd. came to hands of Extx. ELIZABETH DAVIS and Extr. JACOB DAVIS and in what it consisted and value?
2) What might have come to Extx. by use of proper diligence?
3) What disbursements Extx. has made in payment of Est. debts?
4) What advancements made to Complnts. intestate out of Est.?
5) Ascertain rents and profits of lands belonging to said Est. since the marriage of Complnts. intestate that might have come into hands of Extx.

JAMES PORTER et al. Vs: WILLIAM A. SHENON et al. Dec. 1, 1859. Chancellor of opinion exception well-taken. O.A.D. exception sustained. Rep't. set aside. C&M to rep't. to next term of Ct.

Pg. 33 JAMES HENRY et al. Vs: ALEXANDER KENNEDY et al. Chancellor of opinion exception well-taken. O.A.D. exception be sustained rep't. set aside. C&M rep't. next term Ct.

T. D. TILLINGHAST et al. Vs: HEIRS & CREDITORS of JOHN HENRY and JAMES WILSON Vs: JOHN HENRY'S

HEIRS. In this cause ordered AZRO A. BARNES be appt'd. Spec. Comm'r. to take and state an acc't. since C&M of Ct. is Admr. of JOHN HENRY, Dec'd. and party Defdt. to these suits.
1) What amt., if any, of personal property or assets still in hands of Admr.?
2) What are individual liabilities of Est. still unpaid?
3) What amt. assets belonging to firm MCTEER, PRIDE & HENRY and MCTEER, HENRY & CO. are still on hand and undisposed of?
4) What are unpaid liabilities of said firms?

Pg. 34 B. W. & J. P. FORCE & CO. et al. Vs: J. A. HOUSTON & CO. Ordered that C&M summons J. A. HOUSTON, one of the Respdts. to say under oath what monies he has collected belonging to the said firm of J. A. HOUSTON & CO. & to pay them over to C&M.

Pg. 35 Monday, May 28, 1860. Special Term of Chancery Court. Hon. SETH J. W. LUCKY, Chancellor presiding by interchange w/Hon. T. NIXON VAN DYKE, Chancellor of 5th District.

S. J. MCREYNOLDS Vs: JACOB SUMMY. Purchase money for which land sold has been paid by S. J. MCREYNOLDS, the purchaser. Ct. considers that lien retained upon land has been discharged.

SAMUEL PRIDE, C&M Vs: GEORGE RAMSEY & C. P. SAFFLE. Respdts. in this case are endebted to SAMUEL PRIDE, C&M by note of $275.00 - purchase money for house and lot in town of Louisville called the Bonham Lot under a decree in Chancery Ct. in Maryville as the property of A. L. and S. S. GILBERT, Dec'd. 21st Jan'y. Said note remains due and unpaid. Ordered by Ct. C&M recover of GEORGE RAMSEY & C. P. SAFFLE $275.00 int. and costs.

Pg. 36 SAMUEL PRIDE, C&M Vs: WILLIAM CUMMINGS & C. P. SAFFLE. CUMMINGS and SAFFLE endebted to C&M by note in hand, "Six mos. after date promise to pay C&M $53.00 w/int. - two town Lots #2 and 15 in town of Louisville sold as property of A. L. and S. S. GILBERT, Dec'd. and GEORGE D. GILBERT, a minor heir of GEORGE GILBERT, Dec'd. April 16, 1859. Note remains due and unpaid. C&M recover from Respdts. $53.00 plus $3.56 int.

SAMUEL PRIDE, C&M Vs: THOMAS EVIER, WILLIAM JEFFRIES and JAMES H. HENRY. Defdts. endebted to C&M by note: 6 mos. after date promise pay C&M $72.00 w/int. for two town Lots #3 and 14 in town of Louisville sold as propery of A. L. and S. S. GILBERT and GEORGE D. GILBERT, a minor, heirs of GEORGE S. GILBERT, Dec'd. Apr. 16, 1859. Appears note remains unpaid and due. C&M recover from Respdts. $72.00 plus $4.82 int.

Pg. 37   Tuesday, May 29, 1860. Ct. met Hon. S. J. W. LUCKY, Chancellor, presiding.

JOSEPH TEDFORD Vs: JAMES WILSON et al. Leave granted JAMES WILSON make new plea.

LEONARD A. WOOD & O. Vs: WILLIAM P. WOOD & O. Respdt. H. STEPHENS allowed until Friday of July special term to file his Ans. by consent of parties ordered by Ct. that injunction hereupon granted in this cause be dissolved to allow M. H. STEPHENS to use any fallen or dead timber of any kind upon the ground, on lands leased by said STEPHENS and described in bill for purpose of running his still.

GREENWAY, HENRY & SMITH Vs: S. T. COX & O. Leave granted Respdts. to file Ans.

THOMAS L. UPTON Vs: SAMUEL L. YEAROUT. Defdts. have until next term to demur or plead.

WILLIAM D. MCGINLEY & R. L. CATE, Extrs. & O. Vs: WILLIAM AMBRISTER & O. Since last term Ct. negro woman, MORIAH, who is in contest in this case, has given birth to another child, a male named GEORGE. The Ct. is pleased to Order that JAMES W. HUMES, Esq. be allowed until next term Ct. to Ans. as n/f for said GEORGE, as well as for his mother, MORIAH, and her other Ch. as he was authorized to do by Order of this Ct. Further Ordered by Ct. that a copy of original bill be substituted since original lost.

Pg. 38 B. W. & J. P. FORCE & O. Vs: J. A. HOUSTON & O. Offered for sale on Jan. 27, 1860 at C.H. door lands mentioned in decree belonging to SAMUEL L. YEAROUT and ISAAC N. YEAROUT being the highest and best bidder for tract of land sold to him at $2,163.00. Lot adjoining sold to J. M. TOOLE for $923.00. Pd. into
Pg. 39 hands of C&M. All rights of said SAMUEL YEAROUT in these tracts be divested and land in District #9 adjoining lands of M. H. THOMPSON, JOHN R. FROW, ANDREW EASLY and O. Said tracts consituting one farm and containing 461 A. M/L. and be vested in ISAAC N. YEAROUT and his heirs, the said sale embraces 3 1/2 undivided shares in said tract of land which descended to the heirs of ISAAC YEAROUT, Dec'd.
Ct. pleased to order and decree title, land and tenament in the lot of land containing 1/2 A. lying on the McGhee Ferry Rd. near Maryville adjoining lands of SAMUEL PRIDE on 3 sides and said road on the other - be divested out of said SAMUEL L. YEAROUT and be vested in JAMES M. TOOLE, the purchaser.

GREENWAY, HENRY & SMITH Vs: S. T. COX & O. HYATT MCBURNIE & CO. have leave to become party Defdts.

Pg. 40 Court adjourned to the 1st Wed. after the fifth Mon. of July when a Special Term of Ct. will be held. SETH J. LUCKY.

Pg. 41 Wed. Aug. 1, 1860. Be it remembered that at a Special Term of Chancery Ct. for Blount County - it being the 1st Wed. after the fifth Mon. of July 1860, the Hon. T. NIXON VAN DYKE, Chancellor, present and presiding.

ROBERT M. LINN Vs: JOSHUA O. HAYS & JOHN R. HAYS, JOHNSON JONES. Respdts. JOSHUA O. HAYS and JOHN R. HAYS executed to Complnt. promissory notes: 1) Due Oct. 2, 1857, for $770.00. 2) Other due Sept. 1, 1857, for $500.00. JOSHUA O. HAYS on Apr. 13, 1857, signed a lien-mortgaged premises in favor of Complnt. His Honor pleased to A. & D. Complnt. have and recover of JOSHUA O. HAYS and JOHN R. HAYS sum of $986.40 balance due. If not pd. by Sept. 1st, C&M to advertise for 40 days in Brownlow's *Knoxville Whig* and in 3 or more places in Blount County and proceed to sell house and lot in Louisville and if that not enough, sell tract of land of 50 A. described in mortgage deed and rep't. to next term Ct.

Pg. 42 WILLIAM & JESSE ELMORE Vs: EPP EVERETT. Case con't. by consent.

L. B. LIPPINCOTT & O. et al. Vs: S. J. MCREYNOLDS & O. Cause dismissed by Complnt.

WILLIAM L. PORTER Vs: L. D. FRANKLIN & O. Respdt. WILLIAM MCTEER, who has been served - to Ans. Complnt. bill within one month.

H. C. SAFFLE & BRO. Vs: WILLIAM MCTEER et al. By consent - case is cont'd.

Pg. 43 JAMES PORTER & O. Vs: WILLIAM A. SPENCER & O. There was due Respdt. W. A. SPENCER the sum of $6,256.49 w/int. of $62.56 or $6,319.05. Respdt. recover from said WILLIAM MCTEER, JAMES PORTER, JAMES M. HENRY, JASPER HENRY, SAMUEL MCCAMY, WILLIAM D. MCGINLEY, PLEASANT M. BOWERMAN and JOHN SINGLETON sum of $6,319.05 together w/court costs in this Ct.

CHARLES M. MCGHEE, Extr. of JOHN MCGHEE, Dec'd. Vs: B. M. RUSSELL & O. All charges of bill and amended bill are met and ans. Therefore decreed that the two bills be dismissed and Complnt. C. M. MCGHEE and ALEXANDER KENNEDY, his Security, pay costs.

Pg. 44 SAMUEL HENLEY Vs: HEIRS of A. H. HENLEY, Dec'd. ARTHUR H. HENLEY departed this life having first made a will and also by an instrument of writing, or article of agreement, entered into on 3rd Oct. 1847 between himself and his son, DAVID HENLEY. Had put son, DAVID, in full possession and absolute ownership of one of the farms of said Testator containing 478 1/2 A. valued at $4.00 A. Testator further orders and directs in his will that if any of the rest of his sons who were, or might become, of age after his death should desire it - each of his sons who might so wish should have the same number of A. of any other lands of said testator - other than the homestead place set aside to heirs and valued in same proportion. Thus, DAVID was to account on the final settlement. It appears to the Ct. that Complnt. is a son of said Testator and has attained the age of 21, and has elected to comply w/will provisions. There are lands in Blount County belonging to Est. of Testator - Complnt. entitled to relief prayed for - to value of that of DAVID HENLEY.

Pg. 45 Ordered that JAMES M. HENRY, SAMUEL TULLOCH, STEPHEN S. PORTER, J. C. M. BOGLE and BENJAMIN F. DUNCAN be appt'd. Comm'rs. to lay off said land in 6th District adjoining lands of GEORGE W. HENRY, HENRY HAMIL and O. and rep't. to next term Ct.

JOSEPH H. TEDFORD Vs: JAMES WILSON. Exceptions taken by Complnts.' Sol. be sustained and an acc't. be recommitted to C&M to follow procedures outlined at Nov. 1859 term Ct.

THOMAS SARTAIN & WIFE Vs: W. W. BAYLESS & O. On 17th of Jan. 1860, C&M sold negro slaves in pleadings mentioned where upon S. W. J. NILES, by his agent, CHARLES M. MCGHEE, became the purchaser of all of the said negroes to wit: The woman and child for the sum of $1,765.00; the oldest boy, SAM, for $600.00; the youngest boy, PRESTON, for the sum $411.00; for which notes were executed for 12 mos. Note signed by C. M. MCGHEE and D. W. LATTIMORE for $1,676.75. One note signed H. BRADLY, C. M. MCGHEE and D. W. LATTIMORE for $530.00 and another signed C. A. GURLEY, C. M. MCGHEE and D. W. LATTIMORE for $390.45. Title divested out of SARAH BAYLESS and the interest of the said THOMAS C. SARTAIN by virtue of his ----- have in said slaves be divested out of him and into the said S. W. J. NILES forever.

Pg. 46 Judge orders 1st: WILLIAM BAYLESS the Gdn. of the minor heirs in this case, who has had the slaves in possession shall be chargeable with their hire.
2) What BAYLESS entitled to for nursing and taking care of said slaves and for nursing and taking care of the slaves which died in his possession, belonging to said heirs?
3) What amt. was pd. by Gdn. WILLIAM BAYLESS in order to transfer the negroes in the division among the heirs of JOHN BLACK, Dec'd.? What amt. is yet due him,

if any?

Pg. 47

ROBERT WEAR Vs: JAMES D. WEAR & O. Aug. 1, 1860 - on the bill Ans. and exhibits proof and rep't. of C&M and the exceptions of Respdt. JAMES MCCONNELL and Wife and JAMES D. WEAR to the same. It appears to the Ct. that said TILDA was given in the lifetime of HUGH WEAR to his daughter, MARTHA E. MCCONNELL, absolutely, and was not a loan, it is ordered by the Ct. that Respdt. MCCONNELLS' exception be sustained and that the Master's rep't. be informed in that regard. It appearing to the Ct. that MARTHA E. MCCONNELL and her husband, JAMES MCCONNELL held and claimed said girl and has an advance possession of the same for more than 3 yrs. after the said gift and upon the death of HUGH WEAR. It is therefore considered by the Ct. that the said TILDA, be regarded and taken as an advancement by HUGH WEAR to MARTHA E. and because the Ct. is not advised as to the value of said girl when the said MARTHA E. took her into possession the C&M will take and state an amt. concerning same and rep't. to next term Ct.

Further considered by Ct. C&M restate his acc't. so as to show what would be a fair and reasonable compensation to JAMES D. WEAR for nursing and attending the sick negroes while in his possession. Respdt. is only allowed to retake the testimony of DANIEL TAYLOR and the Complnt. be allowed to cross-examine and take rebutting testimony. Upon rep't. of C&M made in May 1860 Term of the sales of the land and slaves in the pleadings mentioned which rep't. is in all things confirmed. C&M sold said land and slaves on the premises of the Dec'd. on the 19th day of Jan. 1860 to the highest bidder on 12 mos. time w/Int. except for 5% purchase money pd. down; and the JAMES D. WEAR became the purchaser of the land for $2,155.00 and executed his note w/JAMES MCCONNELL and MOSES ELLIOTT as security for $2,047.25 retaining a lien upon said land for the purchase money.

His Honor is pleased to O.A.D. that C&M will make a deed to JAMES D. WEAR for the 130 acres of land adjoining MARGARET WEARS' Dower, MOSES ELLIOTT and O. whenever the purchase money is pd.

Pg. 48

And it further appearing that JAMES D. WEAR became purchaser of the girl RACHEL and her 2 Ch. to wit:

HARRIS and PHILIS for the sum of $1,415.00; and also up the boy, BILL, for $200.50; and up the boy, TOM, for $455.00 and that for the said 5 slaves he executed his note at 12 mos. w/Int. with JAMES MCCONNELL and MOSES ELLIOTT as his Security for the sum of $1,966.98 amt. of purchase money less 5% and that MARY her Ch. was sold to MARGARET WEAR for the sum of $1,400.00; AISY to the said MARGARET for $801.00; and the girl, LOTTY, to MARGARET for $25.00; and MARGARET executed her note for said 4 slaves w/ROBERT WEAR and EDWARD GEORGE and N. G. VINEYARD as Sureties for the $2,114.70 purchase money less 5% (cash) and that JAMES MCCONNELL became purchaser of the boy, SAM, at $1,180.00; and also boy, PETER, at $931.00 and he executed his note at 12 mos. w/int. for sum of $1,937.05 purchase money less 5% cash - with JAMES D. WEAR and N. B. MCCLAIN as Security.

His Honor pleased to O.A.D. that all title and claim which the heirs and distributees of the said HUGH WEAR, Dec'd. held in and to said slaves above named be divested out of said heirs and vested in the purchasers, forever.

C&M to ascertain and rep't. next Term Ct. what would be reasonable compensation to the several Sols. who have engaged in this cause.

Pg. 49 B. W. & I. P. FORCE & CO. Vs: J. A. HOUSTON & CO. Aug. 1, 1860. Complnt. brought into Ct. a note given for the land in pleadings mentioned executed by ISAAC N. YEAROUT, THOMAS J. FROW and JOHN R. FROW for $1,081.50. - 6 Mos. after date promise to pay C&M of Blount County, $1,0811.50. Note due and unpaid. Complnt. asked for jdgmt. Ct. orders it to be pd.

THOMAS L. UPTON Vs: L. L. YEAROUT et als. Ordered Complnt. bill be dismissed and that he and his Security be taxed with court costs.

Pg. 50 H. HEARTSELL & J. G. WALLACE, Admrs. of GILBERTS Vs: HEIRS & CREDITORS. Ordered that Admrs. pay over to C&M all monies in their hands - before next term Ct. C&M to make pro-rata distribution of assets of estate among creditors. It appears a large amt. of outstanding debts due said Est. cannot be collected. Admrs. will hand over the same to C&M and he will proceed to sell same at public sale to highest bidder for cash in hand. C&M to make title to purchasers.

Pg. 51 JOHN GRIFFITTS, Extr. of ENOCH KEENE, Dec'd. Vs: WIDOW & HEIRS of E. KEENE and J. B. JACKSON & WIFE Vs: ROBERT HUGHS & O. Bill and X Bill. In the year 1856, ENOCH KEENE departed this life after having made and published his last Will & Testament where in he appointed Complnt. GRIFFITTS his Extr. and said Complnt. files his bill to have construction of same. Complnt. entitled to relief sought. It appearing to Ct. that Testator after making will and before death of Testator, sold and conveyed by Deed the tract of land on which he then resided and which he had specifically devised and disposed of in his Will to one ROBERT HUGHS for the consideration of $2,000.00. Testator, by said sale, revoked his Will. From the proceeds of the sale, Testator furnished his son, JAMES W. KEENE, with the sum of $700.00 to purchase for Testator's own use, one negro man, FRANK, mentioned in the pleadings. And that appearing that the same JAMES W. did with the money so furnished purchase the said negro and took title to same in his own name.

It is therefore considered by the Ct. that a resulting trust arises in said slave in favor of the Testator and belongs now to his personal estate. And it appearing to the Ct. that on the -- day of ---- 185-, and before the Testator's death, there issued to him by the Federal Government a Land Warrant #79251 for 120 A. of land under an Act of Congress of March 1815 which was not specifically directed. It appears to the Ct. that the Testator constituted his widow, MARY INAMY? KEENE, general and residuary legatee of all the rest and residue of his personal estate not otherwise specifically disposed of. It is considered by the Ct. that the proceeds of the land sold, as before mentioned to ROBERT HUGHS together with the negro boy, FRANK, and the said land warrant and all other of the personal estate not otherwise specified passes to and vests in the said MARY KEENE absolutely as Legatee in said Will. It is further considered by the Ct. that Complnt. JACKSON & WIFE are not entitled to relief prayed for. The X bill is dismissed and Complnt. JACKSON pay court costs.

Pg. 52 C&M take and state an acc't. and rep't. next term Ct.
1) What amts. belonging to said Est. have or should have

come to Est.?
2) What disposition has been made of same?
3) What amt. remains in his hands?

Made arrangements to see W. D. MCGINLEY pd. for his council - for the Extr. and JESSE G. WALLACE, council for MARY KEENE, be entitled to a lien on her portion of said Est. for his fees.

W. D. MCGINLEY & R. L. CATE, Extrs. & C. Vs: WILLIAM AMBRISTER & O. Aug. 1, 1860. Bill of Complnt. and Ans. Respdt. except NANCY SPILMAN and husband, WILLIAM SPILMAN, nonresidents and JOHN C. GALLIHER and wife, MARY GALLIHER. Chancellor pleased to O.A.D. that slaves BETSY, MORIAH, HENRY and RILEY and infant child of MORIAH, named GEORGE, are entitled to their freedom under last Will & Testament of GEORGE AMBRISTER, Dec'd. The emancipation of said negroes being construed and adjudged to be the primary object in this clause of said Will. Chancellor pleased to free this order - Slaves entitled to the bequest of

Pg. 53 $1,000.00 each, the same to be pd. to them in equal parts by Extrs. Said Slaves entitled to compensation for their time and services since death of Testator, GEORGE AMBRISTER. Ct. further A.& D. in favor of JAMES W. HUMES, Sol. for said slaves - a lien upon amt. they receive for his services. Ct. further pleased to A.& D. that LORETTA F. AMBRISTER is not chargeable w/any monies expended for her in lifetime of Testator and her portion of the estate of Testator is not liable to ademption. Widow of Testator, ELIZABETH AMBRISTER, is entitled under the Will to $6,500.00 to be pd. first out of notes of JOHN CHANDLER and B. M. CHANDLER mentioned in 1st clause of Will. If not sufficient, then out of other Est. of

Pg. 54 Testator. She is further entitled to the land already belonging to her and to crop growing thereon, at death of Testator and also negro boy, FRANK, and the personal property that belonged to her before marriage.

Slaves b/n/f JAMES W. HUMES pray appeal to Supreme Ct. Holston Conference of the Methodist Episcopal Church (South) entitled to $4,000.00.

Respdts. WILLIAM AMBRISTER, JOSEPH AMBRISTER, ASA AMBRISTER, JOHN N. BLACKBURN and Wife, ELJA BLACKBURN, LORETTA AMBRISTER and ELIZABETH AMBRISTER may appeal to next term of Supreme Ct.

Pg. 55   JAMES KEY Vs: WILLIAM STEELE & BRO. Aug. 2, 1860. C&M to take and state an acc't. and ascertain what amt. purchase money still due and rep't. to Ct. this term.

JAMES KEY Vs: WILLIAM STEELE & BRO. Case confirmed $600.00 due Principal, $144.80 Int. purchase money for tract of land described in bill. Defdt. has 2 mos. pay-.

Pg. 56   GREENWAY, HENRY, & CO. Vs: J. B. COX & O. Leave given Respdts. 2nd Sept. file Ans.

JAMES H. GILLESPY, Extr. of MATTHEW WALLACE, Dec'd. Vs: LEGATEES of MATTHEW WALLACE. C&M sold house and 2 town lots in Maryville on Aug. 9, 1856 and T. A. POPE of firm TOOLE BROS. & CO. purchaser for $750.00 note executed by J. M. TOOLE, WILLIAM TOOLE, JR. and T. A. POPE. Land on Pistol Creek containing 125 A. and that Gen. WILLIAM WALLACE became purchaser for the sum of $732.00 which he pd. down in cash.

Pg. 57   WOOD, ABBOTT & CO. Vs: S. T. COX & O. Complnt. not entitled to relief sought. Same to be dismissed. Complnt. and Security, HORACE MAYNARD, pay costs.

JAMES HENRY & O. Vs: ALEXANDER KENNEDY & O. It is considered by Ct. that ALEXANDER KENNEDY, Respdt., recover from WILLIAM MCTEER, JAMES HENRY, WILLIAM S. PORTER, JAMES M. TOOLE, DAVID CHANDLER, WILLIAM KIDD, JOHN SINGLETON, ANDREW MCCLAIN, WILLIAM A. SPENCER - $5,253.24.

Pg. 58   S. J. MCREYNOLDS Vs: A. GRISHAM & J. K. DUNCAN, J. A. MCCAMY & JOHN A. STRANGE. Cause in all things confirmed except that portion which attempts to show the amt. due J. A. MCKAMY, J. A. STRANGE, J. K. DUNCAN and A. GRISHAM from said firm. It appears to Ct. an acc't. should be taken O.A.D. that C&M take and state an acc't.
1) What amt. of monies, notes, acc'ts. and other property has come into hands of J. A. MCKAMY belonging to firm GRISHAM, STRANGE & CO. and what disposition made?
2) What amt. remaining in his hands?
3) Amt. of sales made by said Recv'r., to whom made and

what amt. remains uncollected?

Pg. 59 SAMUEL PRIDE, Admr. of JOHN HENRY, Dec'd. Vs: WILLIAM MCTEER & O. Complnt. has leave to file an amended bill for purpose of transferring the settlement of his administration from County Ct. to this Ct.

H. & B. DOUGLAS & O. Vs: S. J. MCREYNOLDS & C. Aug. 1, 1860. On Bills, Ans., Exhibits, Proof as to JOHN E. GLASS and JAMES W. WHITEHEAD from all which it appears that on 27th of Feb. 1857, H. & B. DOUGLAS recovered sundry jdgmts. agnst. S. J. MCREYNOLDS before SAMUEL YEAROUT, J.P., for Blount County amounting in all to $1,216.18 of which $166.00 has been pd. and on which Respdt. JAMES A. HOUSTON is *stayor?* and also on 22nd May 1857, HUGH DOUGLAS recovered a jdgmt. agnst. S. J. MCREYNOLDS for $327.28 on which HOUSTON is also *stayor?* and also May 22, 1857, STRICKLER & ELLIS & CO. recovered a jdgmt. agnst. MCREYNOLDS FOR $289.00, J. A. HOUSTON, *Stayor?* -

Pg. 60 jdgmts. remain unpaid, except about $700.00. It appearing to Ct. that D. C. GHORMLY, SAMUEL GHORMLY, THOMAS HARDIN, ESTHER LEEPER and H. HUGH B. LEEPER are indebted to S. J. MCREYNOLDS by jdgmt. in Circuit Ct. of Blount County in sum of $652.70 on May 27, 1859. It appearing to Ct. that GEORGE W. TEFFETELLER is indebted to the said MCREYNOLDS and J. A. HOUSTON for about $300.00 by several notes secured by deeds of trust, one by a house and lot in Maryville and other property. The land of JACOB SUMMY was sold by this Ct. for $350.00 to MCREYNOLDS and retaining a lien on same for purchase money. MCREYNOLDS agreed in writing that if within 4 yrs. SUMMY would repay the purchase money and interest. JOHN E. GLASS and JAMES W. WHITEHEAD are indebted to MCREYNOLDS in sum of $11.00 by jdgmt.
Ct. O.A.D. that H. & B. DOUGLAS, HUGH DOUGLAS, and STRICKLER ELLIS & CO. are entitled to have said monies now in hands of this Ct.

Pg. 61 Complnts. entitled to have deeds of trust in favor of said MCREYNOLDS and HOUSTON on the property of GEORGE W. TEFFETELLER, MCREYNOLDS, and HOUSTON to have title. Complnt. Bill be dismissed as to Respdts. ELIJAH NELSON, SAMUEL M. and J. D. HICKS,

JOHN POTTER, Z. HARRIS and B. F. DUNCAN, A. W. EMMITT, JOSEPH L. HACKNEY, DAVID A. STEELE, JOHN STEELE and JOHN SINGLETON and that they pay all costs in their behalf expended. S. J. MCREYNOLDS and J. A. HOUSTON pay all other costs.

Pg. 62　ROYSTON & O. Vs: J. D. WEAR & O. Aug. 2, 1860. Leave granted to amend bill.

SAMUEL PRIDE, Admr. Vs: WILLIAM MCTEER & O. - #2 Q. M. COX & J. MCHENRY Vs: WILLIAM MCTEER & O. - #3 T. D. TILLINGHAST Vs: HEIRS & CREDITORS of JOHN HENRY. - #4 JAMES WILSON Vs: HEIRS of HENRY. - #5 JAMES PORTER Vs: JOHN S. PRIDE & O. Cases consolidated. JOHN HENRY, Dec'd. at time of death a partner in firm MCTEER, HENRY & CO. Other partners being: WILLIAM MCTEER and formerly partner in firm MCTEER, PRIDE & HENRY CO. - JOHN HENRY, WILLIAM MCTEER, JOHN S. PRIDE.

Pg. 63　The creditors firms whose debts are hereinafter stated have agreed to assume debts of other company - $260.00 debts of said firm.
The personal assets of JOHN HENRY, Dec'd. have been exhausted in payment of his individual debts.
Decreed by Ct. that JAMES HENRY, of JOHN and JOHN C. CHILDS be app't'd. Comm'rs. to sell the tract of land in pleadings mentioned at public sale to recover $2,780.00.

Pg. 64　Monies rec'd. by C&M to be used to pay debts and costs of JOHN HENRY, Dec'd. and T. D. TILLINGHAST, HYATT MCBERNIE & CO., B. W. & J. P. FORCE & CO., W. H. NEWBOLD, assignee of REED BROS. & CO., BENJAMIN F. FREDERICK, PRATT & REATH, HENDERSON & FRIBLES, RODOLPHUS KENT, STEPHENS & LEAVETT, and HARRIS-HALE & CO. all creditors of said firms of MCTEER, PRIDE & HENRY and their Sol., O. P. TEMPLE, Esq. (Sums to be apportioned to each firm listed.)

Pgs. 65-67 (Provide a continuation with enumeration of settlement figures for each of the above companies.)

Pg. 68　Creditors of said company enumerated: WILL WALLACE, JAMES PORTER, JAMES A. PORTER and G. W. HAZEN (Their payments are listed.)

Pg. 69-71 (Continuation of payments due from above creditors).

Pg. 72   R. & S. SAFFELL Vs: J. C. M. BOGLE, Gdn. & O. Bill & X Bill. Complnt. entitled to relief sought. J. C. M. BOGLE - have property divided and Est. settled as the property can be divided. O.& D. that F. POPE, B. F. DUNCAN, ALEXANDER COOK can be appt'd. Comm'rs. to partition all the real estate and to divide the negroes belonging to said Est., equitably. O.& D. that WILLIAM HEADRICK, Surveyor of Roane County, BENJAMIN F. BRATON and JAMES LUCKY be appt'd. Comm'rs. to partition and set apart real estate in Roane County subject to lease exhibited by R. M. SAFFELL in his Ans. to the X Bill and rep't. to next term Ct.

Pg. 73   Court adjourned until Court in Course.
         T. NIXON VAN DYKE.

Pg. 74   Tues. Nov. 6, 1860.
         Be it remembered that in pursuance of an Act of the General Assembly passed on the 19th Jan. 1860, a Ct. of Chancery was opened and held at Courthouse in Maryville, Tennessee, on Tues. the 6th day of Nov. in the year of our Lord One Thousand Eight Hundred and Sixty being the first Tuesday after the first Monday of the said month and the Chancellor not being present, by order of the C&M. Ct. adjourned until tomorrow morning at 8:00 A.M.
         SAMUEL PRIDE, C&M.

         Wed. Nov. 8, 1860 - Ct. met and adjourned until tomorrow A.M. at 8:00.
         T. NIXON VAN DYKE.

         SAMUEL PRIDE Vs: WILLIAM MCTEER & O. Cause coming for final hearing and upon D. made by Supreme Ct., State of Tennessee. Knoxville - 2nd Mon. Sept. 1859 modifying and confirming a D. of this Ct. of May 1859 Term.

         The 3 town lots containing 1/4 A. known in plan of Town as Lots #7, 8 and 40 which belonged to SAMUEL PRIDE, WILLIAM MCTEER, RANKIN DURYEA & CO. and STE-
Pg. 75   PHEN S. PORTER - Maryville College had a lien on same to secure payment of $300.00 note drawn by W. P. L. CUMMINGS, SAMUEL PRIDE, WILLIAM MCTEER as

Securities. All have sold their respective interests to MINERVA MCTEER and that by direction of RANKIN DURYEA & CO., the Sheriff of Blount County by Deed bearing date 7 July 1860 conveyed their interest in Lots 7 and 8 to MINERVA MCTEER and MINERVA MCTEER on the 14th Nov. 1859 pd. $300.00 on said debt to Maryville College. Deed vested in MINERVA MCTEER.

W. D. MCGINLEY & R. L. CATE, Extrs. Vs: WILLIAM AMBRISTER & O. Ordered by Ct. that C&M inquire and rep't. instantly: What is the fair and reasonable fee of JAMES HUMES, Esq., for his services in this and Supreme Ct. as counsel of the negroes who were formerly the slaves of the Testator, GEORGE AMBRISTER, Dec'd.

Pg. 76 JAMES TAYLOR et al. Vs: JAMES WALKER and SAMUEL PRIDE Vs: JAMES TAYLOR et al. In this cause the death of CATHERINE EDGEMOND is admitted. Cause revived in name of ELIZABETH EDGEMOND, her child and heir. Cause cont'd. until next term of Ct.

WILLIAM MCGINLEY & R. L. CATES, Extrs. & C. Vs: the HEIRS of GEORGE AMBRISTER, Dec'd. This cause came to be heard on D. of Supreme Ct. - for services rendered by JAMES HUMES, Esq. as counsel for persons of color who were slaves of GEORGE AMBRISTER, Dec'd. He entitled to $250.00 to be taken from $1,500.00 awarded to these former slaves. Cause retained upon docket to execute D. of Supreme Ct. to superintend the deportation of said persons of color to the coast of Africa. Remainder of $1,500.00 to be paid Treasurer of State and notify the Governor pursuant to Section 2705 of the Code.

Pg. 77 SAMUEL GHORMLY Vs: H. & H. L. STEPHENS. Cause is cont'd. Ans. of HENRY STEPHENS has been filed. Respdt. has until Feb. Rules to substitute his Ans.

S. J. MCREYNOLDS Vs: RUFUS M. CONLY & J. S. M. EVERETT. Nov. 8, 1860. RUFUS M. CONLY is indebted to Complnt. S. J. MCREYNOLDS $60.00 note of Sept. 29, 1859 and due Dec. 25, 1859 and also a Jdgmt. rendered by L. L. YEAROUT, Esq. of May 15, 1855 for $28.00 plus costs. RUFUS CONLY pd. all but $60.00 of purchase price of land and then fraudulently for purpose of evading the payment of said debt, proceeded to sell said land to J.

S. M. EVERETT. O.A.D. the C&M sell said tract of land at public sale and pay to claimant his due and RUFUS M. CONLY and J. S. M. EVERETT pay costs.

H. C. SAFFELL & BROS. Vs: WILLIAM MCTEER. Cause cont'd.

Pg. 78 SAMUEL HANLEY Vs: HEIRS of A. H. HANLEY, Dec'd. Nov. 8, 1860. Cause cont'd.

ROBERTSON, HUDSON & PULLIAM Vs: S. J. MCREYNOLDS & CO. This cause dismissed by Defdt. paying all costs.

JAMES KEY Vs: W. M. & J. A. STEELE. Parties compromised this cause.

S. W. ROYSTON et al. Vs: JAMES D. WEAR et al. Cause cont'd.

C. P. SAFFLE Vs: B. L. WARREN et als. This cause is dismissed. The Respdt. recover of C. P. SAFFLE & C. GILLESPY, his Security, all costs of this cause.

SAMUEL GHORMLY & ANN GHORMLY, Admr. & Admx. W. JAMES, Dec'd. Vs: ROBERT GARNER & O. Ordered that C&M take testimony and rep't. what a reasonable allowance be made Admr. and Admx. for services attending the business of said estate and rep't. next term of Ct.

Pg. 79 JOSEPH H. TEDFORD Vs: JAMES WILSON. Nov. 9, 1860. There remains in hands of Complnt. $535.60 proceeds of property belonging to Defdt. WILLIAM MCTEER levied to satisfy jdgmt. in favor of Defdt. JAMES WILSON. O.A.D. JAMES WILSON recover of TEDFORD $535.60 plus interest.

CLARK HYDE & CO. Vs: J. A. HOUSTON et als. The demurrer is overruled and Respdt. MCREYNOLDS allowed until March to file Ans.

CHAMBERLAIN, MILER & CO. Vs: JAMES A. MCCAMY & O. Respdt. has until next term Ct. to file Ans. The Respdt. has 1 mo. to file w/C&M books, notes, acc'ts., bonds, jdgmts. etc. and other evidence of debts of firm

Pg. 80   MCCAMY & HARB. C&M to be appt'd. Recv'r. and directed to proceed to collect same.

H. T. COX Vs: R. P. BOWERMAN, JAMES HENRY & W. D. MCGINLEY. Papers in this cause have been lost. Complnt. has leave to file copy of his bill. To take proof and prepare cause for hearing.

ROBERT M. LINN Vs: JOSHUA O. HAYS & O. Nov. 9, 1860. $95.00 bid for 50 A. tract of land offered for sale by C&M. This is an inadequate consideration. Same shall be set aside and M. shall cancel the note executed by M. W. MCNUTT the purchaser & repay him. M. to advertise and sell premises containing 70 A. The 70 A. may be sold at Campbell Station in Knox County. The proceeds aris-
Pg. 81   ing from sale shall be first applied to payment of amt. re ferred to due to E. HATFIELD. Int. hereafter to in satisfaction of Jdgmt. rendered agnst. JOSHUA O. HAYS by THOMAS C. COSTER, a J.P. of Roane County. C&M to rep't. next term Ct.

NICHOLAS BREWER, Gdn. JOHN CHAMBERS, a Lunatic, Vs: RHODA CHAMBERS & O. Filed Sept. 6, 1858. Upon Ans. of RHODA CHAMBERS and her Ch. and upon jdgmt. Complnt. NICHOLAS BREWER, Gdn. of JOHN CHAMBERS - it appears that JOHN CHAMBERS is a confirmed lunatic and permanently and hopelessly insane, at time of his derangement he possessed an estate both real and personal and also was owing bills. Complnt. to be pd. Wife, RHODA, and Ch. entitled to be provided for out of estate as in case he were dec'd. RHODA assigned dower rts. J. C. M. BOGLE, Surveyor for Blount County, JARVIS A. ROREX and JOHN WHITE be appt'd. Comm'r. to assign dower out of 15th Civil District adjoining lands of JOSEPH LAMBERT, the HEIRS of HOWEL LAWSON,
Pg. 82   JOHN CALDWELL, J. C. M. BOGLE and O. containing 160 A. One other tract in same District adjoining lands of JOHN MCCAMPBELL, J. W. H. TIPTON and O. containing 256 A. and another tract of 160 A. in 16th District in Hiwassee District, 8th Range East of the Meridian 2nd fractional township of Lot #7. Further ordered that Comm'rs. lay off and set apart to RHODA out of the money, stock and other provisions on hand of said estate, a sufficiency for support of RHODA and Ch. under 14 yrs. age for 12 mos. C&M to show:

1) What amt. debts of estate and due whom?
2) Gdn. make sale of personal property.

Pg. 83 ESTHER LEEPER & HUSBAND, HUGH B. LEEPER Vs: Admr. & HEIRS of JOHN P. HARDIN, Dec'd. Nov. 8, 1860. Cause heard and determined in Bills, Ans., Exhibits, proof of jdgmt. agnst. MARTHA HOWARD, JOHN H. HOWARD, THOMAS S. HARDIN, MARTHA A. HARDIN, JOSEPH HARDIN, MARGARET S. PORTER and her husband, H. ANDREW PORTER. In month of Oct. 1854, JOHN P. HARDIN departed this life in Blount County intestate seized and possessed of a large real estate, to wit: A tract of land of 600 A. granted to HARDIN by Grant #4694. Also another tract of land on which he last resided before his death containing 1,200 A. conveyed by JOHN CRUSE to said HARDIN on the 3rd Mar. 1845 and another tract of 80 A. granted to JAMES CALLAWAY and JOHN ISBILL by Grant #4061 and another tract of 28 A. granted to JOHN P. HARDIN by Grant #4083 and another tract of -- A. granted to JAMES CALLAWAY and JOHN ISBILL by Grant #4060 and another tract of 80 A. granted to JOHN and M. W. MCGHEE by Grant #41127. Also a tract of land containing 240 A. granted to JOHN CRUSE by Grant #1450. It appears to Ct. that Complnt. ESTHER was the widow of JOHN P. HARDIN and entitled to dower rts. out of said lands. A portion of their Ch. were minors under age 21 yrs. Dower was assigned by appt'd. Comm'rs. in 1854 Nov. term Ct. A surveyor appt'd. was the brother of one of Admrs. - thus null and void.
New surveyor appt'd. Feb. 1855 - to lay aside dower, etc. J. C. M. BOGLE, Surveyor, ANDREW KIRKPATRICK and G. W. P. RUTLEDGE appt'd. Comm'rs. to assign dower for ESTHER LEEPER, widow of JOHN P. HARDIN, Dec'd.

Pg. 84 JAMES WILSON & O. Vs: JOSEPH H. TEDFORD & O. By consent of parties leave granted Respdts. to Feb. rules to plead Ans. or demur to Complnts. bill.

JOHN GRIFFETHS, Extr. of ENOCH KEENE Vs: WIDOW & HEIRS of KEENE. Nov. 8, 1860. Ordered by Ct. that JOHN GRIFFETHS, Extr. of ENOCH KEENE, Dec'd. pay into Office of C&M all cash and O. personal property of said Estate so same may be pd. to MARY KEENE, widow, according to former decree. It appears that there issued to E. KEENE in his lifetime a Land Warrent # ----- for 80

A. which was undisposed of by him and has been said to belong to said widow. C&M to offer land warrant for sale according to the laws of the U.S. Interior Department of Government and pay widow.

Pg. 85 THOMAS C. SARTAIN & WIFE Vs: WILLIAM W. BAYLESS & O. Nov. 8, 1860. WILLIAM BAYLESS, Gdn. for minor heirs in this case is not chargeable anything for the hire of the slaves, nor is he entitled to anything for nursing and taking care of said slaves, but he is entitled to recover out of funds arising from sale of said negroes the sum $171.62 due for funds expended to equalize division of slaves among heirs of JOHN BLACK, and for taxes, Sol. fees, etc. C&M to take money for sale of said slaves - then pay to said Complnts. the 1/5th of said sum and that he pay over in 5th's to WILLIAM BAYLESS, Gdn. for other Respdts. who are minors.

JAMES HENRY & O. Vs: SAMUEL PRIDE & O. Leave granted to Ans. in Feb. Term Ct.

Pg. 86 WILLIAM C. & RICHARD L. CRESWELL & ANDREW CRESWELL Vs: WILLIAM C. & RICHARD L. CRESWELL. Nov. 9, 1860. Bill and X Bill. SAMUEL L. CRESWELL, Ancestor of Complnts. departed this life in Blount County in yr. 1853 after having made and published a will which was dated Jan. 4, 1853. Left his lands charged w/support of his wife, NANCY L. CRESWELL, during her life, together w/other incumberance in favor of his two daughters, SARAH C. and ELIZABETH J. CRESWELL. When these obligations complied with, he willed his landed estate to his two sons, WILLIAM C. and RICHARD L. CRESWELL. Balance of his personal property to be devised and bequeathed and equally divided between 2 sons at their becoming of age of the younger. One tract of land 189 A. in 13th Civil District adjoining lands of JOHN SPARKS' heirs, ANDREW CRESWELL and O. being the same purchased from THOMAS BOHANNON and on which he resided at his death. It appearing to Ct. from Exhibit "B" that ROBERT PICKENS, Admr. of SAMUEL M. CRESWELL, NANCY CRESWELL, widow, and WILLIAM L. CUMMINGS, the Gdn. of the Complnts. in the yr. 1853 at

Pg. 87 Sept. Term Ct. of Blount County instituted a proceedings to have land sold by D. Land cannot be sold until youngest son is 21 yrs. but land WAS sold 5th day Dec. 1853,

Pg. 88 WILLIAM A. WALKER, Clerk of Ct. sold it to ANDREW CRESWELL for $689.00 and made rep't. to Jan. term Ct. 1854. Final decree rendered divesting title in Circuit Ct. That sale is Null and Void. - Had no rt. to sell land. CRESWELL has rt. to be reimbursed. He got no title to land when bought. Ordered that his purchase money be returned and money for improvements made to property. Complnt. entitled to an acc't. of the rents and profits of same tract of land since ANDREW CRESWELL came into possession. What is a fair fee for WILLIAM D. MCGINLEY and J. G. WALLACE the Sols. of said WILLIAM C. and RICHARD L. CRESWELL for services?

Pg. 89 SAMUEL PRIDE Vs: JAMES PORTER & O. On application of Complnt. jdgmt. taken agnst. HANNAH M. PORTER, ELIZA TAYLOR, STEPHEN SMITH, MARY SMITH, NICHOLAS C. PORTER, JAMES E. PORTER for want of Ans. Process having been served on them and also agnst. J. P. H. PORTER, NANCY BROOKS, JESSE BROOKS and LORENZO PORTER - nonresidents as to when publication has been made. Ordered that alias process issue to MEIGS CO. to be served on CAMPBELL PORTER. It being suggested that WYATT PORTER and PROCTOR PORTER are nonresidents it is ordered that publication be made as to them. The death of JOHN P. TAYLOR is suggested. Leave granted JANE PORTER 2 mos. to file her Ans.

GREENWAY, HENRY & SMITH & O. Vs: H. T. COX & O. On application of Defdt. JOHN B. COX injunction granted is dissolved as to note in pleadings executed by H. T. COX in favor of JOHN B. COX to collect same on condition he execute to C&M a bond.

R. M. & S. S. SAFFELL Vs: J. C. M. BOGLE & WIFE, SARAH J. SAFFELL, HEIRS of JOHN & C. A. SAFFELL. Nov. 9, 1860. Div. of slaves of JOHN and CLEMENTINE A. SAFFELL, Dec'd. Comm'rs. appt'd. by Ct. rep't.

Pg. 90 1) We have allowed and apportioned to RICHARD M. SAFFELL a portion of said lands called Lot #2 known as the MCREYNOLD'S Tract (description given) Montvale Rd. corner DEARMAND, D. CUPP corner to GODDARD and DUNCAN 107 A. valued at $1,498.00, also the following negroes: NANCY, ALFRED and HUGH valued at $2,850.00. Allotted to SAMUEL SAFFELL land Lot #1 known as BONHAM Tract lying in 10th District (description given) 115 A. valued at $920.00 and following negroes: LEWIS, MOLLY, ISAAC and FLORENCE valued at $3,350.00. We have allotted to SARAH J. SAFFELL two parcels of land - Lot #3 known as the MURRY Tract in District #8 and designated as Lots #2 and 4.

Pg. 91 In rep't. of Comm'rs. of partition between JAMES WILSON and heirs of JOHN SAFFELL (description of lot) Lot #1 now owned by JAMES WILSON - one lot 99 A. worth $975.00 and following negroes: ANNETTA, DEORIX, POLLY, ANN and SANDY valued at $2,900.00. We have allotted to BESSIE C. BOGLE, formerly BESSIE C. SAFFELL, who intermarried with J. C. M. BOGLE, a portion of land Lot #4 known as the CALDWELL and MCCAMPBELL Tract, District 15 (description given) 209 A. valued at $700.00 and the following negroes: WASHINGTON, JANE and PHILIP valued at $2,950.00. Also to R. M. SAFFELL and SARAH I. SAFFELL Lots #1 and 2 of

Pg. 92 the tracts known as the SIMMERLY Tract on Crooked Creek District #8 (description given) 146 A. valued at $800.00 or $1,600.00 for the two individual fourths; and we allotted to SAMUEL SAFFELL and BESSIE C. BOGLE Lots #3 and 4 of the same SIMMERLY Tract (description given) 160 A. worth $800.00. Comm'rs. having rec'd. information that RICHARD SAFFELL, SAMUEL SAFFELL and SARAH SAFFELL had each sold their undivided interest in and to 5 certain town lots belonging to the estate on which J. C. M. BOGLE now resides, to the said J. C. M. BOGLE, the husband of BESSIE C. SAFFELL BOGLE, the Comm'rs. leave her undivided 1/4th to be held in common and undivided with the other 3/4ths which her husband now owns and holds. Comm'rs.

Pg. 93 equaled land values out of prices for slaves.
Comm'rs. B. F. DUNCAN, F. POPE, and A. COOK
(A map of lots distributed among heirs drawn on this page).

Pgs. 94-95 Information given in process of vesting both lands and slaves from the Estate of JOHN SAFFELL and wife, CLEMENTINE A. SAFFELL, and into the possession of the heirs of same.

Pg. 96 H. & B. DOUGLAS et al. Vs: S. J. MCREYNOLDS et al. Nov. 9, 1860. S. J. MCREYNOLDS and J. A. HOUSTON indebted to Complnts. for $580.00. C&M sold to J. E. TOOLE highest bidder property belonging to MCREYNOLDS known as SUMMY Property for sum of $50.00 -

Pg. 97 applied to debt. District 14 on waters of of Ellejoy Creek described as follows: East half of the Old Dutch JOHN GARNER farm containing 124 A. adjoining lands of heirs of JOHN HENRY, Dec'd. GEORGE LATHAM, WILLIAM ELLIGE, A. DUNLAP and O. w/tenament to be vested in JOHN E. TOOLE and his heirs forever, subject never the less to the equity of redemption of the said JACOB SUMMY for 2 yrs. from the 11th March 1859. GEORGE W. TEFFETELLER indebted to said MCREYNOLDS for $280.00 - town lot belonging to TEFFETELLER in town of Maryville. C&M to sell town lot at public sale and apply it to note.

C. W. C. NORWOOD & WIFE, MALINDA NORWOOD Vs: E. & I. GEORGE & O. AND WILLIAM S. JOHNSON & WIFE Vs: E. & I. GEORGE & O. Sat. Nov. 10, 1860. Bill and X Bill.

Pg. 98 Documents as submitted unclear. Ct. appoints THOMAS A. POPE, a Spec. Comm'r. to take and state an acc't. The mortgage executed by MALINDA THOMPSON, now NORWOOD, and her husband, JESSE B. THOMPSON for the benefit of B. D. BRABSON and O. was not valid and binding upon her, the said MALINDA, but the sale of the slaves named in that mortgage to pay the debt to B. D. BRABSON as set forth was valid. E. GEORGE had no rt. to pay any other debt than the debt secured by the mortgage and any part of the purchase money for the slaves remaining in his hands after paying the mortgage - he is decreed to acc't. to her together w/Int. since sale of said slaves. The Ct. further D. that Complnt. MALINDA shall not be charged with any other debt of her former husband THOMPSON, except mortgage debt above alluded to.

The Extrs. shall be charged w/note upon ANDREW KIRKPATRICK w/Int. in that they did not use due dilligence in having said note collected and JOHNSON and Wife will be charged w/Int. they have rec'd.

Ct. O.& D. that Complnt. JOHNSON and Wife have sustained their X Bill and that negro woman, EDY, was not willed by SAMUEL GEORGE to any person by his will and

Pg. 99 that he died intestate as to said girl - nor had any disposition of said girl been made and that title set up by EDWARD GEORGE to the said EDY as to the Complnt. JOHNSON and Wife is void and pretended claim and shall not prejudice in any manner their rt. to said negro and her increase and hire as an heir-at-law and daughter of JOSIAH GEORGE, Dec'd. and granddaughter of SAMUEL GEORGE, Dec'd. The proof shows that ARMAND M. JOHNSON has been under disability and the statute of limitations has no application so as to prejudice her rts. to said slave and her increase and hire.

Ct. of opinion, and so D. that JOHNSON and Wife have a rt. to have a collection of the advancements made by SAMUEL GEORGE in his lifetime and by his will and otherwise to his heirs-at-law in order to ascertain the Int. of the Complnts. Commission should determine:

1) What amt. assets came to hands of EDWARD or I. W. GEORGE, Extrs. of SAMUEL GEORGE, Dec'd.?

2) What amt. of said assets were pd. out and to whom?

3) What amt. pd. to Widow BARBARY GEORGE or should have come to her by will of SAMUEL GEORGE, Dec'd.?

Pg. 100 4) What amt. assets came to hands of EDWARD GEORGE, Admr. of BARBARY GEORGE, Dec'd.?

5) The Comm'r. should state the acc't. between Extrs. and Legatees under will of SAMUEL GEORGE and the distribution of BARBARY GEORGE.

6) Comm'r. should ascertain amt. of all advancements made by SAMUEL GEORGE by will or otherwise to his heirs and shall state the amt. separating the advancements in land from negroes and those in personal property?

7) Comm'r. will hear proof and rep't. value of EDY at death of SAMUEL.

8) It being admitted that EDY has died since filing of the bill of JOHNSON and Wife that she had several Ch. The Comm'r. will rep't. their names and ages.

JOHN C. CHILDS & WIFE, JAMES HENRY & O. Vs: SAMUEL PRIDE, Admr. & W. J. HENRY. Moved Ct. to dismiss Complnts. bill.

1) SAMUEL PRIDE, Admr. Vs: WILLIAM MCTEER.

2) M. COX & J. M. HENRY Vs: WILLIAM MCTEER.

3) T. D. TILLINGHAST & O. Vs: HEIRS & CREDITORS of JOHN HENRY, Dec'd.

4) JAMES WILSON Vs: HEIRS of JOHN HENRY.

5) JAMES PORTER Vs: JOHN S. M. PRIDE & O.

Report of Comm'rs. JAMES HENRY and GEORGE C. CHILDS appointed by D. to sell the tract of land mentioned in pleadings.

Pg. 101 Sat. Nov. 10, 1860. HEIRS of JOHN HENRY, JAMES PORTER Vs: JOHN M. PRIDE & O. Undersigned to sell lands of JOHN HENRY, Dec'd. Sold land 25th Sept. 1860 to JACKSON ISH for $13,250.00 and executed his note. WILLIAM HENDERSON, Esq./Securities. Signed: JOHN C. CHILDS, JAMES HENRY, Commrs.

Pg. 102 SAMUEL PRIDE, Admr. of JOHN HENRY, Dec'd. Vs: WILLIAM MCTEER & O. SAMUEL PRIDE, C&M, produced in open court, a note by N. L. PORTER and R. J. WILSON for $3,130.23 - to pay C&M the amt. - witnessed June 12, 1860. Note was not pd. Now ordered to pay note and Int.

ROBERT WEAR Vs: JAMES D. WEAR & O. (Heard 11/8/1860). It appears the rent of land and hire of negroes in possession of JAMES D. WEAR and his sisters from death of HUGH WEAR to time sold - less taxes and

Pg. 103 other amts. to sum of $488.29 and rent of land and hire of negroes in possession of ROBERT WEAR. The Complnt. and his mother and her family for the like period amts. to $416.39 and it appearing that "TILDA," decreed at last term to be an advancement to JAMES MCCONNELL and MARTHA MCCONNELL was worth at the time given by HUGH WEAR the sum of $350.00. His Honor pleased to O.A.D. that the sum of $350.00 should be charged to the JAMES and MARTHA MCCONNELL be acc'td for and settled by them in distribution of assets of said estate. Each of above to acc't. for the above amts. in settlement of estate. The widow is not entitled to receive any portion of the advancements so ascertained, but is entitled to, but is entitled to distributive share of net hire of the negroes, $150.00 each, to Sol. J. G. WALLACE and J. E. TOOLE and $125.00 each to O. P. TEMPLE and J. W. D. MCGINLEY.

Pg. 104 C&M to pay Sols. from funds of said Est. in his hands.

DAVID CUNNINGHAM Vs: ALFRED CUNNINGHAM. At hand a transcript of D. of Supreme Ct. of Tennessee at Knoxville and the proceedings hereafter which D. as follows: "DAVID CLAIBORN CUNNINGHAM Vs: ALFRED & MARGARET CUNNINGHAM." Complnts. filed to establish mental capacity of MOSES CUNNINGHAM at time of the execution of the conveyance. To ALFRED the relief is denied as far as cancellation of the Deed and consideration of $1,200.00 along w/support of the old man and his wife. So far as regards the sum of $400.00 alleges to have been pd. by the transfer of the note which the Defdt. held on JOHN CUNNINGHAM of Missouri, the Ct. is of the opinion that the Ans. is vague and unsatisfactory and the Complnts. are not included absolutely by the recital in the deed nor the declarations of the old man. Ordered to the Master to enquire and report whether:

Pg. 105 1) Defdt. at time of execution of Conveyance held any Bona fide valid and unsatisfied notes on JOHN CUNNINGHAM of Missouri?

2) If so, amt. and whether the same were transferred to and agreed to be recinded by the old man in part satisfaction of purchase money for land. If no such notes in existance, or not accepted by the old man, then Ct. is of opinion and D. the Defdt. should acc't. for purchase money w/Int. Other considerations - a mare and colt and field of corn $300.00. A distribution of assets of estate cannot be pd. during lifetime of old man. The case is remanded for taking an acc't. of Est. Costs to be adjudged to Complnt. and his Securities in the Appeal Bond, J. BONELLS and by Defdt., ALFRED CUNNINGHAM and ELIJAH HATCHER.

Pg. 106 WILLIAM M. STEELE, Admr. & O. Vs: ELIZABETH DAVIS & O. Nov. 10, 1860. It appears that upon death of Testator, said ELIZABETH and her Ch. continued to live on land to use and enjoy the property until 1860 when they referred the matter of settlement to Arbitration of WILLIAM BICKNELL, SAMUEL TULLOCH and JAMES R. COX. An amt. found due said O'CONNOR, the Gdn. of his Ch., the sole distributee of his wife which thru opinion of Chancellor, not obligationary as an award is conclusive upon the parties in interest of family settlement there being no creditors of Testator. Chancellor O.A.D. that the Bill be dismissed and costs pd. as follows: One-half by said O'CONNOR, one-fourth by Respdt. ELIZABETH DAVIS, and remainder by JOHN C. DAVIS or MYERS for which execution is awarded.

C. W. NORWOOD & WIFE Vs: E. & I. W. GEORGE AND W. L. JOHNSON & WIFE Vs: E. & I. W. GEORGE. Need determination what compensation the said GEORGE is entitled to for raising the Ch. of the said EDY and Ct. will

Pg. 107 rep't. value of service and hire EDY from death of

SAMUEL GEORGE to his death and he shall have permission to examine the parties.

W. D. MCGINLEY & O. Vs: HEIRS, LEGATEES of GEORGE AMBRISTER, Dec'd. Master to hear proof value of fees for JESSE G. WALLACE for his services in this case as Sol. of LORETTA AMBRISTER, a minor. Fee $40.00 reasonable.

Pg. 108   H. HARTSELL & J. C. WALLACE, Admrs. of GILBERTS, Dec'd. Vs: HEIRS & CREDITORS of said GILBERTS. It appears that amt. of $1,520.40 in hands of Admrs. of Ests. of GEORGE S., A. L., and S. S. GILBERT, Dec'd. Remaining sums to collected $777.31. Other claims belonging to Est. proved to be either onerous or satisfied - other goods sold at C.H. steps for $22.75 sums in hands of C&M - $2,694.78. Debts of three intermingled, the three having conducted business together and they being jointly liable for various debts. C&M to make distribution of moneys after satisfying costs. Ct. adjourned until next regular term. T. NIXON VAN DYKE.

Pg. 109   Tues. May 7th, 1861. C. GILLESPY, Admr. Vs: WIDOW & HEIRS of WILLIAM A. GILLESPY, Dec'd. Minor heirs exist. Ct. not advised as to whether slaves must be sold to facilitate distribution of assets. Question referred to C&M that he take an acc't. and hear proof and rep't. to next term Ct. whether necessary to sell slaves for partition. C&M to hire out slaves until next term Ct. Respdt. JAMES F. GILLESPY filed his Ans. and requested all advancements be collected and heirs named on original bill - all being present and represented in Ct. and entered their appearance without service of process.

NORWOOD & WIFE Vs: EDWARD GEORGE & O. & JOHNSON & WIFE. C&M to take slaves into his custody and make disposition for their support and upkeep until further order of Ct. as may be cheapest and least expensive to those who may be entitled to them. Due regard being had to their safety and comfort. If any of them can be hired out, he will do so. If however, EDWARD GEORGE will agree to keep them all free of charge then they will be permitted to remain with him. If he will not do so then W. S. JOHNSON will be permitted to take them on the same terms. If neither will do so they will be disposed of as directed above to whoever will take charge of them on best terms.

Pg. 110 R. I. WILSON & WILLIAM S. PORTER Vs: SMITH MURPHY & CO. & O. Complnts. came and dismissed their bill. Ct. O.A.D. that Defdt. SAMUEL PRIDE, C&M, recover from Complnts. R. I. WILSON and WILLIAM S. PORTER, THOMAS E. OLDHAM and J. R. LOVE, their Securities, in the injunction bond $3,207.44 plus $97.29 Int.

MARCUS D. BEARDEN et als. Vs: GRINSFIELD TAYLOR. Final D. Complnts. claim is barred by Statue of Limitations. Complnts. to pay costs of cause. Allowed 2 mos. to make appeal.

Pg. 111 JOSIAS GAMBLE Vs: SAMUEL HENRY. On motion of Respdt. 2 mos. allowed to plead Ans. or demur.

SAMUEL PRIDE Vs: JANE PORTER et al. On motion of Respdt. JANE PORTER, has time of 2 mos. granted her to file Ans.

GREENWAY, HENRY & SMITH et al. Vs: H. T. COX & CO. & O. On appl. HYATT MCBURNEY & CO. have leave to file X Bill in nature of original bill on entering into bond and security for costs.

HYATT MCBURNEY & CO. Vs: H. T. COX et als. Defdt. allowed 2 mos. to plead Ans. or demur.

W. S. PORTER Vs: L. D. FRANKLIN et als. In this case death of Rspdt. L. D. FRANKLIN is suggested and admitted.

CHARLES LONES Vs: WILLIAM ROREX et als. Respdt. has 2 mos. time to file Ans.

ESTHER LEEPER & HUSBAND Vs: W. W. HOWARD & O., HEIRS of JOHN HARDIN, Dec'd. PATRICK MCCLUNG appt'd. Commr. to lay off Dower to the Complnt. in place of G. P. RUTLEDGE and the two other Commrs. heretofore appt'd. Rep't. next term.

Pg. 112 H. FOSTER Vs: W. M. STEELE et als. Leave granted Respdt. 2 mos. to file Ans.

SAMUEL PRIDE, C&M Vs: JAMES D. WEAR, JAMES MCCONNELL & MASON ELLIOTT. It appearing to Ct. JAMES D. WEAR, JAMES MCCONNELL and MASON ELLIOTT are indebted to SAMUEL PRIDE, C&M, by two notes at hand in words and figures to wit: $2,047.25. 12 mos. after date w/Int. we promise to pay SAMUEL PRIDE, C&M, Chancery Ct. at Maryville, $2,047.25, the purchase money for land of late HUGH WEAR as inventoried in D. of said Ct. and ordered to be sold. Jan. 19, 1860, JAMES D. WEAR (Seal), JAMES MCCONNELL (Seal), MASON ELLIOTT (Seal).

$1,966.98. 12 mos. after date w/Int. we promise to pay SAMUEL PRIDE, C&M. of Chancery Ct., Maryville, Tennessee, $1,966.98, the amt. of purchase money, less 5% for the slaves RACHAL and her twin Ch. TOM and BILLY - sold under a D. of the Chancery Ct. is the property of HUGH WEAR, Dec'd. Given under our hands and seals 19 Jan. 1860. JAMES D. WEAR (Seal) JAMES MCCONNELL (Seal) MASON ELLIOTT (Seal) and it appearing to satisfaction of Ct. that said notes remain due and unpaid it is therefore O. by Ct. the said SAMUEL PRIDE, C&M, recover from JAMES D. WEAR, JAMES MCCONNELL and MASON ELLIOTT the sum of $4,014.23 Principal on said two notes and the further sum of $351.91 for which execution may issue.

Pg. 113 SAMUEL PRIDE, C&M, JAMES MCCONNELL, JAMES D. WEAR and N. B. MCCLAIN. It appearing to Ct. that Defdts. indebted by note to Complnt. - the following words and figures, to wit: $1,937.05. 12 mos. after date w/Int. we promise to pay SAMUEL PRIDE, C&M, $1,937.05 the purchase money less 5% for the slaves SAM and PETER - sold under a D. of said Ct. as property of HUGH WEAR, Dec'd. Given under our hand and seal this 19 Jan. 1860, JAMES MCCONNELL (Seal) JAMES D. WEAR (Seal) N. B. MCCLAIN (Seal) and it further appearing to Ct. that note remains due and unpaid, it is therefore O. that the Complnt. SAMUEL PRIDE, C&M, recover of the said JAMES MCCONNELL, JAMES D. WEAR and N. B. MCCLAIN the sum of $1,937.05 and further the sum $150.44 Int.

SAMUEL PRIDE, C&M Vs: JAMES HENRY, ANDREW KIRKPATRICK, SPENCER HENRY & JOHN F. HENRY. Appears to Ct. Defdts. are indebted to Complnt. by note in

Pg. 114 hand in words and figures following to wit: $3,131.41. One day after date, we, or either of us promises to pay SAMUEL PRIDE, C&M, $3,131.41, this being bal. of Principal and Int. of a Jdgmt. rendered 25th Nov. 1857 in Chancery Ct. Blount County agnst. ROBERT JAMES, JAMES HENRY and O. in favor of SAMUEL and ANN GHORMLY, Admr. and Admx. of WILLIAM JAMES, Dec'd. on which Jdgmt. execution issued and was levied on lands of JAMES HENRY in Blount County and the same was sold by Sheriff of Blount County on 20th Nov. 1858 and purchased by the said Admrs. and this note is given for security and payment of said Jdgmt. and to redeem the said lands. JAMES HENRY (Seal) ANDREW KIRKPATRICK (Seal) SPENCER HENRY (Seal) JOHN F. HENRY (Seal).

And it further appears said note remains due and unpaid. Therefore O. by Ct. that SAMUEL PRIDE, C&M, recover of the above the sum of $3,131.41 Principal and further sum of $87.16 Int. and costs.

SAMUEL PRIDE, C&M Vs: JAMES HENRY & S. HENRY. Respdts. indebted to Complnt. by note of hand - words and figures as follows, to wit: "One day after date we promise to pay SAMUEL PRIDE, C&M, $1,591.36. It being the consideration of a note w/Int. executed 30 Nov. 1859 to SAMUEL and ANN GHORMLY, Admr. and Admx. of WILLIAM JAMES, Dec'd., for $1,486.33, Feb. 4, 1861. JAMES HENRY (Seal) SPENCER HENRY, Security. It further appears note remains unpaid, therefore O. that SAMUEL PRIDE, C&M, recover from JAMES HENRY and SPENCER HENRY, Security, $1,591.38 Principal and $24.67 Int.

Pg. 115 S. J. MCREYNOLDS Vs: RUFUS M. CAULEY & J. S. M. EVERETT. This case coming for final hearing on 7 May 1861 before Hon. T. NIXON VAN DYKE, Chancellor and upon Rep't. of C&M. which rep't. being unexcepted to in all things confirmed. C&M in obedience to a D. order made at last term Ct. after advertising to the reassignments of said Decree proceeded on 27 Apr. 1861 at C.H. doors in Maryville to sell lands mentioned in proceedings at public sale to highest bidder and S. J. MCREYNOLDS became purchaser for sum of $90.00, that being the highest and best bid. Court pleased to O.A.D. that all right, title, int. or claim that RUFUS M. CAULEY and J. S. M. EVERETT, or either of them have in and to the tract of land set forth and specified in pleadings - 31 1/2 A. M/L, lying in the 4th Civil District, Blount County, adjoining lands of HENRY CLEMENS, J. S. M. EVERETT, CYRUS CURTIS and O. bounded as follows: (Survey report given... Line common to CYRUS CURTIS, to corner w/HENRY CLEMINS, to a stake in line w/JOHN LOWERY) title to same without rt. of redemption be vested in S. J. MCREYNOLDS his heirs and assigns forever. C&M to issue a Writ of Restitution to place S. J. MCREYNOLDS in possession of land and C&M to make out certified copy of this decree.

And it further appearing to Ct. that Respdt. RUFUS M. CAULEY is indebted to S. J. MCREYNOLDS, after deducting the proceeds of the sale of land in the sum of $14.22. Ct. pleased to O. that S. J. MCREYNOLDS have jdgmt. agnst. RUFUS M. CAULEY for $14.22 together w/costs of Jdgmt.

Ct. adjourned until tomorrow morning 7 O'Clock.

T. NIXON VAN DYKE.

Pg. 116 Wed. May 8, 1861. B. W. & J. P. FORCE & CO. & O. Vs: J. A. HOUSTON & CO. Complnts. produced before Ct. following note executed in this cause and moved for jdgmt. $1,081.50 - "Six mos. after date we promise to pay SAMUEL PRIDE, C&M of Chancery Ct. at Maryville, $1,081.50 w/Int. 27 Jan. 1860. ISAAC N. YEAROUT, THAD. J. FROW, JOHN R. FROW." which note was executed as part consideration for lands in the pleadings. The note is due and unpaid. O.& D. by Ct. that ISAAC N. YEAROUT, THOMAS J. FROW and JOHN R. FROW pay SAMUEL PRIDE, C&M, sum of $1,081.50 plus $94.30 Int. making in all $1,175.80 together w/costs.

A. DYER Vs: ALLEN ANDERSON. On motion of Complnt. it is O. by Ct. that Master investigate state of Title to the land in controversy and rep't. next term Ct. whether the Respdt. can make a good Title to the Complnt. and he is directed if it is deemed necessary to have a survey of the land w/plot of same and rep't. next term Ct.

LEONARD A. WOODS Vs: M. A. STEPHENS & O. & M. A. STEPHENS Vs: L. A. WOODS & O. Leave granted to Respdts. in X Bill 2 mos. to file Ans.

Pg. 117 CLARK HYDE & CO. Vs: J. A. HOUSTON & O. Respdts. S. J. MCREYNOLDS and J. A. HOUSTON having Ans. for sufficient reason discovered to the Ct. They are ordered to be filed and the jdgmt. Pro Confesso heretofore taken is set aside for nothing held.

W. C. & R. L. CRESWELL Vs: ANDREW CRESWELL. Bill and X Bill. These causes coming on for further hearing on 8 May 1861 upon rep't. of C&M made to present time of Ct. is being unaccepted to is in all things confirmed. It appears ANDREW CRESWELL has pd. on land in pleadings mentioned, including int., betterments and taxes, $638.15 and that rents and profits of land since he came into possession of it amts. to sum $332.50 which subtracted from the amt. pd. leaves due to said ANDREW CRESWELL the sum of $305.65 w/int. from 8 Mar. 1861. His Honor pleased to O.A.D. that Complnts. WILLIAM C. and R. L. CRESWELL pay to ANDREW CRESWELL $305.65 w/int. from Mar. 8, 1861 until pd. and if the same is not pd. within 4 mos. from this date then the C&M, after advertising 30 days, shall sell the land in the pleadings at C.H. door. As to the said bal. due ANDREW CRESWELL, it is O. by Ct. that if land sold - no equity of redemption and O. that C&M make rep't. next term Ct.

Pg. 118 S. J. MCREYNOLDS Vs: GRESHAM STRANGE & CO. On rep't. of C&M to wit: "In obedience to an O. of Chancery Ct. Nov. Term 1860 - C&M to rep't. and show what amt. of debts may be due and unpaid agnst. said firm.
    Amt. collected............$8,812.29
    Amt. disbursed............$4,575.44
    Amt. in Recv'rs hands.....$4,226.85
Submitted May 8, 1861.   SAMUEL PRIDE, C&M.
Because it appears to Ct. that there are still debts outstanding and uncollected due firm GRESHAM STRANGE & CO. amounting to $2,062.96. JAMES A. MCCAMY, the Rec'vr., is about leaving State of Tennessee and by consent of the parties, JAMES A. HOUSTON is now appt'd. Recv'r. and he directed to proceed w/collection of debts still owed the firm GRESHAM STRANGE & CO. Rep't. next term Ct. and that he enter into Bond w/Security in the sum of $2,500.00 for the performance of his trust.

DAVID CUNNINGHAM, Admr. & O. Vs: ALFRED CUNNINGHAM. Be it remembered this 8 Day May 1861 before

Pg. 119 the Chancellor upon all proceedings heretofore had in this case, this cause came up for hearing and upon transcript from Supreme Ct. of Tennessee at Knoxville and upon rep't. of C&M. Ct. being of opinion that the exceptions are well taken and are therefore sustained, but the rep't. is confirmed so far as not excepted to and it appearing from said rep't. that the mare was worth - on the day demand was made by the Admr. the sum of $55.00 and at the same time the horse was worth $125.00 and that the day of demand was Apr. 3, 1868 and that the int. on the two above sums of money to this date is $33.42. And it further appearing from transcript of Supreme Ct. that there was $400.00 of the purchase money which the Respdt. ALFRED CUNNINGHAM pretended in his Ans. to the bill was pd. in notes upon JOHN CUNNINGHAM of Missouri from the Supreme Ct. transcript it appears that under the peculiar circumstances of this case that the admissions of the old man, MOSES CUNNINGHAM, and the recitals in the deed are excluded as evidence and the Ct. is further of opinion that the Ans. of Respdt. ALFRED in relation to said note is vague and unsatisfactory and he has failed to establish proof of fact that there were notes of the amt. specified or that they were rec'd. fairly by the old man in payment for the land, or any part thereof and it appears further that the land was conveyed and the deed date 30 Sept. 1854 and from that date until the present the said sum of $400.00 at rate of 6% Int. - the sum of $158. The Ct. therefore O.& D. that Complnt. DAVID, Administration to recover of Respdt. ALFRED the said several sums of money amting. to $771.95 together w/all costs which have not heretofore been adjudged for which execution is awarded and Respdt. ALFRED therefore comes and prays an appeal to next term Supreme Ct. at Knoxville, Second Mon. Sept. 1861 and same is granted. He has 2 mos. to file an appeal bond.

Pg. 120 H. T. COX Vs: JOHN MCCULLY & O. Complnt. having obtained settlement of his claims involved in cause comes into Ct. and dismisses suit. Respdt. assumes costs.

N. BREWER, Gdn. & O. Vs: RHODA CHAMBERS et al. Came to be heard and determined before Chancellor, 8 May 1861 upon rep't. of Commrs. appt'd. to lay off a yr. support for RHODA CHAMBERS and her Ch. under 14 yrs. and also lay off Dower to her as wife of JOHN

Pg. 121 CHAMBERS, Lunatic, made their rep't. as follows: We the Commrs. being unconnected to either by affinity of consanguinity w/the parties in this cause - to lay off Dower and one yr's. support. (There follows a detailed rep't. of the Estates assets and those which were awarded to RHODA CHAMBERS. The land was then surveyed and the Dower portion was suggested to be awarded to her, as a widow.) The land lying in Blount County, Tennessee, District #15 on waters of Little River bounded by LAWSON

Pg. 122 heirs, to corner w/LAMBERT and SAFFELLS heirs - another stake w/LAMBERT TIPTON and LAWSON which contains 1/3 of real estate of JOHN CHAMBERS, Lunatic. Given under our hands and seals this -- of Nov. 1860.
JAMES A. ROREX (Seal) JOHN WHITE (Seal) J. C. M. BOGLE (Seal).
The rep't. of Commrs. being unexcepted to was in all things confirmed and Ct. O. the plat be spread upon the record and D. that said RHODA have a title to her said Dower as described. Title to be divested out of heirs of JOHN CHAMBERS and into RHODA CHAMBERS. Rept'd. of N. BREWER, Gdn. made to this term Ct. being unexcepted to is confirmed. Ct. orders Widow pay cost of laying off her dower for which execution is awarded and

Pg. 123 by consent of parties this cause is retained for further action as may be necessary.

DAVID CUNNINGHAM, Admr. & O. Vs: ALFRED CUNNINGHAM et al. On motion, leave granted to Respdt. ALFRED CUNNINGHAM to withdraw the note filed by him w/his Ans. agnst. DAVID CUNNINGHAM in order that he may proceed to collect same upon his leaving a copy of note w/Master.
Court adjourned until Court in course.
T. NIXON VAN DYKE

Pg. 124 November Term 1861
Be it remembered that in pursuance of an Act of General Assembly passed 19th Jan. 1861, a Ct. of Chancery was opened and held at Courthouse in Maryville, Fri. 5th Nov. 1861. Chancellor not present. C&M adjourned Ct. until tomorrow.
SAMUEL PRIDE, C&M, by T. A. POPE, Dpty. C&M.
Wed. Nov. 6, 1861. Ct. met pursuant to adjournment. No Chancellor being present, Ct. adjourned until tomorrow morning at 8 AM.

Thurs. Nov. 7th, 1861. Ct. met pursuant to adjournment and the Chancellor not being present after remaining open until 4 O'clock and still no Chancellor appearing until Ct. in course.

Pg. 125 At Chambers, 20th Jan. 1862.
For sufficient reasons appearing to me from written application of JESSE G. WALLACE, Esq. Sol. for Creditors in the case of heirs of JOHN HENRY, Dec'd. agnst. the Widow and Admr. of said Dec'd. pending in Chancery Ct. at Maryville, O. that C&M be, and is hereby appt'd. Recv'r. and Commr. to receive recp't. for purchase money due, and become due, for an acc't. of sales made of real estate made by said Chancery Ct. in above cause, to be held by C&M subject to the order of Chancery Ct. Further O. that C&M rep't. next Term Ct. what he shall have done in the premises.
Given under my hand a.c. this 20 Jan. 1862. T. NIXON VAN DYKE, Chancellor.

Pg. 126 Maryville, Tues. May 6, 1862.
H. & B. DOUGLASS & O. Vs: S. J. MCREYNOLDS & O. C&M shows that on 18 Dec. 1860, house and lot in E. Maryville of Respdt. G. W. TEFFETELLER was sold to JOSEPH T. MCREYNOLDS, who gave note and security - accepted by C&M. The Ct. decrees that sale be confirmed and purchaser have title to property. C&M make him Deed for house and lot when purchase money pd. and purchaser to have writ of possession.

NORWOOD & WIFE Vs: E. & I. W. GEORGE, Extrs. AND JOHNSON & WIFE Vs: E. GEORGE & O. By consent of parties, time given until next term Ct. for both parties to file exceptions to the Master's rep't.

ROBERT WEAR Vs: JAMES D. WEAR & O. The Ct. orders that money already pd. into Ct. be pd. out by him to those entitled to the sum and that C&M receive from those yet owing the Estate the common circulating currency of the country. Because it appears to Ct. that such was the contract made day of sale.

Pg. 127 Tues. May 6, 1862.
H. B. LEEPER & WIFE Vs: HARDIN'S HEIRS. By consent - time given until next term Ct. both parties to except to

rep't. of Surveyor and Commrs.

MARGARET CUNNINGHAM Vs: ALFRED CUNNINGHAM. In this case the death of Complnt. MARGARET CUNNINGHAM is suggested and admitted and this cause to be named in the name of her Admr.

JOSEPH H. TEDFORD Vs: JAMES WILSON. In this cause O. by Ct. that C&M pay out money in this case to those adjudged entitled thereto.

WILLIAM S. PORTER Vs: L. D. FRANKLIN et als. In this case the death of Complnt. and Defdt. L. L. FRANKLIN is suggested and admitted and the cause named in names of the Admrs.

W. C. & R. L. CRESWELL Vs: ANDREW CRESWELL et als. In this case the rep't. of M. being unexcepted to is in all things confirmed. Master directed make Deed for land sold to ISAAC HINDS when purchase money pd.

ISABELLA S. MARTIN Vs: HEIRS of JOHN MARTIN & JOHN C. MARTIN, Dec'd. In this cause leave granted Defdts. to file Ans. within 2 mos.

S. J. MCREYNOLDS Vs: YEAROUT & CRAIG. In this cause 2 mos. given Defdt. J. G. WALLACE to file Ans.

R. S. MCNUTT & CO. Vs: J. A. HOUSTON, Trustee. In this cause Defdt. HOUSTON allowed 2 mos. to file Ans.

Pg. 128 S. J. MCREYNOLDS Vs: GRESHAM STRANGE & CO. Rep't. of Recv'r. JAMES A. MCCAMY made to May term 1861 which rep't. is unexcepted to and is confirmed. It appears Recv'r. has collected $8,802.29 and dispersed sum of $4,575.44 leaving a bal. $4,226.85 which money is O. to be pd. into Ct. and the Ct. hereby renders a diem? agnst. Recv'r. JAMES MCCAMY for said sum of money and the Int. thereon. It appearing to Ct. on Dec. 1856 the said Recv'r. gave a bond for his performance as Recv'r. in penalty of $1,000.00 w/JAMES K. DUNCAN and WILLIAM MCCAMY as Securities. The Ct. therefore D. that the said Securities pay the sum of $1,000.00. This D. agnst. said Recv'r. which execution may issue and execution may issue agnst. Recv'r. for whole amt. of this D. which if he pays will relieve the Securities.

SAMUEL PRIDE, Admr. of JOHN HENRY, Dec'd. Vs: HEIRS of JOHN HENRY, Dec'd. In this case the M. who is now Commr. for sale of said Real Estate mentioned in pleadings is directed to receive in payment of purchase money any bankable currency of the country.
All orders made at former Terms of this Ct. not already executed are hereby revived and cont'd.
Court adjourned until Ct. in course. T. NIXON VAN DYKE.

Pg. 129 Nov. 4, 1862.
The Hon. A. G. WELCHER, Chancellor, not being present Ct. adjourned until tomorrow morning at 8 O'Clock A.M. SAMUEL PRIDE, C&M.
Nov. 5, 1862.
Ct. met pursuant to adjournment. Present and Presiding the Hon. A. G. WELCHER, Chancellor.
WHEREUPON the Hon. A. G. WELCHER, Chancellor, presented and ordered the following Commission and endorsement thereon to be placed on record:

STATE OF TENNESSEE

To All Who Shall See These Presents - GREETINGS.

Where as it appears from the official returns of an Election held in our counties composing the "Second Chancery District" in said State on the 22nd day of May 1862 for the purpose of electing a Chancellor for said district that A. G. WELCHER received the highest number of votes polled in said Election.

Therefore I, ISHAM G. HARRIS, Governor of the State of Tennessee, do hereby commission the said A. G. WELCHER, Chancellor, as aforesaid during the term and with all the powers, privileges and emoluments authorized by law.

In testimony whereof I, ISHAM G. HARRIS, Governor as aforesaid have hereto set my hand and caused the great seal of the State to be affixed this 12th day of July 1862.
By the Governor I. G. HARRIS
J. E. R. RAY, Security.

Pg. 130 State of Tennessee Be it remembered that on this 15th
Blount County day of August 1862 the Hon.
ALBERT G. WELCHER, the person named in the within commission Chancellor of the Second District in the State of Tennessee approved before me and in due form of law took and subscribed the Oath prescribed by law to support the pursuant Constitution of the Confederate States of America and the Constitution of the State of Tennessee and the Oath of office as Chancellor and the oath more especially to prohibit duelling.

JOHN C. GAULT, Judge
4th Judicial Circuit
State of Tennessee

W. S. PORTER Vs: L. D. FRANKLIN & O. Death of Complnt. suggested and admitted. Leave granted to revive suit in name of CAMPBELL GILLESPY, his Admr.

S. & A. GHORMLY, Admrs. of WILLIAM JAMES, Dec'd. Vs: ROBERT JAMES & O. Suggested to Ct. papers mislaid or lost. After diligent search, cannot be found. O. by Ct. parties have leave within 2 mos. to supply same for filing other bills, Ans. etc. in their place.

CLARKE HYDE & CO. & O. Vs: J. A. HOUSTON & O. Death of Respdt. S. J. MCREYNOLDS suggested and admitted. Case revived as to J. A. HOUSTON, his Admr.

S. J. MCREYNOLDS & O. Vs: JOHN & W. R. YEAROUT. Death of Complnt. suggested and admitted. The same is revived in name of J. A. HOUSTON, his Admr.

MARGERET CUNNINGHAM Vs: ALFRED CUNNINGHAM. The death of Compnlt. suggested and admitted. Same is revived in name of DAVID CUNNINGHAM, her Admr.

Pg. 131 SAMUEL B. HENDERSON et al. Vs: WILLIAM HENDERSON, M. RUSSELL et als.

M. RUSSELL Vs: WILLIAM HENDERSON & O. Bill and X Bill. In these cases leave of 2 mos. granted Defdt. WILLIAM HENDERSON to file Ans. and Bill and X Bill.

R. L. MCNUTT & CO. VS: J. A. HOUSTON, Trustee et al. Defdts. having failed to ans. judgement by confession is therefore taken.

S. J. MCREYNOLDS Vs: YEAROUT & CRAIG. Death of Complnt. being suggested and admitted. Same revived in name of J. A. HOUSTON, his Admr.

WILLIAM C. WALLACE Vs: JAMES W. BICKNELL. Complnt. by his counsel comes and dismisses his suit and agrees to pay costs of same.

HU B. LEEPER & WIFE Vs: HEIRS of JOHN P. HARDIN. Commrs. appt'd. in former Ct. to lay off and assign Dower to Complnt. ESTHER LEEPER, formerly the widow of JOHN P. HARDIN, Dec'd. They made following rep't.: Commrs. commissioned to set off to ESTHER LEEPER, the late ESTHER HARDIN, her dower out of Est. of said Dec'd. husband, JOHN P. HARDIN. The following lands w/erections thereon to wit: A tract of land lying in Blount Pg. 132 County on waters of Little Tennessee River containing 436 A. and 3 Roods, bounded as follows: Little Tennessee River near the Narrows - One of original corners of Grant - to corner w/J. H. PARSONS, to head of an Island, to stake on bank of Sluice, to a large barn - leaving barn outside dower, thence with center of Rd. to a stake on a Mt. to corner w/WILLIAM WRIGHT - to stake corner of HARDIN HEIRS back to stake of J. H. PARSONS - to a rock in a small patch north of the dwelling which constitutes 1/3 of real estate of JOHN P. HARDIN, Dec'd. Dec. 11, 1861. PATRICK MCCLUNG, (Seal), A. L. ANDERSON, (Seal), J. C. M. BOGLE, Sheriff of Blount County (Seal).
The same being unexcepted is to in all things confirmed. Ct. O.A.D. that dower be divested out of heirs of JOHN P. Pg. 133 HARDIN and be vested in ESTHER LEEPER during her natural life and costs be shared between Complnt. and Respdt.

SAMUEL PRIDE, C&M Vs: ROBERT MCLIN, J. A. MCLIN, R. M. SAFFELL. Defdts. in case indebted by note to Complnt. in following words and figures: $399.00 Six mos. after date we promise to pay SAMUEL PRIDE, C&M $399.00 par value, 25 Jan. 1861 and it appearing note unpaid. O. by Ct. SAMUEL PRIDE, C&M, recover from said ROBERT MCLIN, J. A. MCLIN and & R. M. SAFFELL the said amt. w/$30.49 Int. plus costs.

SAMUEL PRIDE, C&M Vs: ISAAC HINES & THOMAS PICKENS. Defdts. in case indebted by note to Complnt. in following words and figures $315.48 "6 mos. after date we promise to pay SAMUEL PRIDE, C&M, $315.48 for value rec'd. being part of purchase price on ANDREW CRESWELL land. Oct. 19, 1861. ISAAC HINES (Seal) THOMAS PICKENS (Seal) it further appearing note due and unpaid. O. by Ct. SAMUEL PRIDE, C&M, recover from ISAAC HINES and THOMAS PICKENS $315.48 plus $10.72 Int. plus all costs.

Pg. 134 W. C. & R. S. CRESWELL Vs: ANDREW CRESWELL. In this case C&M O. to pay any monies in hand from sale of land to parties interested and also fees of WILLIAM D. MCGINLEY and JESSE G. WALLACE, Sols., and take receipt for same.

S. & A. GHORMLY, Admrs. & C. Vs: ROBERT JAMES, JAMES HENRY et als. It being represented to Ct. that since filing amended Bill the purchaser of said propty. under Deed of Trust had sold and disposed of said propty. to JOHN C. M. BOGLE, THOMAS A. POPE, D. C. GHORMLY and O. No payments made by purchaser to Trustee. Leave granted Complnts. to file supplimental Bill bringing all other proper parties before Ct. to the end purchase money may be enjoined in the hands of 2nd purchaser and titles decreed.

MALINDA EVERETT Vs: JOHN EVERETT. Petition for Divorce. In this case, Complnt. by her Sol. comes and dismisses her Bill. Respdt. agrees pay costs. Ct. adjourned until 9 O'Clock Tomorrow A.M. A. G. WELCKER, Chancellor.

Pg. 135 Maryville, Nov. 8, 1862.
JAMES ELIGE Vs: EMILY B. ELIGE. Be it remembered that on this 6th day of Nov. 1862 this case comes for final hearing. That upon the proceedings heretofore had and upon Jdgmt. Pro Confesso and upon proof, part of which is written and part in open Ct. and from which it appeared that Respdt. had more than 2 yrs. before commencement of this suit, abandoned maliciously the Complnt. and moved to the State of Texas. Ct. therefore

D. Complnt. divorced from Defdt. and that he be restored to all rts. of a single man. Complnt. pay costs. WILLIAM A. WALKER, Esq., having this day been appt'd. by the Hon. A. G. WELCKER, Chancellor of 2nd Div. of Tennessee, C&M of the Chancery Ct. Blount County, Tennessee, now here appearing in open Ct. w/his Official Bonds and acknowledged before and approved by Chancellor in open Ct. Several Bonds are ordered to be entered of record and are as follows, to wit: "Know all men by these presents that we, WILLIAM A. WALKER, C. GILLESPY, SAMUEL PRIDE, ELIJAH WALKER, JR., D. G. WRIGHT, B. F. DUNCAN and W. D. MCGINLEY are held and firmly bound unto the State of Tennessee, in the penal sum of $10,000.00 for the payment of which will and truly to be made, we bind ourselves, our Extrs. or Admrs. firmly by these presents: Witness our hands and seals this 6th day of Nov. 1862. The conditions of the above obligations is such whereas the above WILLIAM A. WALKER, has this day been appt'd. by the Chancellor of 2nd Div. of Tennes-

Pg. 136 see, C&M. of Chancery Ct. Blount County. Now if the said WILLIAM A. WALKER shall faithfully account for and pay over all monies which shall or may come into his hands, or possession as Spec. Commr. or Recv'r. by Ct. appointment, then this obligation be Null and Void.

Pg. 137 Otherwise to remain in full force and effect. W. A. WALKER (Seal) C. GILLESPY (Seal) JESSE G. WALLACE (Seal) W. D. MCGINLEY (Seal) SAMUEL PRIDE (Seal) B. F. DUNCAN (Seal) E. WALKER (Seal) D. G. WRIGHT (Seal) Signed and Sealed and Acknowledged in open Ct. A. G. WELCKER, Chancellor.

All causes, rules and motions not otherwise disposed at this Term are cont'd. to the next term Ct. Ct. adjourned until next regular Ct. in course.

Pgs. 138-142 are torn from book (Rough edges of torn pages evidence of removal).

Pg. 143 Chattanooga, Tennessee. Aug. 16, 1864.
To All Whom It May Concern:
By Virtue of the Powers in me Vested as Chancellor of the 2nd Div. of Tennessee, I hereby app't. to the office of C&M at Maryville, Blount County, Tennessee, WILLIAM C. PICKENS with all the Rights, Powers and Privileges thereto pertaining. Given under my hand date first above written. D. C. TREWHIT, Chancellor.

Maryville, Tennessee. Nov. 8, 1864.

Be it remembered that on Tues., Nov. 8, 1864, it being the day for which by Law the Chancery Ct. for Blount County was to be held at 10 O'Clock in the morning, I directed the Sheriff of Blount County to open the Ct. which he did by proclamation at the C.H. door in Maryville. I then held Ct. open until 4 O'Clock and no Chancellor appearing I adjourned Ct. until tomorrow, 10 A.M., Wed., Nov. 9, 1864. Ct. met pursuant to adjournment at 10 O'Clock. I opened the Ct. according to Law and no Chancellor appearing I held Ct. open until 4 O'Clock then adjourned until tomorrow morning 10 O'Clock. W. C. PICKENS, C&M.

Thurs., Nov. 10, 1864. Ct. met pursuant to adjournment at 10 O'Clock. I opened the Ct. according to Law and no Chancellor appearing I held the Ct. open until 4 O'Clock then adjourned the Ct. in course believing the public

Pg. 144 interest did not require the present term to continue longer. W. C. PICKENS, C&M. by F. M. HOOD, Dpty. C&M.

Maryville, Tues, May 2, 1865. Be it remembered that on Tues., May 2, 1865, it being the day on which by Law the Chancery Ct. for Blount County was to be held. At 10 O'Clock in A.M. I directed the Sheriff of Blount County to open Ct. which he did by proclamation at C.H. door. I held open Ct. until 4 P.M. No Chancellor appearing I adjourned until tomorrow morning. W. C. PICKENS, C&M.

by F. M. HOOD, Dpty. C&M.

Wed., May 3, 1865. (Same information as May 2).

Thurs., May 4, 1865. Court met pursuant to adjournment at 10 O'Clock. I opened Ct. according to Law and no Chancellor appearing, but being credibly informed that the Chancellor had laid over the present term of Chancery to meet the 4th Mon., 22nd day of May 1865, it being the time of setting of the Circuit Ct. I therefore adjourned Ct. to meet Mon., 22nd day of May 1865 at 10 O'Clock. W. C. PICKENS, C&M, by F. M. HOOD, Dpty. C&M.

Pg. 145 State of Tennessee, Blount County.

Be it remembered that at a Spec. Term of Chancery Ct. at Maryville., Blount County on the 4th Mon., 22nd day of

May 1865, opened and holden according to the Constitution and laws of the United States and of State of Tennessee, Present and presiding the Hon. D. C. TREWHITT, Chancellor of 2nd Div. the following proceedings were had, to wit: The Chancellor produced his Commission as Chancellor and O. the same spread of record which is done and is in the words and figures following, to wit:

State of Tennessee. To all who shall see these presents: Greetings, Know ye that where as a vacancy has occurred in the office of Chancellor of the 2nd Div. of State of Tennessee comprising the counties of Bledsoe, Bradley, Blount, Fentress, Hamilton, Marion, Meigs, McMinn, Monroe, Morgan, Polk, Rhea, Roane and Scott - Now therefore I, ANDREW JOHNSON, Gov. of the State of Tennessee by virtue of power and authority in me vested do app't. and commission DANIEL C. TREWHITT said office of Chancellor of said 2nd Div. of said State of Tennessee until his successor shall have been chosen and qualified and do empower him to execute and fulfill the duties of the same agreeably to the Constitution and Laws with all the powers, privileges and emoluments thereunto appending. In Testimony whereof I, ANDREW JOHNSON, Gov. of the State of Tennessee, have hereunto set my hand and caused the Great Seal of the State to be affixed at Nashville this 25th day of June A.D. 1864.
By the Governor, ANDREW JOHNSON
EDWARD H. EAST, Secretary of State.

Pg. 146 WILLIAM C. PICKENS having previously been appt'd. C&M by the Hon. D. C. TREWHITT, Chancellor of 2nd Div. of Tennesse, and now here appearing in open Ct. w/his Official Bonds and acknowledging before and approved by the Chancellor in open Ct. which several Bonds are ordered to be entered of Record and are as follows to wit: State of Tennessee, Blount County, We, WILLIAM C. PICKENS, A. MARION GAMBLE, THOMAS PICKENS and J. W. FRENCH are bound unto the State of Tennessee in the sum of $25,000.00. Witness our hands and seals this 16th day of Aug. 1864. The condition of this obligation is such that whereas the above bound WILLIAM C. PICKENS has this day been appt'd. C&M of Chancery Ct. at Maryville, Blount County, Tennessee.

Now the said WILLIAM C. PICKENS, as Commr. or Recv'r.

shall truly and faithfully acc't. for all propty. or funds that may come into his hands at anytime as such Clerk as required by Law, then this obligation to be void, otherwise to remain in full force and virtue. WILLIAM C. PICKENS (Seal) A. MARION GAMBLE (Seal) THOMAS PICKENS (Seal) J. W. FRENCH (Seal). Attest: D. C. TREWHITT, Chancellor, a.c.

On the back of which obligation the following oaths were endorsed:

State of Tennessee   I, WILLIAM C. PICKENS, do solemn-
Blount County   ly swear that I will support the Constitution of the United States and State of Tennessee and I have not directly or indirectly given, accepted or knowingly carried a challenge in writing or otherwise to any person being a Citizen of this State either in or out of the State, or aided or abetted...

Pgs. 147-148 torn from book. (Rough edge of missing page attests it was there).

Pg. 149 ...therein since I have been a Citizen of this State and that I will not during my continuance in Office be guilty of either of these acts. That I have not given, nor will I give to any person any gratuity gift, fee or sum and in consideration of my appointment to office of C&M. Nor have I sold, nor offered to sell, nor will I sell my interest in said office and that I will faithfully and without prejudice, partiality, or favor discharge the duties of said office of C&M at Maryville, Blount County, Tennessee, to the best of my ability, so help me God. Sworn and subscribed the 16th day Aug. 1864. W. C. PICKENS... D. C. TREWHITT, Chancellor.

State of Tennessee, Blount County. We, W. C. PICKENS, A. MARION GAMBLE, THOMAS PICKENS and J. W. FRENCH are bound to State of Tennessee in the sum of $10,000.00.

Witness our hands and seals this 16th day of Aug. 1864. The consideration of the above obligation is such that whereas WILLIAM C. PICKENS shall faithfully keep and preserve the Records of said Ct. and shall faithfully discharge duties of said Office, according to law, then the obligation to be void, otherwise to remain in force and virtue.

Signed: W. C. PICKENS (Seal) A. MARION GAMBLE (Seal)

THOMAS PICKENS (Seal) J. W. FRENCH. Attest: D. C. TREWHITT, Chancellor, a.c.

Pg. 150 State of Tennessee, Blount County. We, WILLIAM C. PICKENS, A. MARION GAMBLE, THOMAS PICKENS and J. W. FRENCH are held to State of Tennessee in the sum of $5,000.00. Witness our hands and seals this 16th Aug. 1864. Condition of this obligation - the above-bound WILLIAM C. PICKENS has this day been appt'd. C&M of Chancery Ct., Blount County, Tennessee, if WILLIAM C. PICKENS shall truly and faithfully acc't. for and pay over as required by law all monies from taxes on Suits, Fines and Forfeitures and discharge the duties of said office - then this obligation void - otherwise remain in full force and value. (Signatures of above men repeated with their seals.)

Tues., A.M., May 24, 1865.
Ct. met pursuant to adjournment at 7 O'Clock. Present and presiding, Hon. D. C. TREWHITT, Chancellor.

C. W. NORWOOD Vs: E. & I. W. GEORGE. In this case of death of Mrs. MALINDA NORWOOD was suggested and proven in open Ct. Cause cont'd. to next term.

Pg. 151 JAMES TAYLOR Vs: JAMES WALKER & O. Cause cont'd. next term and Respdt. has leave to file petition making a new party as Trustee in the room of SAMUEL PRIDE whose death was suggested and proven in open Ct.

S. J. MCREYNOLDS Vs: STRANGE & CO. Upon call of docket it appeared that cause was abandoned. The Complnt. and his Counsel (the following is crossed out) hearing docket... as neither of parties appearing by themselves or their Sols. in any manner to prosecute or defend this suit.
It is therefore O. by Ct. - this case be discontinued and stricken from docket and that Complnt. and S. L. YEAROUT, his Security, for prosecution pay all costs.

HARTSELL & WALLACE Vs: GILBERTS HEIRS & O. Neither parties appearing by themselves or Sols. the Ct. is advised of situation as to whether there is any monies in hands of Complnt. - it therefore O.& D. by Ct. - case referred to C&M - he to ascertain from any legal source of proof and rep't. next term if there is any money in hands of Complnt. or either of them and how much and rep't.

Pg. 152 Maryville, Blount County, Tennessee. May 23, 1865.
J. H. TEDFORD Vs: JAMES WILSON. Upon rep't. of C&M in case, both parties have time until next term of Ct. to except to the M. rep't.

H. T. COX Vs: WILLIAM MCTEER. This cause cont'd. by consent of parties.

DAVID CUNNINGHAM, Admr. Vs: A. CUNNINGHAM. By consent of parties - cont'd. Both parties have time to except the M. rep't.

ARCHIBALD DYER Vs: ALLEN ANDERSON. It appears to Ct. this case is abandoned by Complnt., J. D. COUNT ?. It is O. by Ct. that cause be discontinued and stricken from docket. Further considered and D. that the Complnt. pay all costs.

SAMUEL GHORMLY & O. Vs: H. & H. L. STEPHENS & O. This cause upon application of Respdt. is cont'd. next term and O. to remain at Rules to take such further steps as may be proper.

J. H. HOUSTON & O. Vs: J. & W. YEAROUT. Cause cont'd. next term.

Pg. 153 Maryville, Blount County, Tennessee. Tues., May 25, 1865.
JOHN C. CHILDS and JAMES HENRY, Commrs. of JOHN HENRY, Dec'd. Vs: A. ISH, A. J. ISH and WILLIAM HENDERSON. This Decree is vacated by O. of the Chancellor and because the same has been permanently entered. May 25, 1865. (The above is written across the page over the wording of the case. The only discernable part of the entry beneath the above is "the death of A. ISH having been suggested and admitted is ordered that suit be dismissed as to him.")

JOSEPH S. ABBOTT & O., EDWARD H. ABBOTT Vs: SESLER & FAGG. It appears that Complnt. bill filed before last Term Ct. and publication was made requiring Respdt. to appear and defend the same. Respdt. failed to

Ans. O. by Ct. that judgement Pro Confesso be rendered agnst. them and entered as of last rule day of this Ct.

C. GILLESPY, Admr. of WILLIAM C. GILLESPY, Dec'd. Vs: NANCY F. GILLESPY. Case cont'd. by consent until next term.

H. T. COX Vs: JOHN MCCULLY. It appears to Chancellor that Complnt. has taken no steps to prosecute his suit for more than 2 terms past O. that same be dismissed. It is therefore considered by Ct. that Respdt. recover of Complnt. and J. L. COX, his Security, all costs of cause for which execution may issue. (The above is all stricken from record with X's. Under it is written: This cause is cont'd.)

Pg. 154 May 23, 1865.
CRESWELL Vs: MCLIN. Appears to Ct. Complnt. has taken no steps for more than 2 terms to prosecute his suit and has not Ans. same and neither party appearing in Ct. by counsel it O. that same be dismissed. Therefore considered by Ct. that Respdt. recover of the Complnt. and his Security all costs of cause.

JACK MILLER Vs: B. F. OWENS. Petition to become Slave. To satisfactory reasons appearing to Ct. it is O. that this cause be stricken from the docket. Therefore considered by Ct. that Respdt. recover from Complnt. all costs of this cause.

S. B. HENDERSON & O. Vs: M. RUSSELL & O. Bill and X Bill. Death of M. RUSSELL is suggested and proven in open Ct. It appearing that letters testamentary on the Est. of the said M. RUSSELL, Dec'd. have been duly granted to ROBERT RUSSELL to County Ct. of Knox County. It is therefore O. that this cause be revived as to the said M. RUSSELL, Dec'd. in the name ROBERT RUSSELL as his Extr.

Pg. 155 ISABELLA S. MARTIN Vs: HEIRS of JOHN MARTIN, Dec'd. In this cause the death of SAMUEL MCKAMY is suggested and proven in open Ct.

R. L. MCNUTT Vs: J. A. HOUSTON, TRUSTEE & O. On motion of Complnt. cont'd. next term.

JESSE KERR Vs: W. M. COX & O. Upon motion of Respdt. H. T. COX has 3 mos. to Ans. and M. to furnish Respdt.'s Sol. w/copy of the Bill.

JAMES HENRY Vs: H. T. COX. Upon motion Respdt. H. T. COX has 3 mos. to Ans. and M. will furnish a copy of Bill to Respdt.'s Sol.

A. H. RUSSELL Vs: H. T. COX. Upon motion Respdt. H. T. COX has 3 mos. to Ans. and M. will furnish a copy of Bill for Respdt.'s Sol.

JAMES THOMPSON, Admr. of JAMES PORTER, Dec'd. Vs: S. S. PORTER & O. On appeal of Complnt. it is O. that process of subpoena has been served on GEORGE HENRY and JOHN BEAN? and it appearing that process was served on all other Defdts. except ANDREW PORTER and JOSEPH ROBERT PORTER more than 30 das. before Ct. It is O. that jdgmt. Pro Confesso be taken as to said Defdts. and the cause be set for hearing as to them ex parties.

Pg. 156 A. T. BRUCE & CO. Vs: H. T. COX & J. L. COX. The lands of Respdt. having been attached and publication having been made, as required by Law notifying Respdts. to appear at last regular Nov. term Ct. and plead, Ans. or demur to Complnt's. Bill. They have failed to do so. It is O.A.D. by Ct. that same be taken as confessed and set for hearing ex parte. This cause came to be heard before Hon. DANIEL C. W. TREWHITT, Chancellor, presiding. It appears to Ct., Respdts. are indebted to Complnts. including Principal which at 7% per Annum and Exchange in N.Y. at 1% Premium and after allowing all credits - sum of $2,336.88. His Honor please O.A.D. Complnts. have and receive of Respdt. sum of $2,336.88 w/Int. at 6% per annum until pd. and costs of suit and if same not pd. within 60 das. from this date, the C&M proceed to advertise according to law and sell as much of lands, which have been attached as will be sufficient to satisfy this D. before the C.H. door at Public Auction to highest bidder. Upon appeal of Complnts. the sale will be made upon a credit of 6 mos. and in bar of rt. of redemption or any of their creditors to redeem same. The M. will take note and good security from purchaser and rep't. next term Ct. If there be other conflicting attachment in this case the process of sale realized under this decree to be applied according to the privileges of same or as his interest appears.

Pg. 157 WILLIAM MOORE Vs: H. C. SAFFELL. Respdt.'s lands having been attached by process having been issued in this Ct. and publication made as required by law notifying Respdt. to appear at last regular term to plead Ans. or demur to Complnt. bill. He having failed to do so it is O.A.D. by Ct. that Complnt.'s bill be taken as confessed and set for hearing ex parte.

And thereupon this cause came for final hearing upon Complnt.'s bill and jdgmt. Pro Confesso before Hon. D. C. TREWHITT, Chancellor, and because it appears Respdt. is in debt to Complnt. by note as stated in Bill, including Principal w/Int. the sum of $124.94, his Honor pleased to O.A.D. Complnt. have and recover from Defdt. sum of $124.94 w/Int. and costs of suit and in case Respdt. fails to pay same within 60 das. from date, C&M will proceed to advertise according to law and sell lands attached before C.H. door in Maryville at public auction to highest bidder on a credit of 6 mos. taking note and good Security for purchase money and make rep't. next term Ct. Upon application of Complnt. said sale to be made on credit aforesaid in bar of Respdts. rt. of redemption or any of his creditors to redeem same and a lien will be retained on premises for security of payment of purchase money and it being suggested that there are other attachments issuing from this Ct. and levied on same lands attached in this case by consent of parties it is O.A.D. by Ct. that sale

Pg. 158 made under this decree shall be absolute and the purchase money when rec'd. shall be applied as Ct. may hereafter D. according to priority of lien of the respective attaching creditors.

ROCKFORD MFG. CO. Vs: DAVID CALDWELL. Respdt.'s lands having been attached and publication having been made as required by law notifying Respdt. to appear last regular term of Ct. and plead Ans. or demur to Complnt.'s bill. Having failed to do so it is O.A.D. by Ct. that Complnt.'s bill be taken as confesso and set for hearing ex parte and thereupon this cause came to be heard and determined upon Complnt.'s bill and jdgmt. Pro Confesso and because it appears that Respdt. is indebted to Complnt. in sum of $2,627.27 w/Int. from Sept. 2, 1863 until now which added to Principal makes aggregate of $2,878.63. Therefore O.A.D. by Ct. Complnt. have and recover from Respdt. sum of $2,878.53 w/Int. hereafter to accrue and costs. If Respdt. does not pay same in 60 das. from date C&M shall proceed, after due advertisement according to law to sell lands attached at public auction at C.H. door to highest bidder upon...

Pgs. 159 and 160 torn from book. (Torn edges of missing page evident in book binding.)

Pg. 161 ... a credit of 6 mos. taking note and giving security for purchase money and rep't. next term Ct. At request of Complnt., sale herein ordered shall be in bar the rt. of Respdt. or his creditors, to redeem the same under laws of State and as further security M. will secure a lien upon premises sold.

ROCKFORD MFG. CO. Vs: F. M. LAUTER?. Respdt.'s land having been attached and publication made as required by law notifying Respdt. to appear in last regular term Ct. and plead Ans. or demur to Complnt.'s bill and he having failed to do so it is O.A.D. by Ct. that Complnt.'s bill be taken for Confesso and set for hearing ex parte and thereupon this cause came for final hearing and jdgmt. Pro Confesso heretofore taken and entered of record. Respdt. is indebted to Complnt. - 2 promissory notes as stated in bill including Principal $363.96. O.A.D. by Ct. that Complnt. recover from Respdt. sum of $363.96 w/Int. plus cost of suit. If the Respdt. fails to pay within 60 das. and satisfy debt, the C&M will adver-

Pg. 162 tise and sell to highest bidder at C.H. door on a credit of 6 mos. and take note and good security for purchase money and make rep't. next term Ct. At request of Complnt. the sale herein ordered to be made will be in bar of the rt. of Respdt. or his creditors to redeem same under laws of State and as futher security for the purchase money a lien will be retained in the premises sold.

JOHN B. COX Vs: H. T. COX. Upon motion Respdt. has 3 mos. to file Ans. so not delay hearing of cause. M. to furnish said Respdt. and Sol. w/copy of Bill.

LEONARD A. WOOD & O. Vs: WILLIAM P. WOOD & O. May 23, 1865. Motion made in open Ct. by Complnt.'s

Sol. for appointment of Recv'r. The land involved in suit is valuable, has a grist mill and sawmill upon it. There are minors concerned in this case. Case not ready for hearing and must remain at the Rules. Ct. therefore O. and directs that WILLIAM C. PICKENS, C&M, take possession of said land as Recv'r., rent it out, dispose of rents and manage the place in all respects in best interests of parties is cause. That he hold it subject to further O. of Ct. & rep't.

Pg. 163 ANDREW PEERY, Admr. & O. of E. T. DUNLAP, Dec'd. Vs: ALIJAH SIMMONS. May 23, 1865. Heard on bill to Subpoena and Ans. which was served on Respdt. and upon judgement Pro Confesso heretofore taken. It appears to Ct. that intestate, ELIJAH T. DUNLAP, sold to Respdt. a tract of land herein described and took notes of Respdt. SIMMONS for sum of $500.00 to be pd. in yearly installments - all which still due and unpaid, now amt. to $712.86. Intestate bound himself in title bond to make title to Respdt. when purchase money to be made. Tract land situated in Blount County, 14th District on Ellejoy Creek adjoining lands of MANLY KEEBLE, where intestate lived at time of his death and O. containing @ 100 A. and it appearing that no controversy exists about sum of money yet due on said tract - the Ct. is pleased to O.A.D. that said tract to be sold by C&M after giving legal notices and upon application of Complnt. the Ct. O.& D. that the land be sold upon the premises, sold on credit of 7 mos. except 10% required to be pd. in hand and sale made in bar of rt. of redemption on part of Respdt. SIMMONS or his creditors. Sale of land shall be set on lien for purchase until pd.

Pg. 164 WILLIAM O'NEAL Vs: JAMES M. TOOLE & JOHN E. TOOLE. Motion for Jdgmt. upon disposition of Injunction. May 23, 1865. Motion made by WILLIAM O'NEAL, Respdt. in injunction Bill filed by JAMES M. TOOLE in this Ct. agnst. him 25th Jan. 1862. Injunction was granted and served and on 18th April 1865 the Hon. Chancellor LUCKY upon due notice, dissolved the injunction. It now appearing to satisfaction of Ct. that there is no equity upon face of said Bill, and that the rights of said O'NEAL have been seriously prejudiced by the filing of the injunction and further appearing that JOHN E. TOOLE was Security for him, the said JAMES M. TOOLE. Bill filed to enjoin the collection of a jdgmt. at law rendered by the Ct. in favor of WILLIAM O'NEAL and agnst. said TOOLE and O. Jdgmt. was rendered Sept. term 1861 and was for $1,519.64 which jdgmt. is yet unpaid. Ct. pleased to O.A.D. that bill of Complnt. be dismissed at his cost and that said O'NEAL recover of said JAMES M. TOOLE and JOHN E. TOOLE, his Security. The sum of $1,519.64 together w/Int. upon jdgmt. now amts. to sum of $1,853.90 and that they pay all costs of said Injunction Bill.

Pg. 165 SAMUEL & ANN GHORMLY Vs: ROBERT JAMES & O. It appearing it is an old case. Complnts. nor their Sols. appeared to prosecute or take further steps and that they have abandoned same, therefore O. by Ct. that this cause be discontinued and stricken from the docket. Complnts. pay costs for which an execution is awarded.

SAMUEL & ANN GHORMLY Vs: ROBERT JAMES & O. (Apparently the C&M made error and copied the above case a second time.)

GREEN FARMER & O. Vs: JAMES WATERS, Extr. & C. This cause cont'd. by consent of parties to next term of Ct.

R. M. SAFFELL Vs: J. C. M. BOGLE & O. In this cause death of Complnt. suggested.

Pg. 166 CLARKE HYDE & CO. Vs: J. A. HOUSTON & CO. Appears to Ct. cause has been abandoned by Complnts. O. by Ct. to be discontinued and stricken from docket. Complnt. pay all costs.

HEISKELL & BLAIR Vs: J. R LAWRENCE. Appears to Ct. this case abandoned by Complnt. therefore Ct. O. discontinuance and stricken from docket. Complnt. pay costs.

JAMES HENRY Vs: S. K. FINLEY & O. By consent of parties Respdt. has 3 mos. to Ans. (Next suit is faded beyond legibility. It is also stricken from the page with vertical lines drawn through the case.)

Pg. 167 (Ink faded out beyond legibility - apparently part of cause on bottom of Pg. 166. Written from the bottom to top of page are these words superimposed on the case "This Decree is Vacated by Order of the Chancellor because the same has been prematurely entered May 25, 1865." It would appear that someone has wiped a wet cloth over the ink to obscure the entire page as well as the bottom of Page 166 and through three quarters of Page 168.)

Pg. 168 Court adjourned until 7 O'Clock tomorrow morning. D. C. TREWHITT, Chancellor.
Wed. Morning, May 24, 1865.
Ct. met pursuant to adjournment. Present and Presiding Hon. D. C. TREWHITT, as before.

Pg. 169 JAMES W. EVERETT Vs: JOHN E. TOOLE. This cause came to be heard and finally determined upon the Bill, publication and Jdgmt. by Confesso heretofore entered agnst. Defdt. It appears to Ct. that on Sept. 9, 1862, Respdt. JOHN E. TOOLE executed unto Complnt. a title bond which is copied into original bill. Bond is due in legal form and is registered in Vol. 2A, Pg. 1436, Register's Office and from allegations from Complnt's. bill which is taken as confesso as to Respdt. Complnt. has pd. to Respdt. sum of $5,325.00 that being full amt. of purchase price for tract of land. Therefore O.A.D. by Ct. that title unto said tract on which the son, JOHN E. TOOLE, resides at time of sale to Complnt. EVERETT. Land situated in Blount County near town of Maryville and joining lands of WILLIAM KIDD, JAMES PORTER, Dec'd., W. W. LAWRENCE and O. containing 213 A. (M/L.) to be divested out of JOHN E. TOOLE and into JAMES W. EVERETT and his heirs forever. Respdt. is insolvent and irresponsible for costs of the cause. O. that Complnt. pay costs of cause w/leave to have jdgmt. over agnst. Respdt. for the sums for all which execution may issue.

JONES & HARRIS Vs: THOMAS & SAMUEL (HENLEY?). Cause heard May 26, 1865 on Bill and Jdgmt. pro confesso, heretofore taken for want of Ans. Publication having been made for 4 weeks. It appears Defdts. as partners
Pg. 170 are indicted to Complnts. by note dated Nov. 8, 1859 payable 1 da. after date - sum of $65.46 plus Int. to this date is $20.44 making total of $87.90. Ct. pleased to O.A.D. that Defdts. pay to Complnts. the said sum and costs of cause it appearing that the attachment in this

cause has been levied on the interests of Defdt. in a certain tract of land lying in the 6th District of Blount County adjoining lands of GEORGE HENRY, WILLIAM MEANS, JAMES WILSON and O. containing 500 A. (M/L.) Ct. pleased to O. that C&M after giving due and legal notice of time and place of sale expose the Int. of the Defdts. to public sale at C.H. door to highest bidder and on Spec. application of Complnts. he will sell the same on 6 mos. credit and in bar of rt. of redemption on part of Defdt. or his creditors. He shall take from the purchaser a bond for purchase money w/approved security and retain lien on lands and rep't. next term Ct.

JESSE KERR, Sen. Vs: JOHN M. COFFIN & R. I. WILSON. Attachment has only been levied on propty. of one of Defdts. upon application of Complnt. O. that an alias attachment issued to Blount County be levied on propty. of Defdt. R. I. WILSON and on one other propty. Defdt. COFFIN and that an alias counterpart attachment issue to Jefferson City.

Pg. 171 GREENWAY, HENRY & SMITH & O. Vs: SAMUEL T. COX & O. AND HYATT MCBURNIE & CO. Vs: HENRY T. COX & O. On written agreement and compromise of parties, their Agent's Atty's. which was duly proven in open Ct. and in words and figures following: On 19 Mar. 1850, MILER and CHAMBERLAIN filed their bill in Chancery Ct., Madisonville, Tennessee, agnst. SAMUEL T. COX., JOHN B. COX, H. T. COX and O. for settlement of the mercantile firm of COX & DEVER and SAMUEL T. COX & CO. which suit finally determined on Dec. 9, 1858 and resulted in decree in favor of H. T. COX agnst. SAMUEL T. COX for $428.30 and agnst. SAMUEL T. COX and JAMES F. DEVER for $3,200.46. On Jan. 23, 1860, GREENWAY, HENRY & SMITH and RANKIN & DANNEE? & CO. filed their bill in Chancery Ct., Maryville, Tennessee, agnst. SAMUEL COX, JOHN B. COX, H. T. COX and O. which sum is still pending in said Ct. whereas on the -- day of -- 1860, or thereabout HYATT MCBURNIE & CO. of Charleston, South Carolina, filed their bill in Chancery Ct., Maryville agnst. HENRY T. COX, SAMUEL T. COX and O.

Pg. 172 seeking to review said D. in said Ct. in Madisonville and impeaching the same for fraud, which suit is still pending and undetermined and the members of the firms of GREENWAY, HENRY, & SMITH and RANKIN DANNEE? &

CO. and BARCROFT BEAVER & CO. are nonresidents of the Confederate States and alien enemies and their claims have been rep'td. to the Confederate Ct. in Knoxville and are now under control of F. E. CAMBELL, the Recv'r. of said Ct. and the several parties in Int. having met agreed on following terms of Compromise and Settlement to wit: THOMAS C. LYON, Agent and Atty. dismiss said suit at Maryville of GREENWAY, HENRY & SMITH & O. Vs: H. T. COX & O. and pay costs of suit. That O. P. TEMPLE, Agent, dismiss suit of HYATT MCBURNIE & CO. Vs: HENRY T. COX & O. at Maryville and pay costs of same. That T. C. CAMPBELL, the Recv'r., dismiss proceedings in the Confederate Ct. in claims of GREENWAY, HENRY & SMITH AND RANKIN DANNEE? & CO. AND BANCROFT BEAVER & CO. Vs: SAMUEL T. COX, JOHN B. COX & O. at cost of the Government. Said SAMUEL T. COX thru H. T. COX having pd. $1,500.00 this day to said Recv'r. in full satisfaction and discharge of said claims, SAMUEL T. COX is further to advance $1,500.00 (which is hereby done) to be applied as follows: $570.00 to WOODS, the claim of HYATT MCBURNIE & CO. in full - $200.00 in full to discharge claim of WOOD, ABBOTT & CO. pd. over to Recv'r. - and $730.00 pd. to HENRY T. COX, Agent of MILER, CHAMBERLAIN, surviving partners of MILER, CHAMBERLAIN & PECK, E. B. STODDARD & CO. & RULLMAN? & PRICE to be distributed by said Agent pro

Pg. 173 rata among said creditors in full satisfaction to discharge said claims agnst. COX & DEVER, it being object of compromise to satisfy and discharge SAMUEL T. COX and JOHN B. COX from all old debts of COX & DEVER, COX WALLACE & CO. and all liability thereon, in any way whatsoever. Further agreed as pt. of compromise HENRY T. COX release (which is hereby done) SAMUEL T. COX from said D. at Madisonville for sum of $420.30 and for D. agnst. COX & DEVER for $3,200.46 but H. T. COX does not hereby release JAMES F. DEVER from said D. JOHN B. COX released and forever discharged from all liabilities on acc't. of the $1,500.00 Capital Stock in firm COX, WALLACE & CO.

Further agreed HENRY T. COX to have a credit of $1,500.00 placed on his note executed to JOHN B. COX on 1st of Jan. 1856 for $3,414.09 in consideration of the said $1,500.00 this day pd. by him (the said H. T. COX to the said Recv'r.) Further agreed that HENRY T. COX to

Pg. 174 release SAMUEL T. COX from payment of the foregoing claims to wit: That of TRIPE & CO. for $190.00 and that of JOBE CHANDLER & FOSTER for about $90.00 the said H. T. COX being the owner of same. Further agreed as part of Compromise that all the effects of the old firm COX & DEVER of SAMUEL T. COX and of SAMUEL T. COX in firm COX, WALLACE & CO and all individual propty. of SAMUEL T. COX at any time conveyed to HENRY T. COX and JOHN B. COX of HENRY T. COX, in trust for payment of debts of the said firm of COX & DEVER and of him, the said SAMUEL T. COX be released and discharged from all trusts. Others to hand over to SAMUEL T. COX all the old books, papers, notes and receipts belonging to said firm.

On filing this agreement in Chancery Ct., C&M authorized to dismiss said suit.
May 13, 1863. SAMUEL T. COX, JOHN B. COX, H. T. COX, O. P. TEMPLE, Atty., HYATT MCBURNIE & CO. and by T. J. CAMPBELL, Recv'r.
The Ct. is therefore pleased to O.A.D. that said stipulations and agreements in said article of compromise are in all things confirmed and entered as a D. of the Ct. except the pretended stipulations of THOMAS J. CAMPBELL over which the Ct. takes no jurisdiction, said causes are hereby dismissed.

J. S. & E. A. ABBOTT Vs: SISLER & FAGG. Plff. in cause dismisses his suit it being one filed Dec. 15, 1865 and assumes to pay the cost for which execution may issue.

Pg. 175 REED BROS. & CO. Vs: C. A. M. & J. G. WALLACE. Cause came to be heard May 24, 1865 before Chancellor TREWHITT on Bill and Jdgmt. Pro Confesso heretofore taken Defdts. indebted by Jdgmt. to Complnt. sum of $66.67 rendered Feb. 4, 1856 plus Int. of $40.99 making altogether sum of $107.66. O. by Ct. Defdt. pay Complnt. said sum and costs of cause and the cost before J.P. It appearing that interest of C. A. M. WALLACE and JESSE G. WALLACE, the Defdts. in this cause in the Est. of their father, WILLIAM WALLACE, having been attached to this Ct. in the hands of W. C. A. WALKER, Extr. of WILLIAM WALKER, Dec'd. but as said Est. is not yet wound up, or does it yet appear how much if anything will remain after settlement of said Est. for C. A. M. and J. G. WALLACE, or either of them. The Ct. is pleased to cont. such attachment and garnishment until the facts can be ascertained whether there will be anything due to said Defdts. and this case will stand on docket until this fact is attained. In meantime, an execution may issue on the application of Complnt.

Pg. 176 JOSEPH S. KING Vs: STERLING LANIER, SIDNEY C. LANIER, WILLIAM B. LANIER & ABRAIM R. WATT. Bill and Amended and Supplimental Bill. Cause came to be heard May 24, 1865, on the amended bill and supplimental bill. The exhibit and on jdgmt. Pro Confesso heretofore taken as to the Defdts. for want of an Ans. publication having been made for four successive weeks in BROWNLOW'S *Knoxville Whig* before Ct. a newspaper published in Knoxville, Tennessee notifying Defdts. who are nonresidents to appear and defend suit. It appears that on the 23rd day of March 1863? Complnts. purchased from Defdts. who were partners in trading under the name of WATT, LANIER & CO. - Eleven tracts of land in Blount County, Tennessee known as Montvale Springs Property which property is duly described in the Exhibit to their Bill as well as the large amt. of personal property consisting of household and kitchen furniture, wagons, etc. that the prince pd. for said property was $40,000.00 which was pd. down and a deed executed for said real estate. It further appearing that all the Defdts. adhered to the so-called "Confederate States of America" in their rebellion agnst. Government of the U.S. and assisted, abetted and gave aid and comfort to said Rebellion or insurrection both before and after the date of said deed and did not,

Pg. 177 within 60 days after date of the President's Proclamation offer of amnesty, issued July 25, 1862, cease to aid countenance and abet said Rebellion and return their allegiance to the U.S. and the Ct. being of the opinion that under the Act of Congress of the U.S. approved July 17, 1862 entitled "An act to suppress Insurrection, to punish treason and Rebellion and for other purposes said sale of said property was Null and Void. But it further appearing that Complnt. made said purchase in good faith in ignorance of said Law and that he pd. out and advanced his money, therefore this Ct. is further pleased to O.A.D. that Complnt. has a good and valid lien on said property for money so advanced by him, therefore, and that he has a right to subject said property to sale for the satisfaction of

Pg. 178 the money so pd. by him for same and it further appearing that the Defdts. are indebted to Complnt. the sum of $40,000.00 diminished by a credit of $1,000.00 for property use by Complnt. leaving $39,000.00 and Int. thereon to date making altogether $44,070.00 which sum the Ct. is pleased to O.A.D. that Complnt. recover from Defdts. and being opinion of Ct. that Complnt. has equitable lien on said Montvale Property and said personal property. It appearing an attachment has also been levied on same Ct. pleased to O.& D. that unless Defdt. pay said sum of money into C&M within 2 mos. w/costs, C&M to advertise time and place of sale in BROWNLOW'S *Knoxville Whig & Rebel Ventillator* a newspaper published in Knoxville, Tennessee and also in five public places in Blount County one which shall be at Montvale Springs - sale to highest bidder in 6 mos., credit taking from purchaser, bond and approved security for purchase money, and retaining a lien on the Real Estate and on Spec. application of Complnt. said sale will be made on Credit, and in bar of rt. of Redemption of the Defdt. and all other persons, their Agent, or Creditors. C&M to rep't. next term Ct.

JAMES KEY Vs: BARTON L. WARREN. Complnt. brings into Ct. $535.00 of so-called Confederate States Treasury Notes which are deposited with C&M under a rule of this Ct. in this cause to avoid the determination of said cause.

Pg. 179 JAMES THOMPSON, Admr. of JAMES PORTER, Dec'd. Vs: ANDREW PORTER. Defdt. is in Ct. by the attachment of his property and by publication regularly made according to Law, for more that 4 weeks before this Ct. and it is O. that Jdgmt. Pro Confesso be taken agnst. Defdt. for want of an Ans. and the cause be set down ex parte.

JOSEPH S. ABBOTT & EDWARD A. ABBOTT Vs: HENRY SISLER & JULIUS C. FAGG. Jdgmt. Pro Confesso heretofore taken but now entered. Publication has been made for 4 weeks before Ct. in BROWNLOW'S *Knoxville Whig & Rebel Ventillator* and it appearing that Défdts. are nonresidents of the State. It appears Defdts. are indebted to Complnt. by acceptance dated Dec. 24, 1860, due 8 mos. after date and payable w/exchange in New York the sum of $315.19 Int. on which amts. to $70.87 making in all sum of $386.06 with $3.86 exchange or a total of $389.92

Pg. 180 which sum the Ct. is pleased to O.& D. Defdts. pay the Complnts. and also costs of cause. It appearing the Sheriff has levied an attachment on certain real estate of Defdt. FAGG. The Ct. pleased to O.& D. that C&M advertise for 4 weeks in BROWNLOW'S *Knoxville Whig & Rebel Ventillator* in 5 public places in Blount County and shall expose said lands so attached to public sale at C.H. door to highest bidder and sell same taking bond from purchaser w/his approved Security and retaining a lien on said lands. On Spec. application of Complnt. said sale will be made on 6 mos. credit and in bar of rt. of Redemption on part of Defdt. or any of his Creditors. Defdt. allowed 2 mos. time in which to pay said sum into C&M before said sale. Funds pd. in to be held for future order by this Ct. and all other creditors who have liens on the propty. attached will be allowed to come in and set up their liens.

JOHN C. CHILDS, JAMES HENRY et al. Vs: SAMUEL PRIDE, A. J. ISH, WILLIAM HENDERSON AND TILLINGHAST Vs: HENRY HEIRS. On May 24, 1865, Complnt. by Sol. L. C. COOK moved the Ct. for Jdgmt. agnst. Defdt. A. ISH and WILLIAM HENDERSON for sum $14,029.80 being Principal and Int. of 3 notes executed by A. ISH, who is not proceeded agnst. in this motion. Notes were dated Sept. 25, 1860 and due Sept. 25, 1861, Sept. 25, 1862 and Sept. 25, 1863 and all bearing Int. from date.

Pg. 181 They were executed in consideration of real estate in the pleadings sold by Complnts. CHILDS and HENRY as Spec. Commrs. in this cause and also for resale of said lands on acc't. of nonpayment of purchase money and for a D. charging said obligations and purchases w/any deficiency which may arise in a resale of said land. Chancellor being of opinion from proceedings and proof that Complnts. CHILDS and HENRY, under an O.& D. of this Ct. Aug. term 1860, were appt'd. Spec. Commrs. to sell lands in pleadings described to wit: Tract of land known as the JOHN HENRY farm lying in 14th Civil District adjoining lands of JOHN HEADRICK, SAMUEL HENRY and O. on E. side of Little River. Land sold to A. J. ISH and WILLIAM HENDERSON, Defdts. became purchasers at prices shown. Notes unpaid and said Commrs. still have lien. Therefore D. by Chancellor, Complnts. CHILD and HENRY, as Spec. Commrs., recover from A. J. ISH and WILLIAM HENDERSON, Principal sum of $10,070.00

Pg. 182 w/$3,005.00 together w/$3,559.80 making the sum of $14,029.80 w/costs of this motion and further D. by Chancellor unless said money pd. into office of C&M in 60 days w/costs, C&M to advertise in BROWNLOW'S *Knoxville Whig & Rebel Ventillator* and at 5 public places in Blount County one being at most public place where land lies in Civil District and sell to highest bidder on 6, 12, and 18 mos., taking bond from purchaser w/approved Security and drawing Int. from date and retaining a lien to secure payment of purchase money. On Spec. application of Complnts. said land to be sold and a credit and in bar of Redemption on part of A. J. ISH and WILLIAM HENDERSON, or their creditors. Funds derived from sale first applied to payment costs of this cause and second, toward satisfaction of the D. rendered and remainder subject to order of this Ct. If said lands fail to bring amt. of coin of Plff.'s debt, Int. and costs then execution may issue agnst. A. J. ISH and WILLIAM HENDERSON for the residue.

Pg. 183 ELIZABETH M. WALLACE b/n/f GRANVILLE H. REEDER Vs: SAMUEL WALLACE & CHARLES C. NEWMAN & WIFE. Motion made by CHARLES C. NEWMAN first day this Term to dissolve injunction in this cause being argued by Council and considered by Ct. it is O.A.D. that said Injunction be dissolved as to permit Respdt. to prosecute their suit at-law to jdgmt.

JAMES THOMPSON, Admr. of JAMES PORTER, Dec'd. Vs: WILLIAM & J. M. KIDD. C&M to inquire and rep't. next term Ct. on amt. due on the foot of land in pleadings.

ELIZABETH WRIGHT b/n/f Petition for divorce Vs: SAMUEL WRIGHT. Cause abandoned by Complnt. and her Sol. O. to be stricken from docket and Defdt. go hence and recover of Complnt. and her Security all costs and that Complnt. have jdgmt. agnst. husband, the Respdt. for same.

MCBATH & LOVE Vs: JAMES HENRY. O. by Ct. Complnt. take steps in cause on or before next term Ct. or cause will be dismissed at their cost.

Pg. 184 JOHN C. CHILDS & JAMES HENRY, Commrs. Vs: A. & A. J. ISH & WILLIAM HENDERSON. There are sufficient

reasons appearing to Ct. from affidavit of Complnt.'s Sol. Leave granted them to file amended bill. Complnts., by their Sol., dismiss their bill as to A. ISH - the question of costs reserved.
Thurs. A.M. May 25, 1865. Ct. met pursuant to adjournment. Present and Presiding D. C. TREWHITT, Chancellor.

JAMES HENRY Vs: SAMUEL GHORMLY & O. Death of Respdt. SAMUEL GHORMLY suggested and proven in open Ct.

Pg. 185 JOSEPH S. KING Vs: STERLING LANIER, SIDNEY C. LANIER, WILLIAM B. LANIER & ABRAHAM P. WALT. Supplmental Decree. It being suggested that the propty. mentioned in Decree rendered has been in possession of Complnt. since date purchased and the Ct. being of opinion Complnt. should acc't. for reasonable value of rents and profits of property Ct. pleased to O.& D. C&M hear proof and rep't. next term Ct. reasonable value of rents and profits since date of purchase, also amt. taxes pd. thereon by Complnt. for which said property is liable and reasonable value of keeping up repairs. C&M rep't. next term on which side the balance stands, but before taking acc't. he will first give notice by advertisement in some newspaper time of taking the acc't.

CHAMBERLAIN, MILER & CO. Vs: JAMES A. MCKAMY & O. SAMUEL PRIDE, who has appt'd. Recv'r. by a D. rendered Nov. Term 1860 being Dec'd. pleased to O. WILLIAM C. PICKENS, C&M, to proceed as Recv'r. and perform duties formerly assigned to SAMUEL PRIDE, Dec'd.

Pg. 186 Mon. Dec. 25, 1865. Be it remembered that at C.H., Town of Maryville, Blount County, 4th Mon. of Dec. 1865, Present and presiding Hon. SAMUEL R. RODGERS, Chancellor, holding Ct. for 8th Chancery District, State of Tennessee, for County of Blount, pursuant of Acts of Assembly of State of Tennessee, passed at Nashville June 2, 1865, and Ct. being opened in due form of law the following proceedings were had of record, viz:

C. GILLESPIE & W. A. WALKER, Admr. SAMUEL MCKAMY, Dec'd. Vs: MARTHA MCKAMY & O. ALEXAN-

DER KENNEDY, one of Respts. has 2 mos. to make Ans. JAMES M. SHARP Vs: W. A. WALKER, Assignee & C. W. A. WALKER has 3 mos. to Ans.

A H. RUSSELL Vs: H. T. COX. Complnt. has leave to give other Security in room and instead of TILLERY, one of present Sureties and TILLERY thus released of liability.

H. T. COX Vs: WILLIAM MCTEER et al. Cont'd. by consent of parties.

Pg. 187 ROBERT L. WEAR Vs: J. D. WEAR et als. Unless steps taken to prosecute this suit by next term Ct. it will be dismissed at Plff.'s cost.

D. & C. CUNNINGHAM Vs: A. CUNNINGHAM. Death of C. CUNNINGHAM suggested. Cause cont'd.

JAMES TAYLOR et als. Vs: JAMES WALKER et als. AND MOSE GAMBLE Vs: JAMES TAYLOR et als. Both causes cont'd. next term Ct.

GREEN FARMER et al. Vs: JAMES WATERS et al. Unless steps taken agnst. next term Ct. cause will be dismissed at Complt.'s cost.

R. M. SAFFELL Vs: J. C. M. BOGLE et al. Unless steps taken agns't. next term Ct. this cause will be dismissed at Complnt.'s cost.

J. C. M. BOGLE, Gdn. & C. Vs: L. S. YEAROUT et al. The papers having been lost, O. that unless papers in this cause supplied agnst. next term Ct. cause be dismissed at Complnt.'s cost.

SAMUEL GHORMLY Vs: H. & H. S. STEPHENS. Unless steps taken in this cause agnst. next term Ct. will be dismissed at Complnt.'s cost.

Pg. 188 ELIZABETH M. WALLACE Vs: SAMUEL WALLACE, CHARLES C. NEWMAN & WIFE, MARTHA E. NEWMAN. Decree: Death of SAMUEL WALLACE, one of Defdts. admitted to be true and agreed upon by their Sols. - cause shall stand revived agnst. CHARLES C. NEWMAN and wife, MARTHA E. NEWMAN, and proceeded with at present term, and may hereafter be revived by either party, agnst. personal Rep. of SAMUEL WALLACE, if deemed necessary. On Complnt.'s bill an agreement in writing between the parties bearing date of Nov. 3, 1865, as follows: "Whereas on information heretofore filed in District Ct. of U. S. for Eastern Div. of Tennessee at Knoxville agnst. certain lands in Blount County which was sought to confiscate as the property of SAMUEL WALLACE, which suit is still pending and undetermined in said Ct. and whereas 2 claims and Ans. were filed in said Ct. to prevent the confiscation of said property, the one by ELIZABETH M. WALLACE, wife of said SAMUEL in which she set up an equitable claim to said lands and

Pg. 189 other by CHARLES C. NEWMAN and wife, MARTHA NEWMAN, in which they set up a claim to a debt due the said MARTHA E. from the said SAMUEL and certain proceedings by Attachment before a J.P. in Blount County which were returned to the Circuit Ct. and which had been levied upon said lands and ELIZABETH M. WALLACE, in order to enforce her claim b/n/f GRANVILLE REEDER, filed her bill in Chancery Ct. agnst. said SAMUEL WALLACE and CHARLES C. NEWMAN and wife, MARTHA E. NEWMAN, which is still pending and whereas SAMUEL WALLACE departed this life on, or about, Aug. 12, 1865, leaving said ELIZABETH as his widow and MARTHA E. NEWMAN as his sole heir-at-law and whereas as widow and heir being anxious to compromise the suits and settle all matters relative to said Est. did on Sept. 29, 1865, enter into a Bond in which they agreed to select JOHN F. HENRY and EDWARD GEORGE as Commrs. to divide the lands between them and on Oct. 10, 1865, made partition thereof and assigned ELIZABETH M. WALLACE Lot #1 containing 102 A., 3 Roods and 15 Poles and Lot #3 containing 180 A., 2 Roods and 16 Poles and assigned to C. C. NEWMAN and MARTHA E. NEWMAN Lot #2 by Est. 216 A. and 16 Poles and Lot #4 containing Est. 72 A. and on Oct. 25th, 1865, MARTHA and C. C. NEWMAN executed a Deed to ELIZABETH M. WALLACE to join them in a Deed to said WALKER, which she did. MARTHA E. NEWMAN was not privately examined -

Pg. 190 touching her free and voluntary execution of said Bond of Sept. 29, 1865, or Deed of Oct. 25, 1865 and whereas she gave no written assent award or Rep't. of Oct. 10, 1865, made by JOHN F. HENRY and EDWARD GEORGE the attempted arbitration was informal and defective.

It is hereby agreed that the several instruments of Sept. 29th, Oct 10th and Oct. 25th, 1865 are Valid and Effective - same as if prescribed by law.

Pg. 191 CHARLES C. NEWMAN and MARTHA E. NEWMAN executed a receipt to Estate of SAMUEL W. WALLACE for the amt. of note sued on in their Attachment suit bearing date of 26th Sept. 1846 executed by SAMUEL WALLACE, C. WALLACE, THOMAS C. LYON, E. ALEXANDER and ANDREW MCCLAIN which receipt bears date of Oct. 25, 1865 and executed for benefit of ELIZABETH M. WALLACE. MRS. NEWMAN voluntarily and without any coercion or restraint on part of her said husband in carrying out this compromise. Signed: MARTHA E. NEWMAN (Seal), CHARLES C. NEWMAN (Seal), ELIZABETH M. WALLACE (Seal) Witness: DUNLAP SCOTT, ALEXANDER GARDINER, JOHN F. HENRY. State of Georgia, Floyd County.
Floyd Ct. of Ordinary, Nov. term 1865 personally appeared before me, JESSE LAMBUTH, Ordinary of said County, CHARLES C. NEWMAN the within named bargainer w/whom I am personally acquainted and that he acknowledged he executed the within instrument for purposes therein contained and MARTHA E. NEWMAN, wife of said CHARLES having appeared before me privately and apart from her husband's execution of said deed have been done freely. I hereto set my hand and seal this 7th day of Nov. 1865. JESSE LAMBUTH, Ordinary.

Pg. 192 Know all men that ELIZABETH M. WALLACE on one part and CHARLES C. and MARTHA E. NEWMAN on the other part are bound to each other for sum of $6,000.00, Sept. 29, 1865. Above heirs-at-law of SAMUEL WALLACE, Dec'd. and agreed to adjust the Estate as follows:
1) Each party withdraw their suits and each pay own lawyers and costs.
2) The land to be equally divided - according to evaluation and so to give each their respective dwelling houses.
3) Mrs. WALLACE to assume and pay $800.00 of outside indebtedness of Est. and all other indebtedness of the Est. exempting MARTHA's claim and each pay their respective parts.
4) Mrs. WALLACE to have household and kitchen furniture - All other personal property to be equally divided - in

the farm proceeds to be so divided also.
5) Both parties equally held and bound for the KEITH claim.
6) Both parties pay equally charges for dividing land.
7) A bond of $6,000.00 be given by both parties to abide by terms agreed on.
(Signed) ELIZABETH M. WALLACE, CHARLES C. NEWMAN, M. E. NEWMAN Test: ED. GEORGE, JOHN F. HENRY.

Pg. 193 Rep't. of Commrs. Premises divided as follows: Appropriated to ELIZABETH M. WALLACE for her use and benefit 1/2 certain tract of land, 11th Civil District of Blount County adjoining lands of WILLIAM STEPHENS, ROCKFORD MFG. CO., M. E. NEWMAN, HARDIN and O. containing 102 A., 3 Roods, 15 Poles; also Lot #3 adjoining HITCH, HARDIN and E. GEORGE, M. E. NEWMAN and O. containing 180 A., 16 Poles. To CHARLES C. NEWMAN and wife, M. E. NEWMAN, Lot #2 from mouth of Pistol Creek thence up same to E. M. WALLACE line, HARDIN, ROCKFORD MFG. CO. 216 A., 16 Poles.

Pg. 194 Also Lot #4 joining JAMES and ARCHY HITCH, E. M. WALLACE, Est. 72 A. having made partition by survey and satisfaction of parties involved. JOHN F. HENRY (Seal) ED. GEORGE (Seal).

Pg. 195 (Actual description of plots given in each statement above.)
Surveyor of Blount County, H. H. STEPHENS states Ct. description of his survey is correct. Signed: H. H. STEPHENS. (Transfer of said lands then follows.)

Pg. 196 The above described tracts and portions of land we transfer and convey to ELIZABETH M. WALLACE for the consideration of $800.00 applied to the payment of debts of SAMUEL WALLACE, Dec'd. also in discharge of $3,500.00 pending in Suit in Chancery Ct. as "ELIZABETH M. WALLACE Vs: SAMUEL WALLACE." And said CHARLES C. NEWMAN and M. E. NEWMAN by this indenture for themselves and their heirs, Extrs. and Admrs., do warrant and defend the tracts of land into the said ELIZABETH M. WALLACE, her Heirs and Admrs. Signed: MARTHA E. NEWMAN (Seal) CHARLES C. NEWMAN (Seal) Attest: H. H. STEPHENS, JOHN F. HENRY

Pg. 197 State of Georgia, Floyd County, Floyd Ct. of Ordinary, Nov. Term 1865: Personally appeared before me, JESSE LAMBUTH, Ordinary of said County, CHARLES C. NEWMAN and MARTHA E. NEWMAN, wife of said CHARLES and acknowledged the execution of said deed to have been done by her freely and voluntarily. Whereto I have set my hand this 7th day of Nov. 1865. JESSE LAMBUTH, Ordinary.

Rec'd. of the Est. of SAMUEL W. WALLACE the amt. of a note given by the said SAMUEL W. WALLACE to THOMAS WALLACE for the use and benefit of MARTHA ELIZABETH WALLACE bearing date of Sept. 26th, 1846, and signed SAMUEL WALLACE, THOMAS C. LYON, E. ALEXANDER, and ANDREW MCCLAIN this Oct. 25, 1865. Signed: CHARLES C. NEWMAN   MARTHA E NEWMAN.
Chancellor being satisfied compromise is equitable he O.A.D. that it shall in all aspects stand as the jdgmt. and D. of this Ct. and titles shall flow to each other as decreed.

Pg. 198 M. WALLACE entitled to 1/2 of residue of personal estate and MARTHA E. NEWMAN other 1/2. Debts to be equally pd. by parties or acc'td. for under their distributive shares. Amt. of liabilities and distributive shares cannot be ascertained until after the expiration of 2 yrs. from the grant of Admn. and final settlement contemplated by the parties concerned. It is O. that Admr. of SAMUEL WALLACE, Dec'd., shall be made a party Defdt. to this suit and cause be retained on docket until final settlement of personal Est. to be made by Admr. ELIZABETH M. WALLACE has rt. to withdraw deed to her from NEWMAN and wife to the end that same may be registered in the Registrar's Office of Blount County.

ROCKFORD MFG. CO. Vs: DAVID CALDWELL. Upon motion of Complnt.'s Sol. to confirm rep't. of C&M to present Term Ct. D. to sell land on attachment: Chancery Ct. Clerk's Office, Dec. 8, 1865.

C&M rep'ts. 60 days elapsed from rendering D. Respdt.
Pg. 199 CALDWELL failed to pay or satisfy said D. I advertised land levied by attachment and specifically pointed out in D. and after having given legal notice of time, place of sale I did, on Sept. 4, 1865, at C.H. door sell at public outcry to highest bidder in bar of equity of redemption and on 6

mos. credits and at 3rd call, after giving legal time, I struck off the land to ELIAS GODDARD for $1,000.00 for which he executed his note w/WILLIAM GODDARD as Security. I therefore recommend a confirmation of sale. W. C. PICKENS, C&M, by L. WEAR, Dpty. C&M. His Honor O.A.D. that the above be confirmed in all things. Rts. title and interest of DAVID CALDWELL be divested out of premises and into ELIAS GODDARD upon payment of purchase money.

ROCKFORD MFG. CO. Vs: F. M. LASITER. Complnt.'s Sol. asks confirmation of rep't. of C&M in following words. To wit: Decree to sell land on Attachment. Chancery Ct. Clerk's Office, Dec. 8, 1865. C&M begs leave to rep't. that 60 days having fully elapsed from rendition of D. F. M. LASITER having failed to pay and satisfy said D. I advertised land, gave legal notice of time, place of sale and on Sept. 4, 1865 at C.H. door sold at public outcry to highest bidder the said land as directed in D. At 3rd call after legal time, I struck the land off to DAVID GODDARD for $1,000.00 for which he executed his note w/WILLIAM GODDARD as his Security. I therefore recommend confirmation of this sale. W. C. PICKENS, C&M, by L. WEAR, Dpty. C&M.

Pg. 200 There being no exception to rep't. to his Hon. O.A.D. that rep't. in all things confirmed. All rt. title and interest which Respdt. F. M. LASITER had in and to the premises sold is divested from him and into DAVID GODDARD, purchaser. A lien is reserved to secure payment of purchase money and C&M on being furnished w/description of said lands will execute a deed to purchaser upon his payment of expenses.

Pgs. 201 and 202 torn from book. (Rough edge of torn page evident.)

Pg. 203 A. T. BRUCE & CO. Vs: H. T. COX & BRO. For satisfactory reasons appearing to Ct. it is O.A.D. that the rep't. of C&M made to present Term of Ct. showing sale of lands attached in this case to HORACE FOSTER and same is set aside and for nothing held. His Hon. further pleased to O.A.D. that C&M proceed to readvertise and sell same in pursuance of the D. rendered at last Term Ct. Further O. that notes executed by purchaser for purchase money be cancelled and returned to purchaser.

JOSEPH L. KING Vs: STERLING LANIER, SIDNEY A. LANIER, WILLIAM B. LANIER, ABRAHAM P. WATT, W. G. BROWNLOW & JOHN R. HENRY. Be it remembered that on Dec 25, 1865, cause came to be heard and determined before Hon. SAMUEL R. RODGERS, Chancellor, upon bill of jdgmt. Pro Confesso, publication and all other proceedings heretofore had in this case and more particularly upon the rep't. of C&M which is unexcepted to and in all things confirmed. It appears to Ct. since last term in pursuance of a D. rendered at May Spec. Term viz: On the 4th day of Sept. 1865, sold to highest bidder the lands described in the pleadings of C&M the said several tracts of land altogether in a body and without any survey and that Complnt. who bid by his Agent, I. GRAY SMITH, gave

Pg. 204 $40,000.00, therefore considered by Ct. that Complnt. take the said lands by him so bid off, in satisfaction thus far of his D. entered agnst. STERLING LANIER and O. It further appearing from said rep't. that C&M had sold personal property mentioned and described for $2,000.00 also taken by Complnt. in satisfaction of said D., as far as it goes. These lands were regularly attached together w/personal property on Nov. 4, 1864, by the Sheriff of Blount County. C&M was O. to take and state an acc't. in this case as to rents and profits since Complnts. have been in possession of the land and Montvale Springs property described in pleadings. C&M stated the acc't. thus ordered and here rep'td. his proceedings to this term Ct. and it is confirmed. Nothing has been realized from the property since in possession of Complnt. His proof in this case - because of the War going on in the country and the situation of the property as to the North Carolina Raiders - and Complnt. claiming nothing for his expense and trouble in keeping up the property. Therefore considered by Ct. that rep't. in all things confirmed and that expense in keeping up property be taken the one equal to the other. Due in unpaid taxes the sum of $130.00. Ct.

Pg. 205 therefore D. that title which the said STERLING LANIER, SIDNEY A. LANIER and ABRAHAM P. WATT had to said lands described in pleadings be divested out of them and vested in JOSEPH S. KING and his heirs forever. The lands so sold and the title to which is hereby vested and divested situated in Blount County, 8th Civil District and known as Montvale Springs consisting of 11 tracts all joining each other as described in Exhibit A. and registered in Second A (AA) Pgs. 505-508 conveyed heretofore by DANIEL D. FOUTE to ASA WATSON and from ASA WATSON to Respdt. All said property and its erections and appurtenances thereto vested in JOSEPH S. KING and his heirs forever. Complnt. KING pay costs for which execution is awarded.

C. GILLESPY, Admr. Vs: W. C. GILLESPY'S HEIRS. (No writing entered.)

LINDSEY VINEYARD Vs: ROCKFORD MFG. CO. Cause having been settled between parties and costs pd. O. by Ct. cause stricken from docket and cause dismissed.

Pg. 206 J. A. HOUSTON, Admr. et. al. Vs: J. & W. YEAROUT. O. by Ct. cause dismissed. Complnt. failed to appear and prosecute his Suit. Respdt. recover of said J. A. HOUSTON and Securities all costs for which execution is awarded.

SAMUEL PRIDE Vs: JANE PORTER. Death of SAMUEL PRIDE suggested and proven in Open Ct.

JOSIAS GAMBLE Vs: SAMUEL HENRY & O. O. by Ct. that compromise in this cause be brought in next term Ct. cause to be dismissed at Complnt.'s cost.

M. D. BEARDEN et al. Vs: GREENFIELD TAYLOR. D. in this Ct. dismissing Complnt.'s bill. Appealed to Tennessee Supreme Ct. in Knoxville. Has been confirmed by Supreme Ct. O.A.D. Complnt. pay costs of cause.

CHARLES LONAS Vs: W. M. ROREX. Cause cont'd. next term Ct. (This information deleted on page.)

JOHN & ELIZABETH LEVENTORE (?) Vs: ADAM F. WATERS et als. Cause cont'd.

Pg. 207 BAKER & CASWELL Vs: J. A. MCLIN & W. O. MCLIN. O. that unless steps taken to bring cause to hearing in next term Ct. Cause will be dismissed at Complnt.'s expense.

L. B. HENDERSON et al. Vs: HENDERSON RUSSELL et al. By consent by parties this cause cont'd. to next term Ct.

R. S. MCNUTT & CO. Vs: J. A. HOUSTON, TRUSTEE & C. Unless steps taken to bring cause to hearing next term Ct. cause will be dismissed at Complnt.'s cost.

JAMES HENRY Vs: SAMUEL GHORMLY et al. Cause cont'd. next term Ct.

B. F. WALKER & WIFE Vs: A. J. ISH et als. Cont'd. next term Ct.

JAMES HENRY Vs: SAMUEL K. FINLY. By consent, cause cont'd. next term Ct.

JOHN B. COX Vs: HENRY T. COX. Death of JOHN B. COX suggested and proven in open Ct. Suit revived in name of SAMUEL T. COX and A. MATLOCK, Admr. of JOHN B. COX.

JAMES THOMPSON, Admr. JAMES PORTER, Dec'd. Vs: ANDREW PORTER. Cause cont'd. next term Ct.

Pg. 208 CHARLES T. SAFFELL Vs: ISAAC W. COCHRAN. Cont'd. until next term Ct.

JAMES HENRY Vs: HENRY T. COX. Cont'd. at the Rules.

W. A. WALKER, Admr. w/will annexed of SAMUEL PRIDE, Dec'd. Vs: JULIOUS C. FAGG. By consent of Complnt., O. Respdt. J. C. FAGG has 3 mos. plead Ans. or demur.

TRUSTEES of MARYVILLE COLLEGE & W. A. WALKER, Extr. of WILLIAM WALLACE, Dec'd. By Consent of Complnt., Respdt. J. C. FAGG has 3 mos. plead Ans. or demur.

JAMES KEY Vs: B. S. WARREN. On motion of Respdts. Sol. ordered cause cont'd. next term. Leave granted Respdt. A. R. JAMES whose disposition is in file.

JESSE KERR, SR. Vs: W. M. COX et al. Death of W. M. COX suggested and proven open Ct. JAMES HENRY, Admr. Est. of W. M. COX, Dec'd. being present in Ct. - agreed cause be forwarded to next term Ct.

ELIJAH NELSON Vs: JAMES M. TOOLE. O. by Ct. this

cause stricken from docket.

Pg. 209 A. H. KEITH Vs: W. C. WALLACE, W. A. WALKER, Extr. of SAMUEL WALLACE & JAMES M. TOOLE. Death of SAMUEL WALLACE suggested and proven in open Ct. Plff. have leave to file supplimental bill so as to bring new parties before the Ct.

A. R. MCBATH Vs: J. C. FAGG. With Complnt.'s consent, O. that J. C. FAGG have 3 mos. plead Ans. or demur.

ELIZABETH L.(S?) ISH Vs: BENJAMIN A. ISH. Cause cont'd. next term Ct.

WILLIAM BRICKELL Vs: H. T. COX, JAMES BONHAM & O. Respdts. have 3 mos. Ans. and not delay Ct.

ALEXANDER KENNEDY Vs: W. T. DOWELL. By consent parties, cont'd. next term.

SAMUEL TULLOCH, Admr. of ALEXANDER COOK, Dec'd. Vs: JAMES COOK et al. On motion of Respdt. Sol. 2 mos. time allowed Respdts. to Ans.

JOHN STONE & WIFE, ISABELLA E. STONE & BENJAMINE BRIGHT Vs: HEIRS of JOHN P. BONHAM & O. On motion Respdt.'s Sol., M. COX, and GOURLY'S heirs have 3 mos. Ans.

Pg. 210 Monday, Dec. 25th, 1865.
JAMES HENRY, Admr. debonis non of JOHN HENRY, Dec'd. Vs: W. A. WALKER, Admr. SAMUEL PRIDE, Dec'd. et al. Respts. have 2 mos. to Ans.

NICHOLAS BREWER, Gdn. of JOHN CHAMBERS, Lunatic Vs: RHODA CHAMBERS et al. O. by Ct. cause be reinstated on the docket.

ISABELLA S. HENRY & HUSBAND, GEORGE W. HENRY Vs: HEIRS-AT-LAW & WIDOW of JOHN MARTIN, SR., Dec'd. Widow, SARAH K. MARTIN; Heirs: W. B. MARTIN, ELIZABETH J. MARTIN, MARTHA D. MCKAMY, BENJAMIN F. MARTIN, LEONARD MARTIN, GEORGE W. MARTIN, FRANCIS M. MARTIN, ARTHUR A. KENNEDY, SARAH C. KENNEDY, J. C. M. BOGLE, Gdn. for Heirs of JOHN C.

MARTIN, Dec'd. and SAMUEL MCKAMY, Dec'd. viz: ELIZABETH J. MARTIN, JAMES L. and SARAH E. MCKAMY, and GEORGE W. ADNEY, Assignee of LEONARD H. MARTIN, Dec'd. Be it remembered that this 25th of Dec. 1865, cause came to be heard and determined before Hon. SAMUEL R. RODGERS, Chancellor, upon several Ans. of SAMUEL D. and MARTHA B. MCKAMY, SARAH K. MARTIN and of ELIZABETH J. MARTIN and upon Ans. of Gdn. for JAMES L. and SARAH E. MCKAMY and ELIZABETH F. MARTIN the minors names in this

Pg. 211 case, upon notice duly served and upon jdgmt. Pro Confesso, which has been taken agnst. all the parties who have failed to Ans. and upon deposition of WILLIAM B. MARTIN, who had assigned his interest to SARAH K. MARTIN before the same was taken - which deposition was duly taken by and on behalf of the Respdts. and upon all other proceedings heretofore had. It appears further to Ct. that since filing of original Bill Complnt. ISABELLA S. MARTIN has intermarried with the present Complnt., her husband, GEORGE W. HENRY, therefore this suit is revived in his name, the said HENRY and his wife, ISBELLA S. HENRY. Original Bill in this cause has been lost but it appears from Ans. sworn to SARAH K. MARTIN, ELIZABETH J. MARTIN, SAMUEL D. MCKAMY and MARTHA B. MCKAMY that the purpose for which this suit was brought was the confirmation of an instrument of writing which is lost and which was heretofore entered into by the heirs of JOHN MARTIN, SR., Dec'd. and otherwise settling the rights of the parties in interest on the real estate of JOHN MARTIN, SR., Dec'd. and LUCEAN M. MARTIN, Dec'd. one of the distributees of JOHN MARTIN SR., Dec'd. and the Ct. of opinion that the parties are entitled to relief sought - the same is therefore granted and a portion is hereafter directed of the land described in pleadings. The Ans. above-stated being treated as if a X Bill had been filed. It appears JOHN MARTIN, SR., Dec'd. in the fall of 1843 having first published his last Will & Testament which is of record in Blount County. He bequeathed his real estate of near 1400 A. in the 12th District of Blount County and on Nail's Creek adjoining lands of JACOB DOOPS and O., to his 10 sons and daughters share and share alike. But by provisions of

Pg. 212 Will, he did not make adequate, satisfactory, or sufficient provisions for his widow, SARAH K. MARTIN. Soon after, after the Will was proven and within the time she had it in her power to dissent from said Will, the Heirs and her, SARAH K. MARTIN, entered into an agreement by which they agreed to convey to her an undivided share or 1/11th part of the Real and Personal Estate of JOHN MARTIN, Dec'd. to include his Mansion house, Mill and Barn but this agreement was not reduced to writing until afterwards in Nov. 1852. They, the said family, had a meeting at old homestead after LUCEAN M., the youngest son and heir, had arrived at the age of 21 yrs. and they all then able to contract in person - in pursuance of said verbal agreement and agreed in writing that SARAH K. did not dissent from her husband's will - that therefore she should take and receive an equal part including the Mansion house as aforesaid. - share and share alike w/heirs in value of real estate. It was signed and became a binding legal contract and that it is lost. It is hereby D. that SARAH K. have set off for her 1/11th part of said real estate and each one his 1/11th part. It appearing that WILLIAM B. MARTIN had heretofore assigned to his mother his 1/11th part, SARAH by Ct. O. to have this other 1/11th part and the two lots to adjoin each other. SARAH K. is owner in her own right of share of BENJAMIN F. MARTIN. In estate of LUCEAN M. MARTIN, Dec'd. being 1/9th of 1/11th of the entire estate, this fractional share to adjoin lands of SARAH K. It further appearing that ELIZABETH J. has not assigned her share 1/11th part, nor her share as an heir of LUCEAN M. MARTIN, Dec'd. (He having died without issue.) Ct. therefore A.& D. that she shall have alloted to her - her 1/11th part as heir of her father and her share of LUCEAN MARTIN, Dec'd. being 1/9th. MARTHA D. MCKAMY entitled to 1/11th part, her share of lands of JOHN MARTIN, Dec'd. and 1/9th part of Est. of LUCEAN M. MARTIN, Dec'd. SAMUEL D. MCKAMY, in his lifetime purchased at Executor's Sale the share of HENRY L. MARTIN in his father's estate being 1/11th of all lands of JOHN MARTIN, Dec'd. and also the share of him, the said HENRY L. MARTIN in the Est. of land of LUCEAN MARTIN, Dec'd. and that all parties interest had by deed of partition set off by metes and bounds to the said SAMUEL D. MCKAMY and MARTHA B. MCKAMY their shares in the home tract, but they, and each of them are not by said deed precluded from having set off their share of the tract of land in the Tar Kiln Valley known as the Summers Tract. And it appearing that JOHN C. MARTIN in his lifetime had pur-

Pg. 214 chased and was owner of his own share or 1/11th part of the lands of JOHN MARTIN, Dec'd. also his share of 1/9th part of LUCEAN MARTIN, Dec'd. part, also the share of A. A. KENNEDY and SARAH C. KENNEDY, his wife, in the 2 estates of JOHN and LUCEAN MARTIN, Dec'd., also 1/11th part share of L. A. MARTIN, in the estate of JOHN MARTIN, SR., Dec'd., also the shares of GEORGE W. and FRANCIS M. MARTIN in the Ests. of JOHN and LUCEAN MARTIN, Dec'd. He was also owner of share of BENJAMIN F. MARTIN (1/11th and 1/9th) thus making him owner of 5/11ths or 5 of the original 11 shares and 4/9ths or 4 shares in Est. of LUCEAN MARTIN, Dec'd. and upon death of JOHN C. MARTIN these undivided descended to his heirs-at-law. ELIZABETH F. MARTIN and ISABELLA, his widow, now HENRY. The Complnt. in this case has the right of Dower in his lands. Therefore D. by Ct. that his widow and heir-at-law have alloted to them, their shares to include his dwelling house and then part of the old home tract. Shall be alloted all adjoining each other but the land in the Tar Kiln Valley may be

Pg. 215 allotted to the best advantage as the Commrs. may choose. Set off her Dower according to Law - out of the lands so set off. It appearing to Ct. that G. W. ADNEY, who is a Respdt. has purchased at Sheriffs' sale and has deed therefore the undivided share as 1/9th part which descended on part of LUCEAN N. MARTIN, Dec'd. to LEONARD H. MARTIN in the lands of LUCEAN N. MARTIN, Dec'd. Since ADNEY has never had his share set aside, Ct. O. the 1/9th of 1/11th of JOHN MARTIN, SR., of the whole Est. be set aside for ADNEY.
County Surveyor H. H. STEPHENS to set apart the various tracts and shall take w/him THOMAS PICKENS, JACOB DOOPS, WILLIAM GODDARD and ROBERT PICKENS to make partition. They to make rep't. next term Ct. Ct. adjourned until tomorrow A.M. 10 O'Clock.

Pg. 216 Dec. 26th, 1865.
ROCKFORD MFG. CO. Vs: DAVID CALDWELL. For sufficient cause shown Ct. Orders that the Decree ordered 1st day of Present term confirming Master's rep't. of sale of lands is vacated and for nothing held. The bid for the land was totally inadequate a consideration. Complnt. admitting in open Ct. price inadequate. Ct. pleased to O.& D. sale by Master set aside. Master ordered to deliver to ELIAS GODDARD, the purchaser of said sale, his note

148

executed for said land. Respdt. DAVID CALDWELL has pd. the jdgmnt. rendered agnst. him. O. that Complnt. bill be dismissed and Respdt. pay costs.

C. GILLESPIE, Admr. W. S. PORTER, Dec'd. Vs: PHOEBE G. PORTER et als. Respdt. PHOEBE G. PORTER has resigned her Gdnship. of Respdt. ROBERT, ANN H. and JANE L. PORTER and JAMES HITCH has been appt'd. Gdn. in her room and stead by the Ct. That minor Defdts. Ans. by themselves or Gdn. on or before 1st Mon. Mar.

Pg. 217 next and further O. that C&M proceed to hear proof and rep't. amt. assets ought to have gone in hands of Complnt. as Admr. of W. S. PORTER, Dec'd. and take an acc't. and show amt. of outstanding liabilities and unpaid debts agnst. Est. and disbursements made and expenses excused. Rep't. next term Ct.

JAMES MATTHEWS et al. Vs: J. A. HOUSTON & ISABELLA J. JONES, Admrs. of MILAS JONES, Dec'd. et al. AND CROP BILL of GEORGE CALDWELL et al. Vs: J. A. HOUSTON & ISABELLA J. JONES, Admrs. of MILAS JONES, Dec'd. et al. Respdts. HOUSTON and ISABELLA JONES ask for 3 mos. time to Ans. or make defense. Granted by Ct.

C. GILLESPIE, Admr. of W. C. GILLESPIE Vs: NANCY F. GILLESPIE et al. By consent of parties His Hon. O.A.D. that C&M proceed and hear proof and make rep't. showing: Amt. of assets gone into Complnt.'s hands (or should have) also amt. outstanding debts and liabilities agnst. said Est. If any remains unpaid he will furthermore collate advancements made to distributees of said intestate and make rep't. thereof to a full and final settlement and rep't. next term Ct.

Pg. 218 RUSSELL M. PASS & WIFE Vs: JAMES M. TAYLOR, DANIEL TAYLOR & H. T. COX. 3 mos. time given H. T. COX to plead Ans. or demur to Complnts.' bill.

CHARLES LONAS Vs: WILLIAM M. ROREX et al. All Respdts. named in Complnt's. bill served w/Process in Apr. 1861. They have failed to plead Ans. or demur. O.A.D. by Ct. bill be taken as confessed and set for hearing ex parte. C&M to inquire and rep't. amt. due on the several debts secured by deed in trust. Authorized to examine anyone or all parties in interest and rep't. results next term Ct.

JOHN B. COX Vs: HENRY T. COX. Death of Complnt. JOHN B. COX suggested and proven in O. Ct. SAMUEL COX and A. MATLOCK appt'd. Extrs. of JOHN B. COX, Dec'd. Suit be revived in their names, which is done.

Pg. 219 This cause came for hearing and for interlocutory order upon bill and Ans. Appears to Ct. this is a fit case for an acc't. O.A.D. C&M hear proof and rep't. next term Ct. the amt. due from Defdt. H. T. COX to said Extrs. of JOHN B. COX by reason of the premises in his bill set forth. The C&M to show fully the items constituting any credits, if any, to be allowed on debt sued on.

JESSE KERR, SR. Vs: W. M. COX & H. T. COX. (No entry)

WILLIAM C. & RICHARD CRESWELL Vs: ANDREW CRESWELL. At a sale of lands mentioned and described in pleadings made by SAMUEL PRIDE, former C&M of this Ct. in pursuance of a D. rendered in the cause, ISAAC HINES became the purchaser thereof for $720.00 & gave his note w/THOMAS PICKENS, Security. One of the notes is unpaid - one reading $404.52, 12 mos. after date we, or either of us, promise to pay SAMUEL PRIDE, C&M, $404.52 for value rec'd. being part of purchase price of ANDREW CRESWELL'S land. ISAAC HINES (Seal) THOMAS PICKENS (Seal). Attest: T. A. POPE, Dpty. C&M. - and it further appearing that rep't. of sale duly

Pg. 220 made and confirmed. The principal and int. now amts. to $481.87. O.A.D. that W. C. PICKENS, present C&M, to have and recover of ISAAC HINES, Princ. and THOMAS PICKENS, Security, said sum w/Int. hereafter to accrue and costs of this D.

NICHOLAS S. PECK Vs: JAMES M. EAKIN & O. Defdt. ROBERT EAKIN is authorized to take from files the original Power of Atty. from JAMES M. EAKIN to him.

SPENCER HENRY, Extr. of Will of MOSES SCRUGGS, Dec'd. Vs: LEONIDES S. FULKERSON & O. HEIRS & DEVISEES of MOSES SCRUGGS. Ordered by Ct. J. C. M. BOGLE be appt'd. Gdn. ad litem of ANN E. and ELIZABETH E. FULKERSON, minor heirs of WILLIAM R. FULKERSON, Dec'd. 4 mos. given Respdt. FULKERSON

& CONNER and WIFE to Ans.

JOHN MCCULLY & O. Vs: WILLIAM C. CASHION. Respdt. to have been duly brought before Ct. by Attachment and Publication. They have failed to Ans. or demur. O.A.D. by Ct. that said bill shall be taken as confessed and set for hearing ex parte.

Pg. 221 JOHN H. EDMONDSON Vs: WILLIAM C. CASHION. Respdts. JOHN MCCULLY and HARVEY H. C. CARITHERS duly served w/process and that propty. of Respdt. WILLIAM C. CASHION has been attached and publication made. They haved failed to plead Ans. or demur and Ct. being about to close without holding 3 days it is O.A.D. bill shall be taken as confessed as agnst. Respdt. JOHN MCCULLY, HARVEY H. C. CARITHERS and WILLIAM C. CASHION and set for hearing ex parte.

M. E. HARTSELL Vs: JOHN E. TOOLE & O. (No entry)

JAMES HENRY, Admr. & O. of JOHN HENRY, Dec'd. Vs: W. A. WALKER, Admr. & O. In these cases and all cases brought agnst. W. A. WALKER, Admr. of WILLIAM TOOLE, SR., Dec'd. said WALKER is allowed 4 mos. in which to file Ans.

W. A. WALKER, Admr. & O. Vs: JOHN E. TOOLE et al. This is a fit case for an Acc't. at present stage of proceedings. O. by Ct. - C&M hear proof and state an acc't. to next term Ct. showing:
1) What amt. assets of WILLIAM TOOLE, SR., Dec'd. went
Pg. 222 into hands of JOHN E. and B. W. TOOLE as Extrs. of WILLIAM TOOLE, SR., Dec'd., while they acted in said capacity - or what amt. should have come into their hands by exercise of diligence?
2) What amt. they dispursed while in their trust?
3) Amt. of liabilities outstanding - Princ. w/int. and whether or not sale of any real estate necessary for payment of debts. Upon app'l. of ELIZABETH TOOLE, the widow of WILLIAM, by her Atty. 1 mo. allowed her to file Ans.

SAMUEL PRIDE, C&M Vs: ISAAC HINES & THOMAS PICKENS. Death of SAMUEL PRIDE is suggested and proved. Cause to be revived in name of WILLIAM C.

PICKENS, the present C&M. Execution is awarded in said name.

Pg. 223 JAMES THOMPSON, Admr. Est. JAMES PORTER, Dec'd. Vs: WILL KIDD & JAMES M. KIDD. Upon bill and ans. of W. M. KIDD and upon Jdgmt. Pro Confesso taken and entered agnst. JAMES M. KIDD. It appears to Ct. the ans. of WILL KIDD does not sufficiently deny the equity of the bill and it appearing that this is a bill to enforce a widow's lien amt. and further there was due upon the foot of the said land the sum of $2,219.25 which is due Sept. 15, 1865, with further sum of $37.35 making in all $2,256.60. Ct. D. in favor of Complnt. for said sum together w/all costs from Respdt. and if not pd. in 3 mos. C&M to advertise and sell land in bar of redemption and upon 12 mos. credit taking note and security and retaining lien. This land on which Respdt. lives near town of Maryville joins lands of JAMES W. EVERETT, A. MCCONNELL & O.

Pg. 224 HENRYS SMITH & TOWNSEND Vs: W. C. WALLACE & W. A. WALKER, Admr. & O. Jdgmt. Pro Confesso agnst. Respdts. Process regularly served upon JESSE G. WALLACE, MARY WALLACE, SAMUEL L. BICKNELL and wife, MARY B., and publication made as to A. M. WALLACE and WILLIAM C. WALLACE as law requires. All above parties failed to make defense. Ct. about to adjourn without holding 3 days, therefore O.& D. that bill be taken as confessed agnst. said Defdts. and set for hearing ex parte as to them. Because it appears that MARY B. ROBINSON, one of Defdts. is a minor under 14 yrs. age and has no regular Gdn., S. T. ROWAN is appt'd. Gdn. ad libum for said minor and Complnts. by Atty. dismiss their bill as to GEORGE and LIZZIE TOOLE. O. by Ct. that said bill be dismissed as to GEORGE and LIZZIE TOOLE and that they recover of Complnt. and WILLIAM HARRIS, Security, and the prosecution bear costs of making them parties for which execution may issue.

W. A. WALKER, Extr. Vs: MARY L. L. WALLACE & O. MARY B. ROBINSON is a minor under 14 yrs. and without regular Gdn. Ct. appoints J. C. M. BOGLE, Gdn. ad libum for said minor and appearing to Ct. that SAMUEL L. BICKNELL and his wife, MARY B., have been served with process and failed to file ans. and it being suggested to Ct. by Complnt. that discoveries and information sought to be obtained in their ans's. will be material to the attainment of Justice in the case O. by Ct. that Defdts. file their ans. or be in contempt of Ct. - Must file by 1st day of next term Ct. C&M to notify them of O.

Pg. 225 W. A. WALKER, Admr. Vs: MARTHA M. PRIDE & O. O. that an Alias Subpoena issue to GILES CO. and served on JOHN S. M. PRIDE requiring him to come in and ans. this bill. Also process issue to SEVIER CO. to be served on HUGH RODGERS and in case process returned, not found, the C&M will make publication as to said RODGERS as in the case of nonresidents and if it appears S. M. PRIDE has left the State, C&M will in like manner make publication as to him.

J. S. & E. A. ABBOTT Vs: SISLER & FAGG. Land in this case sold by C&M - sold for an inadequate price. O.A.D. said sale be set aside and shall be for nothing held. C&M to readvertise and sell as much of said lands necessary to pay Complnt. D. Rep't. next term Ct.

Pg. 226 ANDREW PEERY, Admr. E. T. DUNLAP Vs: ABIJAH SIMONS. On July 29, 1865, the Master sold the lands to ANDREW PEERY for sum of $176.00. He pd. down $18.00 and Master took a note for balance w/J. D. HEADRICK, Security. Therefore considered to have deed made to purchaser by C&M when balance of money pd. Costs will be pd. out of funds rec'd.

JAMES THOMPSON, Admr. of JAMES PORTER, Dec'd. Vs: ANDREW PORTER. Note filed as evidence of the indebtedness and upon jdgmt. Pro Confesso taken agnst. Defdt. for want of an ans. and which is now entered of record. Note for $866.83 Principal plus $164.01 Int. Total sum of $1,030.84. Ct. O.A.D. that Complnts. have and recover **Pg. 227** from said Defdt. said sum for which execution may issue. A lien on said lands for payment of same and C&M authorized to give notice and proceed to sell said lands after giving due legal notice. If said lands shall not sell for enough to pay debt and costs execution shall issue again agnst. Defdt.

B. D. BRABSON Vs: JESSE KERR. Defdt. has two months to ans.

MICHAEL MISER Vs: WILLIAM L. JOHNSON. C&M to hear proof and state an acc't. at next term Ct. - determine what credits or set-offs the Defdt. entitled to agnst. note of Complnt. and determine true amt. still due and unpaid and rep't. next term.

Pg. 228 JAMES THOMPSON, Admr. JAMES PORTER, Dec'd. Vs: STEPHEN S. PORTER & O. Ct. O. an acc't. at present stage of proceedings. C&M state an acc't. at next term Ct.
1) Amt. of personal Est. and assets of Est. which have come into hands of Admr.
2) Amt. outstanding liabilities.
3) Will a sale of all, or any of lands belonging to Est. be necessary for paying off debts?

JAMES HENRY Vs: THOMAS ROOKER & WIFE. Complnt. HENRY appeared in Open Ct. and admitting claim has been satisfied but costs not pd. Ct. O.A.D. Complnt. recover from Defdt. costs of suit.

JOHN C. CHILDS & JAMES HENRY, Commrs. Vs: A. J. ISH, WILLIAM HENDERSON et al. (No Entry).

Pg. 229 JAMES WILSON Vs: HEIRS of JOHN HENRY, Dec'd. On May 24, 1865, at Spec. Term of Chancery Ct. a D. was rendered in favor of Complnts. and agnst. ISH and HENDERSON for a large sum of money. D. rendered to enforce a Vendor's lien for purchase money. C&M ordered in default of payment to sell the tract known as the JOHN HENRY land in Blount County it being the lower end of HENRY'S bend and containing @ 600 A. joining lands of JOHN D. HEADRICK, the JOHN CLARK farm, the lands of SAMUEL HENRY, SR., JOHN GAMBLE and A. B. GAMBLE. Amt. of purchase money not pd. by Respdt. so C&M having given notice on Sept. 4, 1865, resold the land viz: To Chancellor, Sept. 4, 1865 - The undersigned begs
Pg. 230 leave to rep't. that on this date - to enforce lien for purchase money yet due and owing from ANDREW J. ISH, WILLIAM HENDERSON and ALEXANDER ISH, who is not sued, and Decree rendered for $14,029.80 this amt. to be a lien agnst. JOHN HENRY'S lands being the lower end of HENRY'S bend on Little River containing in all about 600 A. supposed to be about 1/2 Bottom and the balance upland or back land knobs. The bottom land bounded by

Little River and Ellejoy Creek in pursuance of the said decree and according to laws of the State and as I am in possession myself under O. of this Hon. Ct. appointing me Recv'r. and directing said land to be rented, I have given all parties such notice as required by D. - after 4 days and at 1/2 after 12 O'Clock at C.H. door and in presence of a large crowd of persons, I did sell said lands calling forth publicly and by auction and at the call - giving ample time - Struck off the said land to JAMES HENRY, of JOHN

Pg. 231 HENRY, he being the highest, best and last bidder for $14,350.00. I sold it by the group and by the tract and without any new or additional survey - it being a well-known tract of land and I did not regard it necessary to ascertain the boundaries. In my presence JAMES HENRY, the bidder agreed to and did hand over his bid to JAMES HENRY, Esq. and executed to me, C&M, 3 promissory notes - the first for $4,783.00 dated Sept. 4, 1865, due 6 mos. after I retained a lien note signed by JAMES HENRY (Seal) SPENCER HENRY, THOMAS PICKENS, WILLIAM A. WALKER, JOHN E. GAMBLE and MOSE GAMBLE. I took two other notes for same amts. due 12 and 18 mos. after - all signed these notes also - submitted by C&M to Ct. W. C. PICKENS, C&M, by L. WEAR, Dpty. C&M. And by said rep't. it appears to Ct. lands sold for $14,350.00 and that JAMES HENRY, of JOHN HENRY, became purchaser.

Pg. 232 Ct. D. from M's. Rep't. that there is a specific lien upon this land until fully pd. Purchaser to have copy of D. for registration. Services of C&M in this sale worth $150.00. C&M to retain that amt. out of the funds. And it further appearing that the M. of this Ct. was appt'd. Recv'r. by E. L. HALL, Judge of the Circuit Ct. of Blount County and was directed to take into his possession the said JOHN HENRY farm, which he had done, and moved w/his family on it in the last days of Mar. 1865. By this rep't. Ct. realizes that he has realized out of the rents of the farm $602.39 and he has in his possession belonging to

Pg. 233 said Rec'vrship. about 10 loads of hay that has been garnished by the Sheriff of Blount County at the suit of some of creditors of A. J. ISH and that the garnishee was served upon him the 4th day of present month but JAMES HENRY, of JOHN HENRY, filed in this office on this day a deed of quit claim from A. J. ISH by him duly executed 25th Aug. 1865, and duly recorded and registered Sept. 1865 in Registrar's office and by the terms of said Deed, the rents and profits of said tract of land are conveyed to said JAMES HENRY. Ct. therefore D. that M. be allowed the sum of $60.00 for his services and that he take a receipt therefore to JAMES HENRY all the balance of the proceeds and there his said Recv'rship. will end. M. retains costs of case out of funds for which land sold.

LEONARD A. WOOD. & O. Vs: M. H. STEPHENS & O. In this case Complnt. asks leave to file an amended bill which is agreed upon w/payment of costs.

Pg. 234

W. R. HENRY Vs: JOHN GARNER & SAMUEL TULLOCH, Extr. of WILLIAM GARNER, Dec'd. Cause came to be heard on a bill which is a bill making a tender of Federal Treasury Notes they being legal tender notes and upon ans. of JOHN F. GARNER, one of the Respdts. in this case setting up the defense that the contract on which the Jdgmt. mentioned in this case was made before the War and before the passage of the law making said notes a legal tender and that it was for gold but the Ct. is of the opinion and D. that the defense is not good but that Respdts. are ordered to take and rec'v. them in payment of their debt and M. shall take their receipt.

H. FOSTER Vs: W. M. STEELE. Cont'd. by consent of parties.

W. A. WALKER Vs: ROBERT A. WEAR. Death of ROBERT A. WEAR suggested in Open Ct.

REED BROS. & CO Vs: A. M. & J. G. WALLACE. Cause cont'd. next term Ct.

EDWARD GEORGE Vs: JAMES BARNES, surviving partner of PRIDE & BARNES and W. A. WALKER, Admr. of SAMUEL PRIDE, Dec'd. On last day of the Dec. Term of Ct. upon application of Complnt., Jdgmt. Pro Confesso is entered and taken agnst. JAMES BARNES, the surviving partner. Publication having been duly made as to him - he being a nonresident and W. A. WALKER, Admr. has 3 mos. or until April Rules to Ans.

Pg. 235 Court then adjourned until next regular term. S. R. RODGERS, Chancellor.

ABBREVIATIONS

A.	acres
a. & c.	et cetera
a.c.	at chambers
acc't.	account
add'l.	additional
Admr.	Administrator
Admx.	Administratrix
agnst.	against
amt.(s)	amount(s)
Ans.	Answer
app'l.	application
appt'd.	appointed
Atty.	Attorney
Bal.	balance
b/n/f	by next friend
Bro.	Brother
bus.	business
C.	Conservator
C&M	Clerk & Master
C.C.	County Court
Ch.	Child(ren)
C.H.	Courthouse
Clk.	Clerk
Commr.(s)	Commissioner(s)
Complnt.	Complainant
cont'd.	continued
Ct.	Court
Dec'd.	Deceased
D.	Decree
Defdt.	Defendant
Div.	Division
Dpty.	Deputy
Est.	Estate

Extr.	Executor
Extx.	Executrix
Gdn.	Guardian
Int.	Interest
jdgmt.	judgement
J.P.	Justice of the Peace
M.	Master
M/L.	More or Less
mos.	months
Mt.	Mountain
mtng.	meeting
n/f	next friend
O.	Others (or Ordered)
O.A.D.	Ordered, Adjudged & Decreed
pd.	paid
Plff.	Plaintiff
poss.	possession
propty.	property
rec'd.	received
Recv'r.	Receiver
Rep.	Representative
Rep't.	Report
Respdt.	Respondant
rt.(s)	right(s)
Sol.	Solicitor
Spec.	Special
Test.	Testator
Vs:	Versus
w/	with
X	Cross
yrs.	years

INDEX

ABBOTT, 48 86 129 E A 130 153 Edward A 132 Edward H 120 J S 130 153 Joseph S 120 132

ADNEY, 148 G W 148 George W 146

AIKEN, James A 14 James M 18

AIKIN, J M 30 James 23 James M 31 46

ALEXANDER, E 18 138 140 John 22 23 34 44 52 Mrs John 44 52

AMBRISTER, 8 11 Asa 4 5 8 11 23 75 85 Elizabeth 85 George 85 90 101 Joseph 85 Loretta 85 101 Loretta F 85 William 75 78 85 90

ANDERSON, A L 113 Allen 105 120 Barbara 52 Barbary 50 Barbary Rebecca 50 E J 69 Edmond J 50 Edward J 64 74 Elizabeth 69 James 10 23 39 43 James L 50 James M 50 Mary Elizabeth 50

BADGETT, Clementine 50 63 David 50 Donald 50 Romulus 50 Samuel 50

BAILEY, 70

BAKER, 143

BANCROFT, 129

BARCROFT, 129

BARNES, 22 156 Aszo A 52

BARNES (continued) Azro A 77 James 8 9 22 35 156

BAXTER, John 54

BAYLESS, 81 Sarah 73 81 W W 71 81 William 73 81 94 William W 94

BEAN, John 122

BEARDEN, M D 143 Marcus D 102

BEAVER, 129

BECKNALL, Samuel T 71

BECKNELL, Samuel T 43

BELL, 12 13 James 8 12

BERRIRE, 4 James 4

BERRY, 7 Daniel D 15 Letetia 31 Lettetia 16 Lettitia 15 21 Mrs 15

BEST, Christian 17

BICKNELL, J T 23 30 34 James T 17 James W 113 Mary B 152 S T 43 Samuel 19 Samuel L 152 Samuel T 8 William 100

BLACK, 20 J 20 John 81 94

BLACKBURN, Eija 85 John N 85

BLAIR, 126

BLANCHARD, 8 17 19 23 30 34 43 Thomas J 4 12 14 43

BOBLE, J C M 44

BOGLE, Bessie C 96 Bessie C Saffell 96 Hugh 75 J C M 35

BOGLE (continued)
72 81 89 92 93 95 96 108
113 126 136 145 150 152
John 29 John C M 114 Mrs
J C M 95
BOHANNON, Thomas 94
BONELLS, J 100
BONHAM, 95 J 34 J H 24 J S
73 James 20 71 145 James
D 58 James L 46 49 James
S 22 30 49 John P 145
BOOKER, Tell 5
BOWEN, Ann 63
BOWERMAN, 15 A P 33 Michael 14 P M 14 15 74
Pleasant M 15 80 R P 45 64
67 68 75 92
BOYD, 39 Thomas 7 15
BRABSON, 57 B D 4 6 7 9 10
57 97 153 Benjamin 7
Benjamin D 7 Buse P 7
Elizabeth 7 John 4 7 10 Mrs
John 7 Penelope C 7 T C 10
Thomas 7 Thomas C 6
BRADFORD, 8 11 James C 5 8
11 James M 4
BRADLY, H 81
BRATON, Benjamin F 89
BREWER, N 57 107 108 Nicholas 47 92 145
BRICKEL, William M 6
BRICKELL, William 14 145
BRICKEY, Elizabeth 57
BRICKMYER, 18
BRIGHT, Benjamin 145
BRODDY, Joseph 51
BROOKS, Jesse 95 Nancy 95
BROWN, Ann 30 George 58 75
James E 31 John 49
BROWNING, W E 52
BROWNLOW, W G 142
BRUCE, A T 122 141
BURNETT, Haywood 27
BUSUM, 36 H 36 Henry 4 5 7 9
14 20 25 36 Peter 5

CALDWELL, 96 140 David 123
140 141 148 149 George 27
149 John 92
CALLAWAY, James 93
CAMBELL, F E 129
CAMERON, 31-33 39 72 73 L R
39 Marion 43 49 60 S R 28
59 Samuel R 28 49 73
CAMPBELL, David 61 74 Elizabeth 34 51 74 James W 20 T
C 129 T J 130 Thomas J 130
CANNON, William H 73 William
P 48 49
CARITHERS, Harvey H C 151
CAROTHERS, Robert L 53
CARTER, L D 66
CARUTHERS, H H 11
CASHION, William C 151
CASWELL, 143
CATE, R L 9 78 85 90
CATES, 18 R L 18 24 75 90
CAULEY, Rufus M 104 105
CAULSON, John 64
CHAMBERLAIN, 61 70 91 128
129 135
CHAMBERS, John 57 92 107
108 145 Rhoda 47 57 92
107 108 145
CHANDLER, 20 130 B M 85
David 64 86 John 85
CHILDS, 133 George C 98 Jane
63 John C 63 88 98 99 120
133 134 154 Mrs John C 98
CLARK, 6 21 91 106 James 70
John 6 154 R B 6 9 Robert
14 Robert B 21 Thomas N 33
CLARKE, 112 126 Harvey P 70
James 70
CLEMENS, Henry 105 Samuel
29
CLEMINS, Henry 105
COCHRAN, Isaac W 144
COFFIN, 3 57 128 James A 33
John 70 John M 51 57 128
CONER, E E 28

CONGER, Ibijah 17
CONLY, Rufus M 90 91
CONNER, 151 Mrs 151
COOK, 70 A 6 14 20 96 Alexander 89 145 James 11 145 L C 133
COOKE, Alex 4
COSTER, Thomas C 92
COTTER, James 57 William 57
COULSON, Labe 71
COUNT, J D 120
COWAN, Samuel F 70
COX, 37 43 48 55 129 130 H T 23 24 30 33 36 37 45 54 55 64 73 75 92 95 102 107 120-122 124 128-130 136 141 145 149 150 Henry T 128-130 144 150 J B 86 J L 121 122 James R 100 John B 95 124 129 130 144 150 M 98 145 Mad 32 41 48 71 Q M 88 S T 78 79 86 Samuel 128 150 Samuel T 128-130 144 W M 39 45 122 144 150 Will 39 Willeston M 45
CRAIG, 110 113 J S 14 John L 39 John S 4 6 9 17 20 70 72
CRAIGMILES, John H 72 Ples M 72
CRESWELL, 95 121 Andrew 59 94 95 106 110 114 150 Elizabeth J 94 Nancy 94 Nancy L 94 R L 106 110 R S 114 Richard 150 Richard L 59 94 95 Samuel L 94 Samuel M 94 Sarah C 94 W C 106 110 114 William C 59 94 95 106 150
CRISWELL, Andrew 14
CRUSE, John 93
CUMMINGS, 77 John 52 P L 71 W P L 89 William 71 77 William L 94 William P L 64 67
CUNNIGHAM, David 47

CUNNINGHAM, A 120 136 Albert 47 Alfred 60 74 99 100 106-108 110 112 C 136 Claiborne 74 D 136 David 60 74 99 106 108 112 120 David Claiborn 99 John 100 107 Margaret 99 110 Margeret 112 Moses 74 99 107 S 6 Sarah 10 20
CUPP, D 95
CURTIS, Cyrus 105
DANFORTH, Lettitia 15
DANNEE, 128 129
DARRYLL, Henry William 64
DARYLL, Peter L 64
DAVIS, Elizabeth 76 100 George 30 32 44 Jacob 76 John C 100
DEARMAND, 70 95 Campbell 70 Richard 70
DEARMOND, 18 T C 9 T G 24
DEVER, 48 129 130 James 128 James F 129
DONALDSON, 10 L 13 20 Lorenzo 6 10 20
DOOPS, Jacob 146 148
DOTSON, Jeremiah 19 24 28
DOUGLAS, B 73 87 96 H 73 87 96 Hugh 87 R B 71
DOUGLASS, B 109 H 109
DOUTHET, Isaac S 32 Isaac T 28 39 J T 44 76 L 44 Samuel 22 28 32 39 76
DOUTHETT, 49 58 Samuel 19
DOWELL, W T 145
DOWNEY, 17
DUNCAN, 95 B F 48 60 73 88 89 96 115 Benjamin F 81 George 62 J K 86 James K 110 Joseph 52 Rhoda 52
DUNLAP, A 60 97 E T 125 153 Elijah T 125
DUNN, Albert G 50 Daniel 39 John B 50 Mary 50 Rachel 50

DURYEA, 68 89 90
DYER, A 105 Archibald 120
EAKIN, 36 37 James M 41 150
    John 47 62 Robert 150
EARLY, Andrew 72
EASLY, Andrew 79
EAST, Edward H 117
EDDINGTON, Abraham 31
EDGEMOND, Catherine 90
    Elizabeth 90
EDMONDSON, John H 151
EKIN, W L 12
ELDIDGE, William 60
ELIGE, Emily B 114 James 114
ELIZABETH, 10
ELLIGE, William 97
ELLIOTT, Mason 103 Moses 82
    83
ELLIS, 87
ELLMORE, Jess 71 Jesse 47
    William 47 71
ELMORE, Jesse 59 80 William
    59 80
EMETT, A W 39
EMMETT, 39 A W 43 Abijah W
    10
EMMITT, A W 88
EVERETT, 31-33 72 73 127
    Abijah 23 Catherine 48 E 28
    Epaphroditus 73 Epp 43 47
    59 71 80 J 74 J S M 90 91
    104 105 James W 127 152
    John 19 24 28 32 35 42 52
    61 64 65 69 70 114 Malinda
    114
EVIER, Thomas 78
FAGG, 120 130 133 153 Flora J
    63 J C 144 145 Julious C
    144 Julius C 132 Julius N
    63
FARMER, Green 69 126 136
    Greene 69 Lerenah C 69
    Lewis C 69 Rulina A 69
    Sarah A 69
FERGUSON, Andrew 23 34 44

FERGUSON (continued)
    52 Mary C 34 45 57 58
FINLEY, 54 66 L K 66 S K 126
    Samuel K 34 43 55
FINLY, Samuel K 144
FLOVEL, Thomas 11
FORCE, B W 61 70 72 77 79 83
    88 105 I P 70 83 J P 61 72
    77 79 88 105
FOSTER, 6 21 24 130 H 55 102
    156 Horace 21 141
FOUT, Daniel 51 52
FOUTE, 7 Daniel D 41 Martha
    50 64 William 50 64
FRANKLIN, L D 51 59 80 102
    110 112 L L 110
FREDERICK, Benjamin F 88
FRENCH, H L 66 J W 117-119
FRIBLES, 88
FROW, John R 79 83 105 John
    W 72 Thad J 105 Thomas J
    83 105
FULKERSON, 150 Ann E 150
    Elizabeth E 150 Leonides S
    150 William R 150
FURGUSON, Andrew 22
GALLAGHER, J C 12 John C 4
GALLAHER, John C 14
GALLIHER, John C 85 Mary 85
GAMBLE, 38 A B 14 154 A F 53
    A Marion 117 118 Angeline
    65 John 5 6 12 14 18 38 56
    154 John E 155 Josias 31
    69 102 143 Marion A 117
    Mose 136 155 Moses 22 26
    40 53 58 63 65 72 Mr 56
    Mrs Moses 53 58
GARDINER, Alexander 138
GARDNER, Michael 26
GARNER, Allen 14 John 60 97
    156 John F 156 Robert 91
    William 156
GAULT, John 11 John C 112
GEORGE, 38 Barbary 9 98 E 4
    9 17 19 23 35 50 52 69 74

GEORGE (continued)
   97 100 109 119 139 Ed 32
   42 47 64 69 139 Edward 6
   63 83 97 98 101 137 156 I
   97 I Edward 9 I W 4 6 9 17
   19 22 23 35 42 47 50 52 69
   98 100 109 119 Isaac W 6 9
   Josiah 98 Mr 56 Samuel 9
   97 98 101
GHORMALY, D 71 S 71
GHORMLEY, Ann 71 Samuel 71
GHORMLY, A 112 114 Ann 6 8
   9 11 12 17-20 23 35 36 75
   91 104 126 D C 87 114 Mrs
   Samuel 30 S 112 114
   Samuel 6 8 9 11 12 18-20
   23 30 35 36 75 87 90 91
   104 120 126 135 136 144
GIBSON, Peter 11
GILBERT, 29 30 32 36-38 55
   56 66 73 83 101 119 A L 24
   25 28 31-34 36-38 43 54 55
   60 61 65 66 77 78 101
   David 25 38 55 60 65 G S 24
   25 31 34 47 58 George 32 55
   60 77 101 George D 77 78
   George L 61 George S 16 25
   31 37 43 54 65 66 78 Nancy
   15 16 25 28 38 66 Nancy E
   43 54 55 66 S 24 33 S S 25
   31 34 37 38 43 54 55 60 61
   65 66 77 78 101
GILES, 153
GILLESPIE, C 135 149 Nancy F
   149 W C 149
GILLESPY, C 91 101 115 121
   143 Campbell 75 112 J H 51
   61 73 74 James F 101
   James H 3 8 13 14 23 26 29
   31 34 41 46 74 86 Mrs William A 101 Nancy F 121
   Sheriff 7 W C 143 William A
   101 William C 75 121
GLASS, John E 87
GODDARD, 95 David 141 Elias

GODDARD (continued)
   141 148 William 141 148
GOODLINK, D 34 Dennison 45
   Francis 57 Jane 57 Jane W
   57 58 Joseph D 57 Joseph
   W 58 Margarette 57 Martha
   57 Mary Magorite 57 Michael
   57 Mrs Dennison 45
GOODWIN, Newton 63
GOURLY, 145
GRAHAM, 42
GREENWAY, 78 79 86 95 102
   128 129
GREER, John 62
GRESHAM, 106 110
GRIFFETH, John 47
GRIFFETHS, John 93
GRIFFETT, John 62
GRIFFITH, John 15
GRIFFITHS, John 37 62
GRIFFITS, James 15 John 7 62
GRIFFITTS, 84 John 59 84
GRISHAM, 86 A 86
GURLEY, C A 81
HACKNEY, Joseph L 88
HALE, 88
HALL, E L 155 Mary A 18 21
HAMIL, Henry 81 James W 61
   64 65 69 70
HAMILL, James 74
HAMMINS, James W 39
HAMMOND, 38 Jonathan 38 55
   56 Mr 56
HAMONTREE, James 26 P D 26
HANLEY, A H 91 Samuel 91
HANNUM, Ann E 71
HARB, 92
HARDIN, 93 109 113 139
   Esther 59 73 93 113 John
   59 102 John P 93 113
   Joseph 93 Martha A 93
   Thomas 87 Thomas S 93
HARGIS, 20 J T 6
HARGUS, John T 13 14 17 20
HARPER, John 47 Martin 27

HARRIS, 88 127 Isham G 111
 William 152 Z 88
HARTSELL, 58 119 H 101 M E
 151
HARTZELL, H 24 47 Hiram 25
HATCHER, Elijah 100
HATFIELD, E 92
HAYES, J A 49 John 28 John R
 49
HAYS, J A 49 J O 76 John 19
 39 John R 10 17 22 32 44
 58 73 76 79 Joshua O 73 76
 79 92
HAZEN, G W 88
HEADRICK, 15 J D 153 John
 133 John D 154 Will L 15
 William 89 William L 15
HEART, S B 73
HEARTSELL, 28 29 54 56
 Abram 73 H 25 31 36 38 43
 65 66 73 83 Hiram 32 W T
 73
HEARTZELL, H 34 37
HEDRICK, 27
HEISKELL, 126
HEISKILL, John M 52
HENDERSON, 88 154 L B 143
 L D 58 S A 25 S B 121 S D
 59 Samuel B 112 Samuel D
 25 26 29 39 40 Sarah 26 29
 Sarah A 40 58 William 30 55
 60 61 99 112 120 133 134
 154
HENLEY, A H 80 Arthur H 80
 David 80 81 Samuel 64 80
 127 Thomas 64 71 127
HENRY, 16 27 33 38 49 60 67
 75 76 78 79 86 88 95 102
 128 129 133 146 154 George
 122 128 George W 81 145
 146 Hugh 6 9 24 32 42 56
 65 Hugh Jr 21 Isabella 148
 Isabella S 145 146 J 4 7 9
 10 14 20 23 25 36 41 J F 4
 9 10 14 20 23 25 34 36 J M

HENRY (continued)
 32 48 98 J T 41 James 2 4
 24 34-36 38 42 45 46 48 55
 56 60 61 63-65 67 71 74 76
 86 88 92 94 98 99 103 104
 114 120 122 126 133-135
 144 145 151 154-156 James
 H 78 James M 74 80 81
 Jasper 80 John 6 9 10 13 16
 19 24 25 30 33 38 42 49 51
 56 60 62 64 65 75-77 87 88
 97 98 99 109 111 120 133
 145 151 154 155 John F 4 7
 103 104 137-139 John R
 142 Margaret 26 Milley A 60
 Millie Ann 56 Milly Ann 55
 56 Mr 30 56 Mrs John 38 S
 104 Samuel 3 5-7 9 12 17
 19 21 22 26 27 50 102 133
 143 Samuel Sr 154 Sarah 30
 Spencer 103 104 150 155
 Thomas 21 W J 98 W R 156
 William I 74 William J 48 50
 64
HENRYS, 152
HESSER, Clark 31
HICKS, J D 87 Samuel M 87
HILL, Joel 29
HINDS, Isaac 110
HINES, Isaac 114 150 151
HITCH, 139 Archy 139 James
 139 149
HODSDEN, Mary 7 Robert H 7
HOLIMAN, F 31
HOLMAN, F 6 24 F H 19 Fran-
 cis 24
HOOD, Amanda 61 64 71 F M
 39 116 Francis J 51 Hester
 A 51 Hugh A 51 John 51
 Margaret R 51 Samuel B 51
 Sarah A 51 Susan 51
HOOKE, John P 70
HOUSTON, 27 87 110 149 J A
 39 61 70 72 77 79 83 87 88
 91 96 105 106 110 112 113

HOUSTON (continued)
121 126 143 144 149 J H
120 James 27 James A 30
39 87 106 Mary A 30 Mary E
30 Matthew 17 P P 30 39
HOWARD, John H 93 Martha
93 W W 102
HUDSON, 47 59 72 91 Charles
C 72
HUFFSTETLER, 17
HUGH, 9 32
HUGHS, Robert 84
HUME, James W 75
HUMES, James 90 James W 61
78 85
HUNT, James 62
HUTTON, William L 62
HYATT, 18 79 88 102 128-130
HYDE, 91 106 112 126
ISBILL, John 93 Washington 49
ISH, 154 A 5 7 9 10 22 28 31
120 133-135 A J 120 133
134 144 154 155 Alex 21 26
31 Alexander 15 21 24 37 42
154 Andrew J 154 Benjamin
A 145 Elizabeth 15 16 Elizabeth L 145 Elizabeth S 145
Jackson 99 Mrs Alexander
15
JACKIN, James A 31
JACKSON, 84 J B 59 84 Mrs 84
Mrs J B 84 Samuel 5
JAFRIES, Henry H 64
JAMES, A R 144 Ann 3-7 9 16
22 31 44 47 69 Elizabeth 36
Henry 36 Isabella 36 Isobel
12 Robert 5 6 8 9 11 12 17-
20 23 30 35 36 71 72 75
103 112 114 126 Thomas 12
W 91 William 3 5 18 20 23
35 71 72 75 104 112
JEFFRIES, William 78
JOBE, 130
JOHN, 38
JOHNSON, 97 98 101 109

JOHNSON (continued)
Amanda 22 Andrew 117
Armand M 98 Clarissa 15 16
Elkany 51 J K 21 Josiah 15
Josiah K 15 Mrs 97 98 101
109 Mrs Josiah 15 Mrs W L
50 100 Mrs W S 63 74 Mrs
William J 69 Mrs William S
35 97 W L 50 100 W S 63 64
74 101 William 22 William J
69 William L 154 William S
35 97
JOHNSTON, Mrs William 32
Mrs William S 42 William 32
William S 42 47
JONES, 127 Isabella 149 Isabella J 149 Johnson 79
Milas 149
KEEBLE, Manly 125
KEENE, 93 E 59 84 93 Enoch
84 93 James W 84 Mary 84
85 93 Mary Inamy 84 Mrs 93
Mrs E 84
KEITH, 139 A H 145 Alex H 8
12 Alexander 13 Alexander H
12
KENNEDY, 36 45 A A 148 Alex
23 36 46 Alexander 22 45 48
64 67 74 76 80 86 136 145
Arthur A 145 Sarah C 145
148
KENT, 31 Rodolphus 88
KERR, J 31 Jesse 22 34 70 122
128 153 Jesse Sr 144 150
KEY, David 23 James 86 91
132 144 Peter 24
KEYES, 27 Charlotte 3 John 3
27 Moses 27
KEYS, Charles 7 Charlotta 17
19 Charlotte 5 James 71
Margery 12
KIDD, J M 134 James M 152 W
M 152 Will 152 William 64
86 127 134
KING, 143 Joseph L 142

KING (continued)
  Joseph S 131 135 143
KIRKPATRICK, Andrew 93 97 103 104
LAMBERT, 108 Joseph 92
LAMBUTH, Jesse 138 140
LANIER, 131 Sidney A 142
  Sidney C 131 135 Sterling 131 135 142 William B 131 135 142
LANNICAN, 18
LASITER, F M 141
LATHAM, George 60 97
LATTIMORE, D W 81
LAURELL, 33
LAUTER, F M 124
LAVITT, 34
LAWRENCE, J R 126 W W 11 127 Will W 8
LAWSON, 108 Howel 92
LEA, Martha E 40 Samuel 40
LEAVETT, 88
LEE, Samuel 53
LEEPER, Esther 87 93 102 113 H B 109 H Hugh B 87 Hu B 113 Hugh B 21 73 93 L M 6 Mr 102 Mrs H B 109 Mrs Hu B 113 S 19 S M 7 10 Sanders 5 Saunders 5 Saunders M 24
LEGAN, T C 47
LEVENTORE, Elizabeth 143 John 143
LILLARD, 12 W C 8 12 13 William C 12
LINK, 58 E 34 Ephraim 20 22 24 30 46 Ephriam 58 71
LINN, Robert M 79 92
LIPPENCOTT, J B 47 61
LIPPINCOTT, J B 64 L B 80
LONAS, Charles 143 149
LONES, Charles 102
LOTTY, G S Gilberts 24
LOVE, 134 J R 102
LOWERY, John 105

LOWRY, 27 William 27
LUCKERY, Hon Chancllr 19
LUCKY, Hon Chancllr 125
  James 89 S J W 78 Seth J 79 Seth J W 77 Seth W 19
LYON, Thomas C 55 59 75 129 138 140
MALCOMB, John W 26
MARCUM, William 57
MARTIN, Benjamin F 145 147 148 Elizabeth F 146 148 Elizabeth J 145-147 Francis M 145 148 George W 145 148 Henry L 147 Isabella 148 Isabella S 110 121 146 John 110 121 147 148 John C 110 145 146 148 John Sr 145 146 148 Joseph 29 L A 148 Leonard 145 Leonard H 146 148 Lucean 147 148 Lucean M 146 147 Lucean N 148 Mrs John Sr 145 Sarah K 145-147 W B 145 William B 146 147
MATLOCK, A 144 150
MATTHEW, James 149
MATTHEWS, Harlan 7 Harlen 15
MAYNARD, 33 H 22 Horace 24 57 73 86
MCBATH, 134 A R 145
MCBERNIE, 88
MCBURNEY, 18 102
MCBURNIE, 79 128-130
MCCAMPBELL, 96 John 92
MCCAMY, 92 J A 86 James 64 74 110 James A 25 42 91 106 110 Samuel 40 80 William 110
MCCAULY, Theodore Campbell 31
MCCAY, John C 47
MCCLAIN, 29 A 40 Alexander 22 46 50 Andrew 22 26 64 74 86 138 140 John 10 17

166

MCCLAIN (continued)
19 22 49 58 N B 29 83 103
Napolian B 29
MCCLUNG, Patrick 102 113
MCCONNEL, James 14
MCCONNELL, 82 A 152 James
82 83 99 103 Jane 18
Martha 44 72 99 Martha E
82 Moses 18 Mrs 44 Mrs
James 82 Mrs Moses 18
MCCULLOCH, John 10 20
Porter 10 20 R P 20
MCCULLY, John 34 45 57 107
121 151 Joseph 39 45
Martha 58 Mrs John 34 45
57 Samuel 3
MCDONALD, F 22 Wiley 22
MCELRATH, Hugh Mcd 72
MCFALL, F M 70
MCGHEE, C M 80 81 C W 47
Charles M 61 80 81 John 80
93 M W 93 Matthew 17
MCGINLEY, W D 20 65 67 75
85 90 92 99 101 115 William
90 William D 20 58 64 74 78
80 95 114
MCHENRY, J 41 71 88
MCKAMY, James A 135 James
L 146 L F 53 Louisa F 65
Martha 135 Martha B 146
147 Martha D 145 147 Mrs
Robert 53 Robert 53 65
Samuel 121 135 146 Samuel
D 146 147 Sarah E 146
MCKAY, 62 David C 47 George
47 62 James D 47 Jane 62
Margery E 47 Mary Ann 62
Robert 62 William M 47
William W 47
MCKENSEY, Roderick 34 W G
71
MCKENZIE, Roderick 43
MCKINNEY, Robert J 53
MCKINSEY, Samuel 64
MCLIN, 121 J A 113 143 Robert

MCLIN (continued)
113 W O 143
MCMILLAN, Gavin 11 Hugh 11
James C 11
MCNALLY, John 30 32 44
MCNELLY, John 44
MCNUTT, Alexander 70 75
Elizabeth 7 John S 7 M W 92
R L 28 113 121 R S 110 144
MCREYNOLDS, 61 62 64 87 91
95-97 J M 56 Joseph T 109
S J 28 29 32 38 41 42 47 50
55 56 59 60-64 70 71 73 77
80 86-88 90 91 96 104 105
106 109 110 112 113 119
Stephen J 24 25
MCTEER, 10 16 21 25 27 31-33
40 49 60 67 68 70 74-76 88
Maj 7 Minerva 90 Will 63
William 4-7 10 13 16 19 21
23-25 27 30 32 33 40-42 48-
51 53 54 59 60 64 67 69 70
71 74 75 80 86-89 91 98 99
120 136 William Sr 10 20
MEANS, William 128
MEIGS, 95
MILER, 61 70 91 128 129 135
MILLER, Henry 48 63 Jack 121
Joyce 13 Kenny 64
MISER, George 15 George Sr 15
Joseph 14 15 Michael 154
MONTGOMERY, 49 A C 2 47
George 28 32 44 76 George
C 39
MOORE, William 123
MORTON, A H 26 James 26
John 16 20 22 26 Joseph 26
Silas 26 William 16 20 22 26
MURPHY, 102
MURRY, 96
MYERS, 100 Eli 30 Elizabeth
33 45 Henry 49 60 John 6
39 John C 49 Philip 45 76
William 39
NEAL, 20 James 6 14 17 20

NEIL, James 13
NELSON, C W 70 Carick W 54 Carrick W 70 Elijah 48 87 144
NEWBOLD, W H 38 88
NEWMAN, 140 C C 137 Charles C 134 136-140 M E 139 Martha 137 Martha E 136-140 Mrs 138 Mrs Charles C 134 136
NILES, S W J 81
NORWOOD, 101 109 A 74 C A 35 C W 4 6 9 17 19 22 23 42 47 63 69 100 119 C W C 97 Charles 52 Charles W 50 M 19 M R 69 Malinda 9 50 97 119 Matilda 19 Mrs 101 109 Mrs A 74 Mrs C A 35 Mrs C W 4 6 9 17 22 23 42 47 63 100 Mrs Charles 52
NUNN, 40 41 63 E 22 Eli 10 14 17 26 40 41 53 54 58 63 65 72 Martha E 17 40 41 53 63 Martha Elizabeth 63
O'CONNER, 100 G G 49 M E 33 45 Mary Ann 45 76 S W 33 69 Samuel W 30 45
OLDHAM, Thomas E 102
O'NEAL, 125 126 William 125 126
ORR, John 11
OWENS, B F 56 121
PARKER, M C 5 Philance 5
PARSONS, J H 113
PASS, Mrs Russell M 149 Russell M 149
PAYNE, John L 31
PECK, 129 N S 14 18 23 30 31 Nicholas S 41 46 150
PEERY, Andrew 125 153
PENN, G P 31
PHILLIS, 4 5 14 17
PICKENS, Robert 148 Thomas 114 117-119 148 150 151 155 W C 116 118 141 150

PICKENS (continued) 155 William C 115 117-119 125 135 151 152
PIERCE, 21
POPE, F 10 20 89 96 Fielding 71 T A 86 108 150 Thomas A 43 97 114
PORTER, Andrew 122 132 144 153 Ann H 149 Campbell 95 H 95 H Andrew 93 Hannah M 95 James 5 6 14 18 32 34 45 48 51 64 74 76 80 88 95 98 99 122 127 132 134 144 152-154 James A 88 James E 95 James L 5 12 Jane 95 102 143 Jane L 149 Joseph Robert 122 Lorenzo 95 Margaret S 93 N L 99 Nicholas C 95 Phoebe G 149 Proctor 95 Robert 149 S G 34 S S 67 68 122 Stephen S 40 81 89 154 W S 51 102 112 149 William 64 William L 80 William S 59 86 102 110 Wyatt 95
POTTER, John 88
PRATER, B 9 10 Benjamin 5 15 16 26 Benjamin F 15 16 George 15 George W 15 16 21 Hugh 15 16 James 5 7 9 10 15 16 21 26 28 31 John 15 16 Lafayette 15 16 Mary 21 Samuel 15 16 26 31 Thomas 15 21 W 9 10 William 5 7 15 16 21 26
PRATT, 88
PRESSLEY, William 10 23 34
PRESSLY, William 41
PRICE, 129
PRIDE, 16 31 33 49 60 67 75 76 88 156 J L M 64 John L M 50 John M 99 John S 88 John S M 38 98 153 Martha M 153 S M 153 Samuel 1 2 6 9 10 13 16 19 21 24 25 28

PRIDE (continued)
  30 32 33 38 41-43 48 49 51
  55 56 60 61 63-65 67 71 75
  77-79 87-90 94 95 98 99
  102-106 108 111 113-115
  119 133 135 143-145 150
  151 156
PUGH, 4 J D 5 6 9 17 20 John
  D 4 Josiah D 14
PULLIAM, 47 59 72 91 Robert
  W 72
RAMSEY, George 77
RANKIN, 68 89 90 128 129
  Isaac D 64 Isaac N 42 48
  William D 72
REATH, 88
REED, 88 130 156
REEDER, Granville 137 Granville H 134
REID, Robert 11
RHEA, John 47 62 John P 62
RIDER, John 12 18 21 Mrs
  John 18
ROBERTSON, 47 59 72 91
  Richard S 72
ROBINSON, Mary B 152
ROCKFORD, 70 123 124 139-141 143 148
RODGERS, 153 Hugh 153 S R
  156 Samuel R 135 142 146
ROGERS, 20 39 Samuel A 71
  Samuel R 38 39
ROOKER, Elizabeth 42 Mrs
  Thomas 154 Thomas 154
  Thomas M 42
ROREX, James A 108 Jarvis A
  92 W M 143 William 102
  William M 149
ROWAN, J H 27 S T 152
ROYSTON, 88 S W 91
RULLMAN, 129
RUSSELL, A H 122 136 B M 80
  Barkly 61 Bell 47 Henderson
  143 John 29 Lewis 51 M 112
  121 Robert 121

RUTLEDGE, G P 70 102 G W P
  93
SAFFELL, 18 37 38 51 65 66
  73 108 Bessie C 96 C A 23
  24 95 C H 37 66 C P 66
  Charles A 58 Charles T 144
  Clementine A 21 95 96
  Elizabeth 42 44 H C 48 65
  73 91 123 Henry C 34 38 42
  John 73 95 96 R 89 R M 34
  73 89 95 96 113 126 136
  Richard 96 Richard M 30 44
  51 95 S 89 S S 95 Samuel
  42 66 95 96 Sarah 96 Sarah
  I 96 Sarah J 95 96 Thomas
  F 58
SAFFLE, 3 4 61 77 C A 3 6 9 14
  18 19 C P 77 91 Charles P
  46 71 Clementine A 4 5 41
  Elizabeth C 3 H A 25 H C 19
  24 55 59 66 80 Henry C 4 51
  John 3 Mrs 9 Mrs C A 5 R M
  41 Richard 3 Richard M 61
  Sarah J 3
SARTAIN, Mrs Thomas 81 Mrs
  Thomas C 71 73 94 Thomas
  81 Thomas C 71 73 81 94
SCOTT, Dunlap 138 James M
  74
SCRUGGS, Lucy 7 Moses 150
  William 7
SESLER, 120
SEVIER, 153
SHARP, James M 136
SHENON, William A 76
SHEPHERD, Elizabeth 36 Mrs
  Robert 12 Robert 12 36
SHIELDS, Milton 7 Priscilla 7
SILER, 33 P F 72 P L 49 P T 28
  31 33 39 43 59 73
SIMERLY, I 32 James E 42
  Jeremiah 48 Mrs I 32 Mrs
  James E 42 Mrs Jeremiah
  48
SIMMERLY, 96 J 52 Mrs J 52

SIMMONS, 125 Alijah 125
SIMONS, Abijah 153
SINGLETON, John 40 64 74 80 86 88
SISLER, 130 153 Henry 132
SLAVE, Abby 15 Ailcy 46 Aisy 83 Alfred 95 Amy 72 Anderson 26 Ann 96 Annetta 96 Ansen 59 Betsy 75 85 Bill 83 Billy 103 Cloe 40 53 Davis 15 Deorix 96 Edy 97 98 100 Elizabeth 40 53 Florence 96 Frank 84 85 George 78 85 Hannah 73 Harris 83 Henry 75 85 Hugh 95 Isaac 96 Jane 96 Jeff 23 Jefferson 13 14 Jim 7 8 18 Lewis 96 Lotty 72 82 Lucretia 15 Mary 72 73 83 Milly 40 53 Molly 96 Moriah 75 78 85 Nancy 95 Peter 72 83 103 Philip 96 Philis 6 9 20 83 Pleasant 15 Polly 96 Preston 73 81 Rachal 103 Rachel 72 82 Riley 75 85 Sam 73 81 83 103 Sandy 96 Susan 5 6 12 14 18 Tilda 44 72 82 99 Tom 72 83 103 Washington 96 William Sam 72
SMITH, 78 79 95 102 128 129 152 I Gray 9 142 J Gray 5 22 30 31 44 47 James G 16 James Gray 3 4 7 L Gray 69 Mary 95 Stephen 95
SMOOT, 10 John L 5 John T 5-7 10 19 24
SNIDER, Betsy Jane 29 Dorcas 29 Elenor 41 Elinor 29 Isabell 29 John 29 John A 28 M 32 Wilson 29 41
SNYDER, Betsy Jane 29 Dorcas 29 Wilson 29
SPARKS, John 94
SPENCER, 45 W A 45 80 William A 32 34 45 48 64 74 80

SPENCER (continued) 86 William S 74
SPILMAN, Nancy 85 William 85
STANFORD, L L 50 Margaret 48 Margaret J 50
STEEL, Mcclung 8 22
STEELE, David A 88 J 19 J A 91 James 71 John 88 John W 71 M 9 Mcclung 4 W M 91 102 156 William 86 William M 19 71 76 100
STEPHENS, 34 88 H 78 90 120 136 H H 139 148 H L 90 120 H S 136 Henry 90 John 69 M A 105 M H 78 156 Mary 69 William 139
STEPP, James 5 Peny 5
STERLING, Margaret 11
STODDARD, E B 31 129
STONE, Isabella E 145 Jefferson 29 John 145 Mrs John 145
STOUT, David L 61 64 71
STRANGE, 42 86 106 110 119 Gresham 70 106 110 Grisham 63 J A 86 John 25 42 John A 47 86
STRICKLER, 87
SUMMEY, Jacob 55 56 60
SUMMY, 87 96 Jacob 38 77 87 97
SWAN, 76 W H 76 William G 28 30
TATE, Mary 69
TAYLOR, Daniel 55 82 149 Eliza 95 Greenfield 143 Grinsfield 102 James 75 90 119 136 James M 149 John P 95 W B 55
TEDFORD, 4 70 91 J H 120 James H 33 36 John 72 John N 72 Joseph 48 70 78 Joseph H 43 63 64 91 93 110 Robert 27 Robert A 4
TEFFETELLER, 97 G W 109

TEFFETELLER (continued)
George W 87 97 M L 49 76
TEFORD, Joseph H 81
TELLINGHAST, 31
TEMPLE, A A 58 A P 2 James D
73 O P 36 88 99 129 130
THOMPSON, Dorcus 18 James
45 50 57 122 132 134 144
152-154 Jesse B 97 L M 53
Leroy 21 Leroy F 17 Leroy T
18 M H 79 Malinda 97
Martha E 40 Nancy 18 21
Samuel 7 8 17 18 21 Samuel
B 7 8 12 18 21 William H 72
William N 18 21
TILLERY, 136
TILLINGHAST, 133 T D 33 48
50 62 63 69 76 88 98
TIPTON, Benjamin 44 J W H 92
Lambert 108
TOOLE, 57 86 126 B W 151
Elizabeth 151 George 152 I
M 7 J E 96 99 J M 14 48 57
79 86 James M 3 14 57 64
79 86 125 126 144 146 John
E 2 4 5 10 14 17 20 40 41
53 54 63 75 97 125-127 151
Lizzie 152 William 14 151
William Jr 86 William Sr 151
TOWNSEND, 152
TREWHIT, D C 115
TREWHITT, Chancllr 130 D C
117-119 123 127 135 Daniel
C 117 Daniel C W 122
TRIPE, 130
TROTER, Benjamin 7
TRUNDLE, D L 48 73 Daniel L
60
TULLOCH, James M 7 8 12 17
18 21 Samuel 12 81 100 145
156
UPTON, Thomas L 78 83
VANDYKE, 28 Chancllr 23 Hon
41 T N 30 31 T Nixon 8 28
31 41 46 67 69 72 75 77 79

VANDYKE (continued)
89 101 104 105 108 109 111
VINEYARD, Lindsey 143 N G 83
VINSANT, 8 17 19 23 30 34 43
WALKER, 137 151 B F 144 C W
A 136 E 115 Elijah Jr 115
James 75 90 119 136 Mrs B
F 144 W A 72 135 136 144
145 151-153 156 W C A 130
W D 65 William 57 130
William A 17 24 38 42 95
115 155
WALLACE, 14 28 29 54 56 58
119 129 130 A M 55 152
156 C 138 C A M 130 E M
139 Elizabeth M 134 136-
140 I G 36 J C 47 101 J G
24 25 31 32 34 37 38 43 55
63 65 73 83 95 99 110 130
156 Jesse 23 46 Jesse G 25
58 59 66 73 75 84 101 109
114 115 130 152 M 14 31 34
51 140 Martha 51 Martha
Elizabeth 140 Mary 152
Mary L L 152 Matthew 13 14
23 26 34 41 46 51 74 86
Mrs 138 S W 67 Sam 25
Samuel 59 134 136-140 145
Samuel W 67 71 138 140
Thomas 140 W C 67 145 152
Will 8 88 William 25 26 29
33 34 37 39 43 58 59 60 70
86 130 144 William C 67 71
113 152
WALT, Abraham P 135
WARREN, B L 55 91 B S 144
Barton L 132
WATERS, Adam F 143 E L 6 10
20 James 126 136 John 6
10 20 Matilda 10 13 20
Melinda 6 William 6 10 20
WATSON, 12 13 Asa 8 Ira 12 13
WATT, 131 Abraham P 142
Abraim R 131
WATTERS, Enoch 69 James 69

WAYMAN, Edmond 52
WEAR, David 67 Hugh 44 72
  82 83 99 103 Isaac D 7 15
  Isabella 67 J D 44 88 136
  James D 56 67 72 82 83 91
  99 103 109 L 141 155
  Margaret 82 Robert 44 50 52
  56 63 67 72 82 83 99 109
  Robert A 156 Robert L 136
WEIR, Alex 11 James D 32
  Robert 32
WELCHER, A G 111 Albert G
  112 James M 46
WELCKER, A G 114 115 James
  M 31 41
WELLS, S M 71
WEST, Mary 33 Mary A 73
WHEELER, James M 57 Joseph
  24
WHITE, John 92 108
WHITEHEAD, James W 87
WHITTENBERGER, A C 19
  Henry 19
WHITTENBURG, A C 6 Daniel 6
  Hue 6
WHITTENBURGER, A C 11 13
  Ambrose 11 Ambrose C 11
  Henry 11 13 Mrs Henry 11
WILLIAMS, C A 32 M H 25
  Thomas L 1-3

WILSON, 3 18 51 57 61 73
  James 3 9 18 24 30 33 34
  36 38 41-44 48 51 61-64 67
  70 73 76 78 81 88 91 93 96
  98 110 120 128 154 R I 23
  33 38 102 128 R J 57 99
  Rich I 48 Richard I 3 29
  Richard J 51 Soloman 46 T I
  70
WILSTOCK, W P 31
WOOD, 48 86 129 Leonard A
  78 124 156 William P 78 124
WOODS, 129 James 7 Jane 21
  June 18 L A 105 Leonard A
  105 Sam T 18 Samuel 17
  Samuel F 8 Samuel T 7 21
WORD, Samuel G 12
WRIGHT, Archibald 53 D G 115
  Elizabeth 134 J I 12 James
  C 35 Nancy M 50 Samuel
  134 William 113
YATES, William Jr 33
YEAROUT, 72 110 113 Isaac 72
  79 Isaac N 79 83 105 J 120
  143 John 112 L L 83 90 L S
  136 S L 119 Samuel 56 70
  72 79 87 Samuel L 39 41 72
  78 79 W 120 143 W R 112

www.ingramcontent.com/pod-product-compliance
Lightning Source LLC
Chambersburg PA
CBHW050808160426
43192CB00010B/1687